Multifaith Musing:

Essays and Exchanges

Dorothy Yoder Nyce

Foreword by Paul F. Knitter
Paul Tillich Professor of
Theology, World Religions and Culture
Union Theological Seminary, New York, NY

Published by:
Dorothy Yoder Nyce
1603 S. 15th St.
Goshen, IN 46526-4558

Cover art work:
Soot drawing – "Renewal XX"
By Anna Friesen

Library of Congress
Catalog No. 2010904241

ISBN 978-0-692-00865-2

Printed in United States of America

Nappanee, Indiana

Contents

Dedication:

To South Asian friends of diverse faiths,
 most from India, Nepal, and Sri Lanka,
 who have attended Goshen College or lived in Goshen
 and who have shared numerous curry meals in our home.
To know many parents or siblings of these friends,
 visiting Goshen or our being hosted by them in their Asian homes,
 has been John and my special privilege.
With many of these friends,
 contacts continue, along with interfaith respect.
 (With regret for names here missed):

Vishal, Gayatri, Naila, G.B., Harish, Sumitra, Naresh, and Sunil

Jeya, Jorna, Pratiksha, Debbie, Robina, Natasha, and Shashi B.

Sid & Sonal, Vandana, Preeti & Deep, Dinny, Avinash & Grace

Maneesh, Indrani, Rahul, Angelo, Shashi M, Michael, Kathy & Channa

Kavi & Chamindra, Rushika, Thushan, Rana, Fiona, Janaka & Dinali

Sanjay & Rachel, Rita, Elisheba, Jatin, Ram, Rishi, and Nisha T

Veronica, Chandran, Manu, Miriam, Nolin, Shafkat, and Sanjay V

Nisha S, Ranju, Utpal & Prakriti, Tsigi, Kashif, Gunjan, and Abhishek

Gaurav & Lakshmi, Sid S, Dikshya, Sweta, Akansha, and Subhekchya

Benj, Shihoko, Lisa, Chagan, Candida, Jivan, Surinder, Sreekala & Raj,

Ranjita, Pushpa, Lakshmi & Krishna, Hershie, Ramesh, Neela & Ranen.

(Jeevan, Kuldip, Dinesh and Narmin - How we wish they still lived.)

Acknowledgments

With sincere thanks:

Paul F. Knitter – Mentor from whom I have learned the most about being religious interreligiously. His extensive writing has shaped my thought for decades. I value him as professor, peace advocate, and friend.

Judith Davis – Personal friend, professor, writer and medieval scholar notably of the Virgin Mary. She gave good editing advice for the entire book. I remain responsible for any mistakes or neglect.

John D. Nyce – Spouse who has supported my disciplined study, responded to computer 'hitches,' and enabled book layout details.

Christopher Kaiser – Western Theological Seminary DMin Supervisor.

David C. Scott – WTS "outside reader" of dialogues (since revised). Seminary Religions Professor (India). Festschrift: *Spiritual Traditions.*

Eve Ricketts – Recurring exchange about personal Christian-Hindu issues and all things native Indian. Provided housing during WTS study.

Bimla Gour, Gordon Morrison, Judith Davis, Norm Kauffmann, Sid Sahni & Sonal Raj Sahni—Manuscript readers; promotional paragraphs.

Anna Friesen – Visual artist inspired by nature. "Renewal XX" – Front cover art; Soot Drawing—smoke as sacred renewal.

Parents **Bessie L. (King) and Herman M. Yoder** (both now deceased). Mentors with hospitality, reading, Christian faith and church assignments

Gretchen Nyce – Reader (with good critique and humor) of early drafts of major New Perspectives on Faith essays.

John D. Smith - Evangel Press manager who has seen through printing details for this resource.

Mission Focus Annual Review – Permission granted to quote pp. 62-69 of my article: "Sharing God's Gift of Wholeness with Living Faiths: Biblical Examples," vol. 15, 2007, here as Appendix: Texts of Influence.

Foreword

In this collection of essays, Dorothy Yoder Nyce – my friend, student, and fellow searcher – illustrates and embodies a truth that has been dawning on, and calling for reform of, the mainline Christian churches (even many evangelical churches) for the last half century: as the Asian Catholic Bishops have put it: "Dialogue is the new way of being church."

Pentecost, which might be called "the big bang" that launched the *ecclesia*, will continue rippling through the ecclesial universe of the second millennium mainly through the energy of dialogue. In order for the community of Jesus-followers to be faithful disciples in our present world they need to understand "Christian" to mean "dialogical." To continue being the church of Jesus Christ, we will have to be the *dialogical* church of Jesus Christ.

Because of her own life experiences, because of the demands of her own Mennonite Christian faith, because of the friends she has made in other religions, Dorothy Yoder Nyce has felt and responded to this call to live the Gospel in a lived engagement with persons of other faiths. As I read through the essays in this collection – both the more scholarly reflections as well as the living dialogical conversations that she records and imagines – I heard her give expression to two primary reasons why interreligious dialogue has become for her, as for a growing number of Christians, a moral imperative. The world which the church is called to serve, challenge, and transform is a world in dire need of dialogue for two daunting reasons: it is a *pluralistic world*, and it is a *violent world*.

A Pluralistic World

Pluralism – the vast variety of peoples, cultures, religions – has, of course, always colored the fabric of human history. But today, mainly because of the push-button speed of communication and travel, those differing colors have become all the more evident. In fact, for many people, these colors have become bewildering or blinding. This is especially true of the multiple colors of religions. *Religious pluralism* – the abundant, persistent, exuberant diversity of religions – is confronting, often perplexing, Christians as never before. The shapes and colors and even smells of other religions are no longer on the other side of the world. They often emerge from the house next door! In her broadly acclaimed book, Diana L. Eck gives convincing data that there is *A New Religious America* (title), and she describes *"How a 'Christian Country' Has Become the World's Most Religiously Diverse Nation"* (subtitle).

The manyness of religions, therefore, isn't going to go away. It seems that religious pluralism is "as it was in the beginning, is now, and ever shall be." If that's the case, the simple, immediate conclusion is that Christians have to learn to *co-exist,* to live with and be good neighbors to people who are Buddhists, and Hindus, and Muslims, etc. But, as Yoder Nyce makes clear in this book, being good neighbors to each other means more than tolerance, more than just accepting the pluralistic state of affairs. Rather, it means learning about each other, appreciating and valuing each other. Pluralistic co-existence – that is, really living and thriving together as different religions – requires dialogue.

A Violent World

But co-existing and getting to know and value each other are not enough. Because our world is not just a pluralistic world but a violent world, we have to do more together. I'm talking mainly (but not only) about the violence that erupts from the barrel of a gun, the impact of a missile, the explosion of an airplane crashing into a building. I'm talking about military or terroristic violence. The dreams of a new age of peace after the fall of the Soviet Union have turned, it seems, into nightmares. Besides the multiple, rampaging conflicts of ethnic and/or religious groups, the world is witnessing what some call the "clash of civilizations" – a clash fueled by the terrorism of scattered movements pitted against the military might of world powers. As we have seen since 9/11, religion – in this case, both Islam and Christianity – is so easily used to fuel such violence.

But if such "use" of religion for violence is, as is generally said, a "misuse," then the religions of the world will need to do something to prevent that misuse. And they'll need to do it *together.* So, besides co-existence, we also need *cooperation* among the religious traditions of the world. As Yoder Nyce makes clear in her final essay, people of all religions must come together and act together and so prove that religions can be a much more powerful tool of peace than they are a weapon of war. But such cooperation can be realized only through dialogue. The well-known dictum of Hans Küng, therefore, rings true: "There will be no peace among nations without peace among religions. And there will be no peace among religions without dialogue among them."

What Is Dialogue?

But just what do we mean by dialogue? The answer to that question is embodied in the examples of interreligious conversations that are "transcribed" in many of the essays that follow. Playing my role as an academic, I would distill from these essays the following definition of dialogue: it is a relationship between differing parties in which all parties both speak their minds and open their minds to each other, in the hope that through this engagement all parties will grow in truth and well-being. Dialogue therefore is always a *two-way street* that can lead all who travel it to greater understanding and cooperation. All participants in a dialogical encounter have to be ready both to listen and to speak, to teach and be taught. A true dialogue is always both a "give and take" – one gives witness to what one holds to be true and at the same time accepts the witness of what the other holds true and dear. Everyone seeks to convince and is ready to be convinced. And if in the dialogue I come to see and feel the truth of your position, then I must also be ready to clarify, correct, even change, my views. Dialogue is always exciting; it can also be threatening. For many of its readers, this book will be both exciting and threatening.

Christian = Dialogical

So as the Christian church makes its way into the second millennium, this understanding and challenge of dialogue can help Christians to grasp and practice what it really means to be a follower of Jesus. In a sense, the moral imperative of dialogue is calling all Christians to be "catholic" – not Roman Catholic, but truly catholic. "Catholic" means "universal" – embracing of, open to, sent into the whole world with its many peoples and cultures and religions. But for most of church history, this universal quality of the Christian community has been viewed as a one-way street. We bring the saving message to them; we give, they receive.

But "catholic" understood as "dialogue" means that the relationship between the church and other cultures and religions must be *two-ways*. If the church is to grow and be faithful to the Gospel of Jesus, it must not only deliver the Good News but also be open to whatever Good News God may be providing through other religious traditions. Not only by "teaching all nations" but also by learning from all nations can the church cooperate with other religions in the work of overcoming violence and bringing justice to the poor of our planet – and to our poor planet suffering from environmental devastation. To call themselves Christian means that Jesus' followers need others – people and religions who are really different. Only through a dialogical relationship with *others* can the church understand and be faithful to the message of Jesus.

Dialogue *is* indeed a meaningful, challenging "new way of being church." This is what Dorothy Yoder Nyce makes so clear, compelling, and exciting in this book. I expect that it will enable others to share the excitement of this new way of being church, a new way of being human.

Paul F. Knitter
Paul Tillich Professor of Theology, World Religions, and Culture
Union Theological Seminary, New York, NY

Introduction

Questions matter. Is religious plurality vital to the Creator's Wisdom? To what extent does the context (culture) in which one lives determine religious truth for a person? Since elements like beauty, light, and water are key features of religions, might they also contribute creatively to resolving conflicts between living faiths? Do people learn from what they imagine? Does support for or loyalty to one religious tradition justify passing judgment on those for whom another tradition gives deep meaning? Does knowing people of different religions require living with them for an extended time? Since faith traditions provide sense of purpose, enable the practice of moral principles, or grant wisdom and joy, why would members of one not wish to learn from or deeply respect traditions of others? How does scripture enable faith or right living?

On starting to write this piece, my phone rang. A friend from India, visiting his son in Texas, greeted, "Hello, Dorothy; this is Pawate!" Our friendship, as staff members together at a south Indian international school, had grown in part through his and Manju's being Hindu. Earlier that day, an e-mail message reported the death of a Hindu friend's son-in-law; she deserves compassion. A couple of hours later, a Hindu friend from Nepal passed by our house, her second-grade son pedaling his bike. Two weeks earlier, John and I attended a Hindu wedding in Virginia, staying the nights with a young Hindu couple. They invited us to join the blessing ritual with a priest for their new home— our Sunday worship. A week before that, we shared a curry meal with a Hindu family down the street, here from Bangladesh. And recently, a special Sikh friend never responded following lung transplant surgery. She was honored through sacred acts of love that we shared at the hospital, gurdwara, and crematorium. How enriched friendships and musings can be when marked by Divine religions.

This book addresses how people might receive or learn from people loyal to diverse living faiths. Such openness complements being faithful to and growing in personal faith. It credits Divine design for variety in living faiths. As a Hindu friend expresses dependence on God, I affirm without negative comparing personal reliance on Mystery. As Sikhs or Muslims embrace their scriptures with high regard, I honor biblical truth with respect, not claiming it as better. Seeing even modest celebration for the Hindu holiday Holi, I may question the somber quality of Christian thought about Advent. As a person loyal to another living faith affirms its wisdom, I need not apologize for or deny Sophia's strength. Exchange makes possible reciprocal learning and personal growth in belief.

The first dialogue encourages a person to both expect and credit Wisdom from diverse religions, to avoid limiting the Universal Being or Creativity. Principles recur: difference is good; strengths flow from plural faiths; self-exploration is part of the interfaith process. Water, vital to multifaiths, illustrates the symbolic. It prompts finding the sacred in the common and finding common meaning between religions. The sacred in sound, movement and story reinforces how culture and religion ever overlap. While anyone might misunderstand another person, religious tradition or ritual, exchange enables respect for and acceptance of the otherness of the other. The art form of temples engages Mystery; icons and architecture can move a community toward unity. Walking with and finding the Divine in beauty crosses cultures.

Several dialogues examine scripture—Christian and Hindu. Only time and space keep the author from exploring Sikh devotion to their text, the *Guru Granth Sahib*—honored as the present Guru. Whereas Jews, Christians, and Muslims may be called "People of the Book," the quantity of religious texts within Hinduism far exceeds that among those three. Exchange on scriptures involves loyal speakers familiar with their texts. In one setting, partners nudge each other in personal study, while the other exchange finds "insiders" teaching a group of "outsiders." God's universal being matters for Christians. The difference between ancient procedures for worship and epics inspire or teach today's faithful Hindus. Knowing one's scripture requires disciplined study of the world before, behind, and of a text Sandra Schneiders suggests.

A change of format marks "Splitting Differences." Seven characters discuss themes of religion in a one-act play. While content portrays more Hindu and Muslim conflict in India, the link with politics remains near the surface. Sacred rituals, ignorance about others, fear, the tie between memory and revenge, and examples of honesty yet restraint appear. Peace-building efforts apply broadly; food bridges difference.

Two dialogues highlight the female god/goddess image. While most readers expect the goddess of varied forms and names within Hindu mythology, Jews and Christians less likely note "Yahweh and his Asherah." Intent to process information and layered story-telling, readers find response to the figure(s) through history to differ markedly. That fact can be valued without denying ancient religious heritage. Whether to name women and identity as a cultural or religious issue might surface for some readers. The value of a steadfast form to meet fears, of *shakti* (power/energy/Spirit) to enrich being, enters sacred thought—depending on who speaks. People of faith might ponder occasions to gather or celebrate, in light of dialogue. For dialogue involves "talking things through in ways that allow truth to be heard," says Peter Slater. Distinct concepts of Divine Mystery—God of Relationship, Ultimate Being, or Multiple yet One—furthers respect without judgment. For, "religious plurality must be part of the Creator's Wisdom."

Essays offer a style to complement exchange. Chapter nine, focused on how personal experience enlarges vision, might even be read as a Preface. Versions of chapters three and twelve were first prepared for New Perspectives on Faith meetings in Goshen, Indiana. That group's mission: "to foster inter-congregational, inter-denominational, and inter-faith conversations that contribute to new perspectives on faith for a new millennium," is distinct for a small town. It reflects both a need and growing desire.

Max Mueller's observation: "To know one (religion) is to know none" prompts the (Christian) need to be informed about and value sacred meanings and traditions of other living faiths, for its own strength and survival. The paradox of world religions—that both cause conflict and promote peace-building—appears through brief examples. Problems of fundamentalism, scripture that inflicts personal or group pain, and 'just war' issues might be met by nonviolence (*ahimsa* in its broad, Hindu sense), social activism of Engaged Buddhism, or hospitality. Individuals like Thomas Merton, Abdul Ghaffar Khan, a Muslim healer named Amma, and Thich Nhat Hanh model peace-building. Klaus Klostermaier suggests that "only a paradox prepares the mind for a new experience."

In addition to major essays, this book includes a distinct format—imagined, informed, and interreligious dialogues. Dialogue suggests that more than one person contributes. Religious dialogue enables each to recognize truth in the other, a form of hospitality. "Imagined" alerts readers to the fact that examples of exchange are 'creations,' not a reporting of actual conversation. "Informed" indicates that content builds on disciplined study and personal experience, even when imagined. "Interreligious" means that views or practice of more than one religion or ecumenical group receive attention and shape content.

Religious dialogue has multiple formats, as do prayer or study of scripture. While some dialogue takes place within a person—in response to insight read or heard—most is external and expressed between two or more people. Exchange may follow study of another's culture, observance of sacred ritual, or response to emerging questions. When people of diverse religions meet common problems through social service agencies, such action also reflects dialogue. Building healthy relationships is the goal whether through exchange or direct action. Being willing to share beliefs, not intent to debate them, is central to dialogue. Based in self-respect, exchange expects to take risks of disclosure and openness, risks of commitment—to the other and one's own faith. A spirit or attitude toward another evolves whether of goodwill, trust, suspicion, or contrast.

Imagined exchange can express friendship. It cannot achieve what face-to-face encounter might, but it encourages readers to practice direct dialogue. It validates being informed in addition to having opinion. It reveals serious learning through careful listening and honest expression. It claims the integrity of one's own and another's belief. And, hopefully, it motivates mutual action—to address injustice or ill will or to extend friendship. Built on knowledge yet informal, what follows reflects how exchange might proceed. Informed exchange offers a creative outlet, like storytelling, for serious process and worthy content. Information helps partners to overcome ignorance and stereotypes. It counters arrogance of spirit. Being informed of another's point of view follows intentional listening and deep hearing.

Used interchangeably in different settings, the terms interreligious and ecumenical can refer to distinct groupings. The former more often designates world religions while the latter refers to categories like Roman Catholic, Orthodox and Protestant or distinct denominations within the latter. Dialogues within this resource highlight both broad categories. Exchange may imagine Hindu and Christian speakers, two Hindus, or two Protestants depending on the theme. A one-act play finds several Hindu and Muslim college students in conversation. Diversity inherent within religious groupings is also natural. No individual represents a religion. Other members of religions might express different views than those found here. What people of different faiths hold in common serves understanding. Difference is also good, part of Divine Wisdom. As 'hybrid' people—ever connecting and overlapping in new ways—individuals engage distinct others, without negative "othering." Learning from difference strengthens personal commitment.

Each person's present has a past and (likely) future. My religious heritage of Protestant Mennonite within Christianity holds. My living in and returning to India multiple times since 1962 has convinced me of Divine Wisdom inherent within diverse faith traditions and ways of being religious. Friendships developed over forty years and mentors—in person or through writing—teach truth, formal and informal. Being part of a minority, radical Protestant view instills a justice flavor into identity.

Sustained exposure to Hindu, Muslim, Buddhist, or Sikh thought through loyal adherents counters ignorance and arrogance. Further, intra-Christian worship and interreligious exchange convince me of the richness of distinct conviction and loyalty within breadth. No single belief system or practice of corporate praise of the Divine satisfies or expresses wholeness. Max Mueller's axiom, "To know one religion is to know none" holds true. As religious folk assess personal faith claims or grow in openness to truth from others, they discover loyalty expressed in new ways for future being.

However, fears can emerge. Fear of openness may reveal lack of experience with truly hearing others. Or, it might reflect being insulated from exposure to difference. Fear of ignorance might cause one to hesitate welcoming another. Fear of difference defines xenophobia. This fear might prompt disdain for those who differ. Fear also occurs with change. To change one's view of another, when an earlier perspective proves to be wrong, requires effort. To admit the wrong reflects courage. To endorse rather than negate the other affects self-perception too. Fear of conflict, within or beyond the self, can also recur with dialogue. But on seeing difference as strength, partners lessen conflict; each absorbs new insight into personal belief, reducing fear.

Who participates in sacred exchange shapes dialogue here—youth or adult, women or men, being from India, Canada, or the United States. While principles of exchange apply elsewhere, my global experience, and therefore dialogue, centers in India. Its rich religious diversity invites. Being a small minority may enable some Indian and South Asian Christians to honor religious difference, to avoid judgmental absolute claims. However, dialogues here intend to inform partners and shape attitudes, rather than reconcile conflict already active. Academic interest, age, location and extent to which speakers know each other also affect exchange. When more than two people interact, the arts of listening and sharing broaden.

Many voices write about exchange. Paul Knitter names four essential ingredients of dialogue: difference, trust, witnessing, and learning. Aware that "all truth is limited" and that "God is bigger than any religion," Knitter suggests three reasons to dialogue: because we are neighbors, because we need to solve common problems; because peace among nations will only follow peace among religions.[1] While Beverly Lanzetta describes dialogue as "intensely communal," Ross Reat finds it when reading, pondering, and humbly crediting other religions. Raimon Panikkar notes multi-steps for dialogue: from a faithful, critical understanding of both one's own and another's tradition (on-going and new conviction) to internal and then external dialogue, a person tests interpretations in the process.

Religious plurality reflects the Creator's Wisdom and Divine richness. It offers strengths of loyalty and openness to those who practice faith in unique ways. As Thomas Thangaraj suggests, the strength of God-willed diversity finds expression not in how much one tolerates another but in how each embraces the other as an extension of the self.

As Christians enact the rite of baptism or Hindus offer *prasad* (food) during worship, they honor sacred rites. As increasing numbers of Hindu, Muslim, Sikh or Buddhist faithful relocate in the west, how Christians and others receive them activates the universal guideline: "love your neighbor as yourself."

Diana Eck, who lived in India seven years and then extensively researched America's present, diverse religious scene, states, "To attempt to understand the religious viewpoint of someone of another faith is one of the greatest challenges of the human mind and heart, as is the challenge to be understood by the other."[2] As readers engage with themes of sacred traditions, conflict, scriptures, concepts of Divinity, and sources of Wisdom, honest sharing of what gives life meaning grows.

Endnotes:

[1] Paul Knitter. Lecture handout, Dayton, OH, Oct. 14, 2004, 3-4.

[2] Diana L Eck. "Gandhian Guidelines for a World of Religious Difference," in *Gandhi on Christianity,* Robert Ellsberg, ed., Maryknoll, NY: Orbis, 1995, p. 90. See also Eck's *A New Religious America* How A "Christian Country" Has Become the World's Most Religiously Diverse Nation. San Francisco: Harper, 2001.

1

Wisdom from the East

This exchange engages two Christian women, Usha from India and Janet a North American visitor/tourist—in India for an international conference on ecology.

Usha: Welcome! I'm glad you've come to India.

Janet: Thanks. There's so much to observe here; I must miss a lot.

Usha: No doubt. But, you'll alert me to common details that I overlook. From your note, you wonder how the strong interreligious context shapes Indian Christianity, a minor faith here.

Janet: Or, what are some 'givens' for faith, in light of multifaiths?

Usha: Might I first ask you: How often do you meet Muslims? I read that the number of Muslims in the United States about equals the number of Jews there.

Janet: Muslims and Jews: I rarely connect with either, though mosques, temples, and synagogues appear in bigger cities. And Christians share Jewish scripture.

Usha: More U.S. people are Muslim than either Episcopalian or Presbyterian.

Janet: Really? You likely have Muslims neighbors?

Usha: Of course. Their first of five calls to daily prayer wakes me up each morning. I rather like that. More than my alarm, the call from the minaret leads me to talk with the One God too.

Janet: I suppose it could. That's profound, that one faith prompts others to pray.

Usha: All the time. Yesterday, a small Hindu procession stopped traffic in my section of town. Hearing the drums and seeing the adorned, mini-deity carried on a platform, I paused from gardening to thank God for energy. Just last week I had sprained my ankle when my scooter jammed up in traffic.

Janet: Now that's another twist. My first thought on seeing those Hindus might be to wish they'd see the light of Christianity.

Usha: Light? Do you have any idea of the meaning of light for Hindus?
Janet: No. Should I?
Usha: Think about it this way. If your first response to people of another living faith discredits or wishes them to change, without knowing their depth of wisdom about symbols like light, is that fair? Might you bear false witness, when telling your church friends, about Hindu rituals?
Janet: A valid concern, in light of the Ten Commandments.
Usha: Light! Are you aware of India's wisdom-based religious heritage? What you'll absorb on a short visit barely "scratches the surface." What you see when Hindus light candles or offer milk or remove their shoes on entering a temple may fail to notice deeper wisdom.
Janet: I'm sure. How Christians nurture their faith, when present with other religions, interests me.
Usha: Good. Have you heard of the *Vedas*?
Janet: They're ancient Hindu scriptures.
Usha: The religious or reflective tradition of the *Vedas* shapes India's wisdom. *Vedas* means wisdom or science. Serious thinkers pursue Truth.
Janet: How about the common believer?
Usha: Have Luther and Calvin's reforms or views of Aquinas or Augustine shaped your faith?
Janet: Likely so, but I can't explain how in detail.
Usha: In somewhat related ways, the *Vedas* permeate sacred experience here in India, known or not. The *Vedas* expect people to discover Truth for themselves, to pursue ultimate questions: What gives meaning to my existence? Who am I or who are we? Why was I born and what re-birth will follow death? To learn through such sweeping questions helps one to meet or transcend suffering. The Vedic approach also prompts meditation. Here, to practice *yoga* means to develop the mind so that higher realities appear.
Janet: Western Christians may ignore such depth when practicing yoga.
Usha: Patanjali, a sage from north India, noted eight principles of yogic practice, all of which help reunite a person with the divine.
Janet: Principles like breath control and body posture?
Usha: Yes, but also ethical behavior or discipline, plus withdrawing senses.
Janet: Meditation must be a principle. I read Rita Gross, a Buddhist. She sets apart meditation from contemplation. For her, meditation is about resting the mind, while contemplation is a way to work with ideas to foster genuine meaning.
Usha: That's useful. . . . Patanjali follows concentration with ecstatic absorption. The goal is to let go of the ego.
Janet: Buddhists also use the term mindfulness to express spirituality. Intent to slow down, they attend to the present.
Usha: Varied paths or ways move toward union with God. While the

path of good works and compassion in action is called "*karma* yoga," the path of wisdom or "*jnana* yoga" pursues honesty, truth, and self-realization. And a way focused on devotional love is called "*bhakti* yoga," while the path of sacred sound or "*mantra* yoga" highlights reciting or chanting.

Janet: Eastern worship includes a lot of repetition, right?

Usha: Part of the goal is to remember. The Hindu scripture known as The Upanishads is full of rhythm, accent, sequence, and knowledge of letters. Restated, the point is to resonate, to become intimate with sound, with voice. The truth of texts, prayers, and words of power, repeated, absorbs one's self.

Janet: We in the west may tire of repetition.

Usha: You value what is fresh or novel, more than what comes through deep penetration?

Janet: Perhaps. Earlier you mentioned that the *Vedas* permeate Indian culture. Do Indian Christians combine your scripture with eastern culture and religious wisdom?

Usha: Of course. Multi-issues shape the process and outcomes. Westerners often transplanted beliefs here without knowing the *Vedas* heritage. A strange mix followed. Now, informed Indian Christians, aware of that implant and steeped in experience with diverse faiths, honor the wisdom of India's religious heritage—practices and views they might earlier have been told to denounce.

Janet: What else strongly shapes your faith?

Usha: Well, the other major Asian reality—economic hardship. Poverty impacts Asian religions.

Janet: It shapes your spiritual being, your relationship with God?

Usha: Of course. Not first an inward piety, Asian spirituality prompts openness to other religious traditions and engagement with social struggles. Zen Buddhism, for example, states: "Show me." Compassion for those who suffer enables noble kindness, empathy, or joy in a Buddhist.

Janet: Eastern Christians celebrate the plural?

Usha: Not isolated from another's life, spirituality is germane to justice and liberation. To struggle provides meaning.

Janet: The prophet Jeremiah knew that, "To do justice is to 'know' God."

Usha: Someone called it the "*Godwardness* of life . . . seeing God in all things and all things in God." . . . But you wanted to focus interaction between living faiths, right?

Janet: Whatever wisdom you propose.

Usha: Knowing your interest, I began a list of ideas. First: *Here in India religious plurality is a fact of life.* Bishop S. K. Parmar defines plurality as a "gift from God." Believers enrich their commitment through relationships across faiths, through dialogue.

Janet: In the process, your inner truth is tested?

Usha: The process enriches a believer. Pluralism credits the richness of Truth. No one or group has a monopoly on it. Each religious community is obliged or freed to live out its central beliefs with integrity, as it serves humanity.

Second: *Each religion claims unique or distinct features.*

Janet: Like Jesus' uniqueness? Does any other faith have a redeemer who died and rose again?

Usha: Not that I know of. But, as we Christians hold that distinct claim, we with grace expect other faiths to value and explain what is unique for them. S. J. Samartha reminds us that, "In the core of every religion, something belongs to it alone." Buddhists pursue nirvana; Sikhs and Muslims honor their scriptures in most profound ways.

Janet: But is one group's uniqueness "better than" another's?

Usha: Why ask that? Who but God decides quality? Why debate? Whereas debate causes opposition, dialogue calls people to work together. Exchange invites understanding while debate competes. Debate first critiques the other's position while dialogue first looks inward, to discover further ways to reveal God's Way of love. Having heard another's wisdom, each ponders how to enlarge personal insight.

Janet: Useful—dialogue and debate seem to stem from and meet quite different goals.

Usha: People here observe that religions 'fit' the distinct, spiritual competence of those who practice them. While Hindus strive to relate the self (a*tman*) with the foundation of creation (*Brahman*), Christians hope to unite with God through "being in Christ." Hindus might choose paths of selfless devotion to God through work, control of the mind, or absolute knowledge. Samartha advised the church to stress "distinct, not exclusive or only."

Janet: You're stretching my thoughts; give me time!

Usha: How about during your flight home? Third: *Differences will remain and that's good.* Consider Christian Trinity, a concept that offends Muslims because it denies Allah's *one*ness. Rather than debate the point, why not agree to differ? Share convictions on the personal meaning of faith or discuss questions like: "How do you understand integrity in relationships?" Christians can learn from Muslim almsgiving and faithful prayer life, instead of argue over holy difference.

Janet: Accept difference without using it to drive wedges, to estrange people?

Usha: You can't be an effective neighbor and always see difference as negative. Here in India, with Hindu, Muslim, Sikh, or Buddhist neighbors, we live faith by granting others space to be loyal to a religion meaningful to them.

Since I've jotted down numerous points, I'd better move on to the <u>Fourth</u>: *Prayer and scripture matter in religions.* Muslim obedience involves response to five daily calls to prayer.

Janet: Might some Christians say, "But, we're called to pray without ceasing"?

Usha: What motivates that comment? Thinking that we're more pious? Do most Christians pray constantly? Can we welcome public reminders to halt our activity to meet God? Further, how informed of impromptu Muslim prayer are Christians who judge?

Janet: My comment was thoughtless.

Usha: Living among people loyal to other religions calls us to common ground, not first to being over-against. Hindus reveal a strong desire to merge the human spirit with the Divine. With sacred rites, some repeat the Gayatri, a call to contemplation. Christians repeat the Lord's Prayer. And Jews communicate with Yahweh, the God of covenant.

Janet: All connect with one-and-the-same Mystery?

Usha: What do you think? I see prayer as common ground, or breath. Scriptures vary more. Earlier, Christians brought the Bible to India, this country replete with sacred stories. R. S. Sugirtharajah faults those who used Christian scripture to "denigrate Asian peoples' sacred texts." Padmasani Gallup values those who "put the people and their needs at the centre of biblical interpretation." For her, the Bible is one among resources for searching the Truth. You value comments from Indian Christians?

Janet: Sure. I only wish I knew more of their writings.

Usha: My <u>Fifth</u> observation: *No one religion will be decisive for all peoples.*"To know one is to know none," Max Mueller said decades ago. For some Christians, "to be in Christ is the only way to be in God. But in a religiously plural world, to be in Christ is not the only way to be in God." Always expect solid insight from Stanley Samartha or Wesley Ariarajah—that "Asia will never become Christian," for example.

Janet: You welcome that?

Usha: I see that fact as part of divine Wisdom.

Janet: As if God has multiple ways to offer salvation?

Usha: Who knows everything about God's offers? Together, finite people of faith face the Infinite. We work toward harmony and peace. We learn through religious "cross reference."

Janet: "Cross reference"?

Usha: Kenneth Cragg, who lived with and wrote about connecting with Muslims, coined the term. People of faith glean from multifaiths to perceive and express the spiritual more fully.

Janet: Needing each other, a hybrid or porous quality takes root?

Usha: For example, through a term vital to Hindu thought, Samartha notes how God provides *darshana*, "a view of life or insight into the

Mystery of the Divine." Further, God provides *dharma,* "a way of life or motivation to live in obedience." Do we have time for more on the list?

Janet: Sure; I could interrupt less.

Usha: No problem. <u>Sixth</u>: Many *Christians see God at the center of the religious universe; most faiths resonate.* Most Christians pattern Jesus in worshiping God. Motivated by Jesus' example, we serve others. Salvation in Christ means being reconciled with God and neighbor. Again, I value Samartha's word: "Commitment is to God, not to Christianity or the church." Such confession neither insults nor excludes. It welcomes. It witnesses to gospel faith without denying another's dream, without undermining another's integrity of faith in the One God.

Janet: You seem convinced. But not all western Christians would trust your sixth point. To support diverse approaches to God may cause conflict.

Usha: Could well be. What I endorse is keeping <u>God</u> central. Was that not Jesus' main motive? He promoted the kin-dom of God—which highlights relationship or kinfolk—God's inclusive way. Courage to you as you exchange and explain Truth from adherents of other living faiths.

Janet: Might a 'high Christology'—with Jesus at the religious center—overstate his role? Or be a form of idolatry when it replaces God?

Usha: For Indian Christians, Jesus is vital, yes essential. But when we locate God at the center of the religious universe, we expect other pilgrims also to witness to God, to tell their special stories.

Jamet: I heard about an *imam* who guided a missionary orientation group through a mosque. He repeatedly said, "If you don't believe as we do, you're going to hell." That judgment offended the group, until they 'held the mirror.'

Usha: Lessons can be tough to learn; we need grace toward all.

Janet: Would you see God in a healer loyal to another religion?

Usha: Need I limit God? I recall the research of a young American woman with a Muslim female healer who uses storytelling to heal. Located in Hyderabad, Amma exchanges stories. She tells some and expects all patients to bring and tell theirs. She prays with patients, recites verses known for healing power from the Qur'an, and uses Arabic script and a scheme of numbers to diagnose and explain treatments. Do I need to doubt if Allah invades those stories?

<u>Seven</u>: *Indian Christians value their indigenous heritage.* Christian converts were often told to denounce features from their religious past. Some denial and confusion followed. Yet, religions have always borrowed. For example, a classic verse from ancient Shaivite (Hindu) writing states: "God is love, and who so loveth not, the same knoweth not God."

Janet: You mean that isn't just a Christian concept?

Usha: Will we value the universal in Truth? Today, Indian Christian voices plead for understanding. For example, V. C. Chakkarai: "The religious genius of India must form the background of Indian Christianity."

Janet: Such as?

Usha: Believing with Wesley Ariarajah that: "God has always been present, active in a saving way, in Asia." Or Aruna Gnanadason who believes that radical spirituality demands "indigenization of the church's music and liturgy and patterns of ministry." Some Christians wish to ritually include the Hindu lamp—symbol of the presence of God—in their worship settings. Rather than endorse alien cultural expression with some hymns, Satish Gyan encourages worship in India to include chants or *bhajans* and *kirtans* led by a Cantor. He welcomes the use of bells; *prasad* ('eucharist') for all; offerings of fruits, flowers, and cash; plus praising God through *bhakti* (deep devotion).

Janet: Sounds like Wisdom, but . . . I'll ponder points of your conviction when back home. Could I hear the rest of your list tomorrow? I see that my driver just arrived.

Usha: Of course. See you at 9:30. I must go write chapter headings for a new manuscript.

Janet: *Bahut-hi-dhanyawad*!

Usha: And thanks to you too.

Reflection (Christian Speaker)

God of many Faces, Forms, Names, and Nuances,
      embolden us,
      and free us to free others to know You in your breadth.
God of every Tribe and Nation,
      awaken us,
      and broaden our world to include underprivileged before kings.
God of all people of diverse Faiths,
      surprise us,
      and reassure Muslim, Hindu, or Sikh neighbors to trust us.
God of Heaven and Earth,
      expand us,
      and curb our neglect of sky or pollution of land.
God of Risk and Reconciliation,
      engage us,
      and walk with us to confront wrong or negotiate peace.
God of Debate and Dialogue,
      alert us,
      and prod us toward openness to Truth, less bent on being right.
In God we mutually trust.   [Add verses to this prayer, as you like.]

2

Looking Back to See Ahead:

"... to arrive where we started"

This exchange engages two Indian Protestants; a woman teacher (Ms. Lila) and a middle school student (Kamal) have met regularly for two years. They could be called guru *and* sishya. *Thomas Thangaraj explains the* guru's *role within Hinduism as a spiritually mature person who, functioning on God's behalf, removes the* sishya's *(also called* chala) *ignorance. Embodying God's grace and Truth, the* guru *teaches religious knowledge and initiates the disciple into release/liberation/salvation (from rebirth). In a related way Christians understand Jesus as providing salvation or wholeness for the community of loved disciples who then carry on the task of proclaiming God's Way or kin-dom. The following adaptation of the Hindu* guru-sishya *partnership reveals a young Indian mentee's respect for a religious mentor and the mentor's intent to prod the learner toward further Truth.*

Kamal: We're about to begin our third year of meeting. I wonder what theme you have chosen for us to think about today. I like the way you've guided me so far. I only hope that what I learn makes your time spent teaching me worthwhile for you.

Ms. Lila: Have no fear. Your eagerness and perception and questions prod me. I also learn from you.

Kamal: Building on your insight. I'll be indebted for years to come.

Ms. Lila: Let's take a slightly different approach today. We usually focus on a theme, but today let's explore history—history of a theme—of multifaith attitudes among Protestants.

Kamal: Okay. Just how do adults relate when some of their religious views differ a lot?

Ms. Lila: To exchange beliefs requires insight and skill. But that's not all. Often people from *within* the same religion have different views about *how* and *why* to interact with people of another faith.

Kamal: Say more.

Ms. Lila: I'll introduce one book—Wesley Ariarajah's, *Hindus and Christians: A Century of Protestant Ecumenical Thought*. This author brings together Christian views toward Hinduism.

Kamal: Who is he, and why do you value his account of history?

Ms. Lila: Ariarajah is a theologian from Sri Lanka, a Methodist. At one time a leader with the World Council of Churches office on multi-religions and dialogue, he now teaches in a U.S. seminary.

Kamal: From South Asia, he must know lots of people of other faiths.

Ms. Lila: In fact, he thinks that western theology could benefit from Asian spirituality. So, we look at history, informed by a trustworthy person. Remember, the Buddhist religion is prominent in Sri Lanka. Here, seventy-five percent of the people are Hindu. But principles of relating across faiths overlap, whatever the prime loyalty. Are you ready for a quick look at twentieth century ecumenical views of multifaiths?

Kamal: It might have lots of dates, but I'm ready. But first, why did you use the term ecumenical?

Ms. Lila: Good question; don't hesitate to ask. Ecumenical more often refers to exchange or relationships *within* the Christian faith. It might engage Roman Catholics with Protestants, or different Protestant groups, or Orthodox Christians with either of those types. The words multifaith or interreligious then describe exchange among two or more religions. At times ecumenical refers more loosely to either intra-faith or inter-faith, but we'll use it to refer to Christians groups.

Kamal: So, Ariarajah wrote about a century of meetings between Christians?

Ms. Lila: The first World Missionary Conference was held in Edinburgh in 1910.

Kamal: Edinburgh, Scotland?

Ms. Lila: Right. Twelve hundred delegates from mission agencies and young churches met for this landmark event. Planners like John Mott hoped that the group would form a plan of action and set priorities.

Kamal: Were the delegates from all over the world?

Ms. Lila: Most came from the U.S. or Europe, only a few from Asia. Questionnaires had been completed by select missionaries and mission staff people scattered over the world; questions focused on one of eight Commission themes. Commission IV's fine report centered on Christian encounters with other religious traditions. From Asia, Hinduism received good attention with less given to Islam and Animist, Chinese, and Japanese religions.

Kamal: Any names that I should know from that Commission?

Ms. Lila: Perhaps two friends from Scotland: Rev. Cairns who wrote the report that summarized 185 diverse replies, and a professor Hogg from Madras Christian College who sent in sixty pages of response to the ten major questions. The report observed that Christian responses then compared to the early New Testament church as it met Greek and Roman cultures. Some thinkers endorsed and others questioned a book from near that time by a Mr. Farquhar, called *The Crown of Hinduism*.

Kamal: What did he mean by crown?

Ms. Lila: Farquhar believed that Jesus the Savior fulfilled the key longings and ambitions of Hindus. Professor Hogg objected to such a 'ladder' or evolution view—one lower religion beside a higher one. Knowing that Hindus long for *moksha* or release from a cycle of rebirth, he felt that a Christian offer of fulfillment (saving) didn't respond to the basic need felt by Hindus. Another idea addressed was whether having numerous religions was a good thing—in itself. Might plurality have been part of God's plan all along?

Kamal: If God thought that options were good, why do conflicts occur so often between religions?

Ms. Lila: Keep that question in mind. Ariarajah urges Christians to be both faithful to the Gospel and open to the Hindu system that seems deep and true for its followers. For them, 'being saved' means to be freed from this world and to gain unity with the Ultimate.

Kamal: Why question a Hindu's sincere desire to unite with God, even if I find Jesus' teachings about God most helpful?

Ms. Lila: That's worth pondering too. A second ecumenical missionary conference was held at Jerusalem in 1928 and a third here in south India, at Tambaram in 1938. At Jerusalem, difference grew about "spiritual values" of other faiths alongside claims that Christian faith "transcended them."

Kamal: Some presumed that Christianity is clearly better.

Ms. Lila: We might ask: Were they fair to other faiths' values? Was the Muslim sense of God's majesty through reverent worship truly valued? Or, without Buddhists present, was that religion's deep meaning of suffering or its search for emptiness introduced fairly? Or did people who knew few Hindus perceive their desire to be absorbed into God?

Kamal: On what did discussion center at the meeting in Tambaram?

Ms. Lila: A Dutch missionary in Muslim Java, Hendrik Kraemer, had written a book for all to study in advance: *The Christian Message in a Non-Christian World*. It stressed how biblical faith differs from other forms of faith; he described other religions as mere human thought and practice.

Kamal: How did people receive that judgment?

Ms. Lila: Some supported a unique depth for Christianity, while others had reason to dissent. The closing report noted that "Christians are not agreed."

Kamal: Did Christians question their own weaknesses?

Ms. Lila: You raise tough points, like to look inward or back at our own experience. You remind me of a poem by T. S. Eliot: "Little Gidding":

> We shall not cease from exploration,
> and the end of all our exploring
> will be to arrive where we started
> and know the place for the first time.[1]

Have you a quick response? What did you hear? Perhaps I should recite it again, before you reply.

Kamal: I like it. First of all, it supports the idea of exploring, of asking and discovering as you and I do together. It also suggests that our exploring will end. But in the end, exploring brings a person back to beginnings. Perhaps that means back to basics? Or does it mean that exploring just endlessly goes around in circles? I hope not. . . . What intrigues me—in addition to respect for new insight and earlier knowledge—is the idea of knowing for the "first time." That defines discovery, I suppose.

Ms. Lila: A thoughtful response.

Kamal: Thanks. Do I presume that Eliot's verse relates directly to interreligious exploring?

Ms. Lila: That's for you to discover. Let his ideas surface in your mind and comment in your own way, later, about how it connects with history. Further missionary meetings raised further questions.

[Just then a young child on a bike rang the doorbell. "Ma, could you come? My older sister is on fire! I dropped by to visit her. Perhaps her sari got too close . . . or . . . she mumbled the word "dowry." Oh, Ma, I hate to interrupt, but . . . get your bike! Come!"]

Ms. Lila: Of course. I'm on my way. I'll give this copy of Eliot's verse to Kamal to think about this week. Oh, and take a copy of these pages about the Ecumenical Conferences; we'll discuss your questions from today too. Stay as long as you like; here's a pencil and paper to jot down some reflections.

After thinking about the frantic child for a bit, Kamal returned to Eliot's lines. Looking off into a distant, barren field, Kamal wrote some random thoughts and questions.

1. How ironic, those first two lines—"not cease" and "end." They contradict each other, at least on the surface. Does Truth exist more in the one term than the other one?

2. What does "to explore" mean, related to faith—when I explore my faith alongside my neighbor's?

3. Eliot's lines begin with <u>we</u>. Whom do I trust and why? With whom do

I share deep questions?

4.   What about the circling idea—to "arrive where we start"? Is the circling just endless repetition? How does this relate to Hindu *karma* (cause and effect, toward or away from a spiritual goal) or *samsara* (the ceaseless round of birth and death)?

5.   What do I most question about interreligious exchange? Why? Will questions be endless, or pointless? Are some answers 'better' than others? How do we decide? With people of which faith other than mine do I wish to explore?

6.   "Know the place"—what place? Did I begin asking or probing from a place? Can it be defined? How do I describe it?

7.   And what does "to arrive" mean? Do we arrive once or many times? Does arrival suggest ending? How does this relate to Buddhist' *nirvana?* Will I somehow "arrive" with God?

8.   "For the first time"—when was or is or will be the *first?* Is "first" only about sequence? Does it reflect the beginning or imply a time prior to "first," which occurs at the end, after arriving?

9.   Look at those verbs and verb forms—shall cease, exploration / exploring, will be, to arrive, started, know. Action fills the lines, and our lives. And look at the hints of rest: cease, end, arrive. To rest or contemplate is tied to action; together they reflect wholeness.

With those notes in hand, Kamal left.

Endnote:

[1] T. S. Eliot. *Collected Poems*. NY: Harcourt, Brace & World, 1963, 208.

3

"To know one [religion] is to know none." Max Müller

Religious Exchange: Personal and Others'

First, a word about this essay title's author: (Friedrich) Max Müller (1823-1900), the source of the quote, is called the founder of the study of comparative religion. A German, he edited the 50-volume *Sacred Books of the East*. He translated essential writings of seven non-Christian religions. No wonder he wrote "He who knows one, knows none." But, for many Christians "To know one is to know all."[1] Traditions and attitudes do affect interreligious knowledge and respect.

Until my early twenties, I lived a protected life in rural Iowa. My parents instilled respect for others. To respect need not mean to fully accept, as with faith claims. Secondary and college years enhanced faith, both in church school settings. That husband John and I taught at Woodstock School in India for three years shortly after marriage broadened our worldview. There, we worked with ecumenical, Christian colleagues; traveled third class trains; and learned to know Hindus, Muslims, and Sikhs. Visits to their places of worship, conversations, and resources about religion energized me. Learning moved beyond intrigue, in part through seven shorter return assignments in India. The multifaith, sacred spirit of India both beckons me and enriches how I practice Christian being. More than once, a friend has said: "You must have been a Hindu in a previous life." Not believing in re-incarnation, I honor her thought that connects with her holy journey.

Living in Goshen, I know God better through friendships with Asian college students and locals whose religious ties differ from mine. Students of diverse faiths helped me present a chapel focused on saints— of east and west. From the scent of candle and incense, I knew when a guest performed puja before coming to the breakfast table. I received a year's grant to work with local ecumenical events and writing projects.

When visiting the gurdwara (place of worship) in nearby Mishawaka with Sikh friends, the spirit of awe for their holy text ever-shapes my delving into scripture, my inner being. Ways to be religious together exist when not confined to One Way.

Feminist thought and academic work also shape my perspective. Feminist theology and biblical Wisdom engage my study as they counter patriarchal patterns. The study of scripture instills in me respect for what we fail to fully know. God's Reign or order, Kin-dom or Real-ness, while present, is not yet fully achieved. Jesus' life best informs me about the Divine. Yet, Jesus is not 'fullness' or 'final.' Open to "more to come," a person ever-engages with Mystery. Feminism values such breadth; it respects women's personal experience as well as difference. Caucasian feminists do not speak for distinct *womanist* (African American) or *mujerista* (Hispanic) views. With new vision and methods, we interpret history and observe location.

I enjoy study and research. My Doctor of Ministry degree[2] focused on interreligious dialogue. Chris Kaiser advised my disciplined work on quite diverse themes. During the past fifteen years, I have learned the most about "being religious interreligiously"[3] from Paul Knitter. Inspired to credit multifaiths further, I hope in the future to explore the Power or divine Being that pervades multi-religions. *Shekshakshen* is what I call this Energy. *Shek* stems from Jewish Shekinah, *shak* from *shakti* in Hindu thought, and *shen* from Tao insight into Divine compassion or "being at rest." With no monopoly on divine Spirit, though vital to Trinity, Christians often overlook the universal movement, sound, force or Wisdom that guides the cosmos and living faiths. Being alert to *Shekshakshen* might help us claim such breadth. Might "to know only one is to know none" apply also to Spirit vision?

Faith commitment combined with openness to 'otherness' enriches a person. But, insider and outsider reality always exist, even when an outsider may know more about another's faith than an insider. When not allowed inside the holiest sanctum of a Hindu temple, I knew that I was an 'outsider.' When a Malaysian shopkeeper refused to sell me a phrase from the Qur'an in calligraphy, she judged my 'outsider' status to preclude my due honor toward a phrase most sacred for Muslims. Some churches refuse the Lord's Supper elements to those not baptized. Yet, commitment and openness ever intersect.

Christians are challenged: to be as loyal to God in Christ as we are open to faiths that claim the Divine in other worthy ways. To boast "My God is bigger than your God!" distorts God. Shifting from superior attitudes is crucial if we wish to be honest, live together, dialogue, or move toward peace, Paul Knitter says.[4] To abandon claims of being superior need not diminish commitment. To avoid exclusive views need not mean less faith in Christ. To worship with Sikh friends in a gurdwara broadens my view of what is holy. Interreligious exchange can expand knowledge of a partner's religion "from within." Open to learn how Parsis or Hindus honor fire or light can enhance my perception of Jesus' radiating beams of truth. If not open to the universal symbol of light through varied forms, does my vision grow dim?

Experience has limits. I cannot know whether Jesus is the only or 'best' or final savior, not having met all whom God might choose to so endow. Not intent to limit followers, Jesus saves, empowers, or helps me to better know the Ultimate, to move deeper into relating with diverse others. With work enough required to follow Jesus' way of meeting human need, I have no desire to boast of Jesus as superior. I value John Cobb's idea that being faithful to Christ prompts me to look for truth wherever it might be, then integrate it. Because Christ is center for Christians, no boundaries need exist.[5] Expectant, we believe that others have truth that we need.

Stories teach. C. S. Song from Taiwan is noted for Story Theology.[6] In "The Wild Goose Lake," Sea Girl longs for water from the lake to be released to the canals of her drought-hit village. How will she get the golden key needed to open the stone gate? With the stone gate a metaphor for religious faith, the challenge becomes: How will hearts of adherents of diverse religions open up to the depth and riches of each other? Rather than hold God captive—through our presumed right teachings or worship—we discover God beyond our valued limits.

Noah's story of the flood contains God's covenant with all people and creation. Ten generations later God covenanted with Abraham and Sarah. Tension followed. Although caring for *all* nations, God chose Israel to help convey divine care. Election—not for privilege—did not displace other nations. Recall Abraham's encounter from his tent at Mamre. Three strangers appeared on the horizon. Strangers could kill. But Abraham invited them to his tent, and Sarah prepared food for the unknown trio. The story explains that without fanfare, one of the three strangers proved to be Sarah and Abraham's God. Truly, people of other religions can shock us into meeting God.

The call to learn from others does not say that all religions are true, nor that distinct conviction must converge into one religion. But, valuing difference can move toward compassion. Rumi, the great Muslim Sufi, says that the Qur'an's reason for God's having created difference is "so that they can learn to know and compete with each other toward good works." Rather than fear difference, we admit limits to *our* religion and expect wisdom from *other* groups to enrich *ours*.

Alex Kronemer offers another story. During the Middle Ages, a pope and rabbi agreed to have a silent debate about whether Jews needed to leave Rome. If the rabbi won, they could stay. The Pope acted first, raising three fingers; the rabbi raised one. The Pope then gestured over his head; in turn, the Rabbi pointed to the ground. After that pair of actions, the Pope brought wine and bread, so the Rabbi showed an apple. Each then explained the exchange.

After the Pope raised three fingers, referring to the Trinity, he presumed that the Rabbi's one finger noted the one God that they share. After the Pope portrayed God's sitting in majesty in heaven, he thought that the Rabbi's pointing to the ground showed God on earth watching and judging. With the Pope's use of wine and bread to signify Redemption, he understood the Rabbi's apple to remind them both of human sin in creation.

From the Rabbi's perspective, the Pope must have raised three fingers to indicate that the Jews must leave in three days' time, to which the Rabbi replied with one finger: not one Jew would leave. So angered, the Rabbi reported, the Pope swept his hand over his head declaring: Jews must go. Seeing that, the Rabbi pointed to the ground: the Jews would stay right there. When the Pope signaled his desire to have lunch—wine and bread—the Rabbi took out his apple.[7] Their different meanings illustrate how people misjudge each other's sacred symbols and concepts. When a Jewish rabbi, Buddhist nun, or Muslim imam addresses Christians, they reveal their integrity. They also risk not being understood.

This study explores how people of faith receive and absorb diverse faiths while being committed to one. Difference can be so rich. At Hindu temples in India, I observed without trying to intrude. Rather than judge what I failed to understand, I pondered: Why did they tap a bell on arrival or 'baptize' an image with milk or honor holy men clad in ashes and a *dhoti*? I left my shoes at the entrance, moved my hand through a sacred flame of welcome, ate a portion of blessed *prasad*, and talked with the One whom I call God or Mystery. How changed was my faith, on returning to Christian worship?

Not less loyal, I felt that my faith had grown. I wonder why we fear worship alongside a neighbor or stranger whose rituals differ. Do we aspire to limit God to hearing one faith, ours? My goal is not *syncretism* (compromise made by combining beliefs from two religions) or *synthesis* (parts combined to make a whole). Rather, this essay reflects *symbiosis* where people with two different views teach each other important features of their faith as they live or work together for mutual good.[8] Conversion occurs in personal commitment, as each changes because open to values in another.

Jeannine Hill Fletcher refers to the strength of hybrid (or porous) religious identity. Hybrid ties connect sacred distinctions and actions with the result that, "There is no 'Christian identity,' only 'Christian identities.'"[9] Sikhs who call the space sacred where their text lies open or Muslims known for discipline in reciting lengthy Qur'an segments might alert Christians to greater reverence for the First and Second Testaments. Hindus who find awe in *Aum* or Vac (spoken word) or Divine energy in sacred dance steps or a presiding power in the innermost heart of a temple can convey to Christians a deeper sense of the holy. As we value other religions, holding as sacred what marks each uniquely, we learn more of Divine Mystery.

In that, I move toward more wholeness (salvation). Hearing a Hindu friend express intent to pray for me or a given circumstance, I know that Durga may be solicited or Amma may hear the details. Power beyond the routine—Sophia/*shakti*—will engage time or place between us. My friend in turn may absorb a measure of trust in the Divine as I grace a group meal. Together, we honor the sacred in the other. She knows something of my conviction that Jesus' life best informs me of the Real. And I trust her to learn truth from her sacred stories. We move toward unity because we each know enough about the other to trust the One, Ultimate God.

Christians and Buddhists might enrich each other too. A former may probe how attached to things she is and decide to change. She might examine the Fourfold Truths and ponder anew her neighbor's view of suffering. A Buddhist might show devotion to Jesus in addition to Buddha, even though he engages more fully in Buddhist teaching and practice. Paul Knitter's book titled *Without Buddha I Could not Be a Christian* illustrates how a person loyal to one religion "passes over" to another to learn how and why others practice or believe as they do and then "passes back" to integrate and make more effective personal understanding and Truth.

What is Religion?

As we highlight Max Müller's axiom: "To know one [religion] is to know none," we might briefly ask: What then is Religion? Just what is that which we might better not know in the singular? How does the idea that Christianity alone is less than adequate settle? How crucial to wholeness in Jesus the Christ is insight from Muhammed or the *Guru Granth Sahib* or Hindu mystics? From experience, theologian K. P. Aleaz of Kolkata says that Christians need Hindus to help us understand Jesus. For example, Hindu views on renunciation may help explain Jesus' call to give up the self. Others may teach us about life or death.

What does *religion* mean? Claude Geffre suggests that each religious tradition mediates in unique ways the Absolute.[10] Paul Tillich said that "Religion is the soul of culture."[11] While Karl Barth understood religion as human effort to attain salvation, John Cobb questions if there is such a thing as religion.[12] Gordon Kaufman notes that, "Every religious tradition implicitly invokes a human or humane criterion to justify its existence and its claims."[13] Looking at a specific, all religions respond to suffering, though in different ways, Paul Knitter observes.[14]

Sri Lankan Aloysius Pieris notes three levels of religion:
1. Its core experience such as the Jesus story or Buddha's enlightenment;
2. Collective memory, or medium used like story, liturgy, or leadership; and
3. Interpretation—how followers through time explain the core event.

Although religions differ, that fact need not cause conflict. Rather than dispute over difference of doctrine, followers of one faith might ask those loyal to another, How do you witness to truth within or discern Divine will for a situation? As Buddha awakened into enlightenment, Jesus showed love through the cross. Neither channel is superior; both lead to what Christians call salvation. Both enable the "Unspoken Speaker" or Spirit.[15]

The Divine: Mystery/Ultimate/Allah/Jesus—A Glimpse

On first thinking about including a section on Divinity in this essay, I knew the problem of selection. Book titles reveal contrasts: *A History of God* next to *God at 2000* or *She Who Changes* alongside *No god but God*. British writer Karen Armstrong finds agreement about the Ultimate among the great religions. While many people call what transcends us *God*, others use names like Nirvana, Brahman, or Allah, the Arabic word for God. Buddhists yearn for profound emptiness—not being attached to anything—to give life meaning and avoid suffering. For Armstrong, the study of God is something like writing poetry. It attempts to express what cannot fully be expressed. Doing theology, we search into our inner being; we *struggle* (a basic meaning of *jihad*) to find more depth.

Situations might limit engagement. To say that religions are the same loses part of "God's overabundant, incomprehensible mystery," Hill Fletcher suggests.[16] Perceiving religions as too diverse to intersect overlooks their common ground. Muslims staunchly defend God's Oneness and as firmly resist any portrayal of that One. Painted figures filled space in a Buddhist temple ceiling in Sri Lanka. They likely told stories, yet adherents probe Emptiness. I saw the tree in Bodh Gaya (India) under which the Buddha received enlightenment. It shelters holy ground. Caves at Ajunta contain centuries of Buddhist history. Buddhist temples in the States add more visuals for one who enters.

The lens or imagination through which people meet the Divine varies. Christians evoke God's mystery through Trinity, far from simple. Calling the Hebrew name Yahweh ("I AM") too sacred to utter, Jews use an alternate, Greek term—*Adonai*—when reading texts where it appears. While Muslims do not image God in any form, Hindus speak of many gods but mean the same Ultimate One. And Buddhists speak of a "far shore—a reality that we cannot grasp but may awaken to."

Harvard Professor Diana Eck sees objects, names, and images as the lens for meeting the Ultimate.[17] For seven years, she studied religions in India. Both mono and polytheistic strands appear in ancient Hindu tradition; oneness and manyness are not true opposites. Whereas some westerners get 'lost' seeing the array of god and goddess forms, Eck perceives the wisdom inherent. "If something is important, it is important enough to be repeated, duplicated, and seen from many angles."[18] The composite of gods and their descents (*avatars*), multiple paths of salvation (*margas*), systems of thought, scriptures and lore galore—called Hinduism—is rich. In India, life is plural: "diversity unites, rather than divides." The unity of India, a complex whole upon which oneness is based, "is not unity or sameness, but interrelatedness and diversity," Eck says.[19]

Consciousness for the Hindu reveals a person's ability to hold two viewpoints at once. Seeing many god forms, there is One. A well-known quote from the *Rig Veda* states "Truth is One; the wise call it by many names." God's manyness refers to the language used to speak of the Divine. Adherents construct God-language but never exhaust or grasp the Divine.[20] Religious traditions deal with Word (Vac) and deity in diverse ways.

Mystery remains central to thought about deity. Buddhists use an analogy—"a finger pointing to the moon, never the moon itself." Hindus state "neti, neti"—not this, not that—to suggest that there is always more to thought or speech about the Ultimate. Those who talk of Tao fail to know of what they speak: "A way that can be walked is not The Way; a name that can be named is not The Name."[21] Christians who value Holy Mystery do not claim their revelation as final or full. They glean more of Mystery through dialogue with the words, symbols, and rituals of people loyal to other religions.

Jesus, who chose human limits, has for some followers become more central than his message. Yes, Jesus is the one whom Christians confess, through whom they best know God's truth. But Christians who join people of other living faiths to address and remove human or earth suffering look anew at Jesus. Attending to what he preached—living his example of meeting human and kin-dom needs—they know his wish to be One with people rather than King over them. Not intent to form a church or be revered, Jesus called people to practice Yahweh's challenge: "do justice, love kindness, and walk humbly with God."[22] Not confined to building or dogma, Jesus promoted God's new Order of Peace. Jesus the Jewish Prophet proclaimed God's universal love, making starkly clear a preference for those who suffer most.[23]

Second Testament scriptures show Jesus' learning from or complementing those who choose not to follow the Way.

- More than once Jesus commended Samaritans, non-Jews. A Samaritan healed from leprosy alone expressed thanks. A *Good* Samaritan shamed Jewish religious leaders who avoided a victim that he helped. A Samaritan woman drawing water revealed deep theology; she perceived Jesus' Truth and boldly offered hers.
- A foreign, nameless woman called Jewish Jesus to change, to broaden his mission. "Not arrogant or ignorant, she, with courage, referred to broken bread (crumbs), as a way to get through to [him]. Outwitting [his] alibi, she set the story straight."[24]

Central to Divine order is love for the neighbor. "To love God is to do justice," Jeremiah prophesied (22:16). Muhammad expressed much the same for love of Allah. And Buddha warned that those who fail to produce compassion (*karuna*), lack wisdom (*prajna*). Through parables, loving deeds, and deep devotion to God's Kin-dom, or inclusive Way with folk, Jesus prompts faith. But to insist that his way "is the best" can keep us from "doing our best," in "the hard work of loving our neighbor and reshaping our world," Paul Knitter cautions.[25] The faithful believer is open to another's story, another's possible 'Savior' figure. Yet, to credit other saviors in no way doubts that Jesus is *truly* Savior.

The Spirit enables people through universal messages, including words made sacred through Buddha, Muhammad, or the Upanishads. Because Jesus *truly* reveals God does not prove that he alone reveals God. We pursue insight from religions—as Max Müller nudged. Christians walk Jesus' Way alongside travelers who follow other Ways. We "celebrate the power of the Christ-event, not denigrate other events."[26]

Religious Plurality

Religious pluralism suggests liberty, the value of dissent, and positive relationships among faith groups. Early Muslims thought that prior religions had been distorted. For them, Islam became "the full revelation and therefore the norm of all religion."[27] A mission agency took an orientation group of new appointees to a mosque. In the process, the imam and devoted speakers were most adamant that *only* Islam could be called a true faith, that Allah, the One, *alone* is to be worshipped. The appointees gained a perspective about 'only language' that shaped their future encounters. Knitter challenges traditional believers to continue to proclaim what they know to be true and good but without saying that it is the only or last or full word about truth and goodness.[28]

Buddhist-Christian exchange between Rita Gross and Rosemary Radford Ruether appears in *Religious Feminism and the Future of the Planet.*[29] After each tells her life story, each discusses what is most troubling and most liberating about her tradition. The other responds to each section. Then they discuss what inspires them most from the other's tradition. Their exchange led Ruether to greater balance between activist engagement and inner renewal and Gross to new attention to human need along with her disciplined breathing or Buddhist *mindfulness.*

Robert Wuthnow[30] calls being mindful toward what is diverse "reflective pluralism." Knowing oneself is central, alongside attention to others. I 'hear' Raimondo Panikkar's reminder: "To answer the question 'Who am I?' I must ask the question 'Who are you?'"[31] Wuthnow names distinct *traits* of people who practice reflective pluralism.

- "They care about specific issues, teachings, or practices," and what they imply.
- They identify themselves as inquirers. They like to delve into truth claims or features of human nature among religions.
- They examine with care what having a "point of view" means. Culture shapes viewpoint; it needs to be tested and compared.
- They try to soften objections to pluralism by exploring reasons for resistance.
- They stress respect, knowing that beliefs link with identity.
- "They exhibit principled willingness to compromise," to adjust a point in order to work better together.[32]

Pluralists affirm that each religion contains distinct Wisdom. Rita Gross asks how best to live with difference. She asks how people treat each other. Does religion prompt less aggression and more empathy or justice? She sees how exclusive truth-claims can counter compassion. Rather than debate about one savior or a final revelation or correct ways to ponder emptiness, why not focus on what prompts effective living together among religions? People who differ need not converge in thought or practice, but move from ignorance to wisdom. Buddhist insight into how being attached causes suffering applies to viewpoint or doctrine, not only objects, she believes.[33]

Victoria Lee Erickson relates a story from a village in a beautiful mountain area of South Asia.[34] Two days early, arriving at night during a rain storm, and hungry, her group of Christian friends caught a Christian village off-guard. It had no cooked food. After the host prayed, they too prayed, sang, and shared stories in the hut—forgetting somewhat their stomachs. Hearing noise, the host opened the door a crack. A horse appeared; the rider handed the host a bucket and left. Large, blue-shelled crabs dispelled hunger. A near-by village leader, on seeing the visitors and knowing that the Christians were without food, had gone fishing with his Muslim neighbors on their behalf. Villagers of these two religions read their holy books together, share wells and a school, and protect each other. Also, they pray together respecting their diverse voices.

One clear aspect of religious pluralism is scripture. A few details reflect flavor.

- The *Rig Veda*, just one of four Hindu books of revelation, includes over a thousand hymns. The *Mahabharata* epic is much longer than the Bible—whereas one writer says four times as long, another reports six times, and another fifteen!
- Muslims in all times and places view the Qur'an as the direct, recited word of Allah, expressed to the Prophet through Angel Gabriel. People had misunderstood previous revelations; this was the final Divine one.[35] Verse 5:48 states:
  To each of you have we prescribed the law's open way. If [Allah] had so willed, He [sic] would have made you a single people, but [Allah's] plan is to test you in what He [sic] hath given you; so strive as in a race in all virtues. The goal of you all is to [Allah].[36]
- The Buddhist Pali canon contains the *Tripitaka* (meaning three baskets). One basket contains discipline for monks and nuns. Another, called the *Dhammapada*, records Buddha's life and teachings. Discourses include the Buddha's first sermon, Four Noble Truths and the Eight-fold Path. The third basket teaches about interpreting Dharma (Truth).[37] The Buddha nudged monks to see teachings as a raft. Not meant for clinging to, the raft helps one 'cross over' to the other shore.

As stated, I value worship in the gurdwara, with Sikh friends. Adherents bow before their scripture, the *Guru Granth Sahib*, which presides over worship. God revealed the Word enshrined in the Holy Book through a Guru. Giving honor and dignity to the open text, a man, woman, or youth near-constantly waves a fan (*chauri*) over it. The *kathakar* recites and interprets verses of a text opened at random, thought to be the Guru's vak (Word) for that occasion. Sikhs believe that their scripture embodies the eternal Guru. An open attitude allows them to understand other traditions, to differ on some beliefs.[38]

Judaism and Christianity

We turn now to one religion, known to western Christians as their 'cousin.' Asians, being more linked to Hinduism or Buddhism than Judaism, might perceive Christianity as 'Gentile.' Two questions emerge: How might Christians address the falsehood that Christianity supersedes Judaism? And, how does concern for Judaism as a historic religion frame Christian views of Israel as a nation today? Here, reference to Judaism and Israel reflect their history, not present actions.

Christianity depends on Judaism—Jesus was Jewish. His foremost purpose—to reform Jewish life—far outweighed any intent to start an alternative religion. Like major and minor Jewish prophets before him, he wished the people to renew their bond with Yahweh—being faithful to the covenants.

Professor at Union Seminary in New York Mary Boys states, "Nothing in Jesus' teaching compelled a break with Judaism." Despite the ferment he caused, his Renewal Movement, his teaching and life, could have been absorbed within Judaism.[39] Theologian John Howard Yoder agreed: "the schism did not have to be." Neither religion withdrew from or was ejected by the other; the circles of church and Jewry overlapped. Jesus' Sermon on the Mount was not other than Jewish.[40]

Into the second century and beyond, most of Jesus' followers were Jews. Many continued to attend synagogues. John Cobb suggests that Jews and Renewal Movement folk perceived each other as heretics. Each faulted the other for misreading their common scriptures.[41] Those later called Christian came to negate Judaism. Because some Jews rejected Jesus, those who followed him came to usurp Israel's gift of "saving covenant with God." In that, Christians lost the basic idea that Divine covenants are eternal. The Christian claim to supersede Judaism led to false salvation history. It led Christians to see Jesus as against the Law, the Temple, and the people Israel. It led to freedom to hate Jews.

But, Judaism remains chosen to tell others about God's inclusive Kin-dom. "Judaism continues to function as a way of salvation, at least for Jews," Peter Phan notes.[42] Jews long for a coming Messiah and Christians look toward a Second Coming. I wonder if we might partner together in looking, if they approve. We first need to repent of past deeds—racist anti-Semitism, repeated pogroms, and the Shoah (whirlwind/Holocaust). And, non-Jews will expect to denounce current harm that Jews inflict, for example, on Palestinians.

Even works of art convey perceptions. An allegory of sculptures titled "Ecclesia" and "Synagoga" (church and synagogue) appear at the Strasbourg Cathedral in France. A "triumphant Ecclesia stands erect next to a bowed, blindfolded figure of the defeated yet dignified Synagoga." Proud church gazes over the other, the woman "conquered, with her crown fallen, staff broken, and Torah dropping to the ground."[43] Here is supersession set in stone. For Mary Boys' book *Has God Only One Blessing?*, she had an artist create a new "posture" for the two. She believes that the relation between the two will be righted when the church repents of its distortions of Judaism, when Ecclesia sees

Synagoga as her "partner in waiting for the full redemption of the world," Boys concludes.[44]

How certain Second Testament texts reflect on Jews also matters. Mary Boys discusses content from Matthew 23 and John 9 (1-41). The former denounces Pharisees and the latter asks the question about a man born blind, "Rabbi, who sinned, this man or his parents?" Perhaps if we were to read these in the presence of Jewish people, we might 'see' how texts can scorn others. A text prompts Christians to fault Jews for missing God's revelation, while they ignore their pious hypocrisy. Rabbi Hillel summed up Jewish teaching while standing on one leg: "Do not do unto others as you would not have done unto you. That is the torah. The rest is commentary. Go and learn it."

Many Christians have relied on a text translated from John—14:6. It says that Jesus is the Way, Truth, and Life. The second phrase literally judges that no one has access to God except through Jesus.

The context: Judaism and Christianity were deeply at odds. Here appears offence *par excellence*.

The setting: Discourse following the Last Supper. Jesus promises to leave, not taking the Twelve with him. Thomas admits that he does not know the way that Jesus will go, to reach God.

The resolution: Not boasting, Jesus says to follow the way that he's been showing—suffering love. Recall God's pattern of including others when thinking of a Way, or the Truth and Life of it.

The ongoing problem: If this text indeed reflects a later alteration, possibly never spoken by Jesus and counter to the core welcome of biblical theology, how will literal readers alter ingrained actions and attitudes? Why have Christians been so bent to use John 14:6 to exclude others from salvation? What would differ in our relating with other faiths if we claimed this text as *confession* of faith during hard times, not exclusion by narrow judgment?[45]

Theology(ies) **of Religion**(s)

Professor Veli-Matti Karkkainen of Fuller Seminary explains theology of religion.[46] Like Systematic, Liberation, or Feminist Theology, Theology of Religions is a separate field of study. It looks at *value and meaning* within religions. It explores how Christianity *relates* to other religions and what transpires when diverse religions live close together. Theology of religion (or the plural of both nouns) studies *relationships, around themes* like revelation, faith, or salvation. It explores *meaning* for personal, sacred experience through shared rituals, scriptures, history or convictions. It is known by a typology, to note shortly.

Third century, Bishop Cyprian's axiom—"outside the church, no salvation"—had major influence. For more than twelve centuries after

Constantine, Christians believed in only one true religion—its own—and only one savior—Jesus. That classical position *exclusivism,* formulated during the 15th century (Council of Florence), states: "No one remaining outside the Catholic Church, not just pagans, but also Jews or heretics or schismatics, can become partakers of eternal life."[47] Arrogant and likely based on limited exposure to others, that view has shaped Christian thought and action ever since. That view can be as hostile or skewed as false *jihadism.* Triumphal boasts like "God does not speak outside of Jesus"[48] express sin and defensiveness, not faith, notes John Cobb.[49] Dialogue has no chance with such dogma; only one [side] speaks; others must listen. That is monologue.

For Wesley Ariarajah, exclusion with its claim of being superior stems from a context of power. Such power reflects the fourth century legacy; Constantine could not cope with division, with many. Such power also prompted colonialists to insist that God relates in *only* one way. Such power promotes arrogance—"we are right and everyone else must be wrong." Ariarajah observes[50] that the church has yet to credit Jesus' gift of salvation without denying that "God may have many ways to bring people to their intended destiny." God may not wish for people of one religion to transfer to another, Ariarajah hints in Heim's book.

An alternative to the exclusivist stance, the idea of *inclusivism* emerged from the 16th century (Council of Trent). It credits non-Christians with moral actions and belief. More open toward people who do not claim Jesus as Savior, inclusivists still require others to convert to faith in him before death. Christians have tended to shape salvation history around Christ alone.[51] Other adherents are deficient except where they comply with Christianity.[52] After Vatican II, 1962-65, the Roman Church called this model its 'official' one.[53]

Asian theologians see such a typology as western; they try to teach their counterparts. Shaped by daily encounters with other living faiths, many Asian Catholic leaders explain that "unique alone" or "better than" language counters empathy toward their cultures. Since talk about "Jesus as the one and only Savior" creates hostility, some Asians prefer to speak about Jesus as the "Teacher of Wisdom, the Healer, the Liberator, or Compassionate Friend of the Poor." Such titles commend qualities of Jesus' without denying that other religious figures are also special. Convinced that God *truly* calls us in Christ, Christians need not presume that our call is the *only* one that God offers to all people.[54] "To know one [religion] is to know none" comes to mind.

Pluralism, a third, more recent part of the standard typology sanctions multiple ways to know salvation. Early proponents were John Hick and Paul Knitter. Not all religions express the same thing. As Jesus' message of salvation reveals a "universal, active presence of God,"[55] so Buddhist' effort rids the self of desire—to attain nirvana, its holy goal.

Adherents of any religion reflect Divine will as they love the neighbor, work for justice, or bring meaning to life in unique ways.[56] K. P. Aleaz, from Kolkata, urges Christians to enrich their views of Jesus through insight from Muhammed or Krishna; all three reveal the Real. Mutual exchange enriches each. He calls for Pluralistic Inclusivism. He urges affirming faith experience in another while being humble, rather than boastful, of one's own conviction. Openness to relate transforms each one's move toward fuller truth and leads toward converging Wisdom, while holding to the distinct.[57]

Pluralism does not endorse relativism—that all religions are equally true. Pluralism credits religions which value Mystery, provide meaning, uphold solid ethics, and liberate diverse people. Jesus is the way, truth, and life for Christians; other names save or other truth from God may enhance other traditions.[58] Whereas evangelical Karkainen distorts pluralism, saying that it promises that "all will be saved," John Hick explains pluralism as "more than one way to be saved." John Cobb simply declares about pluralism: "all religions have validity."

Paul Knitter published *Introducing Theologies of Religions* in 2002. Intent to enhance study across cultures and religions, he offered alternative terms for the standard categories. He identifies models through the thought of key spokesmen, models that he re-names: *Replacement* / "Only one true religion," *Fulfillment* / "The One Fulfills the Many," and *Mutuality* / "Many True Religions Called to Dialogue." To these he adds a fourth titled *Acceptance* / "Many True Religions: So Be It."

Before 1960 when most Christians presumed that God did not engage other religions, Roman Catholics questioned Protestant and Orthodox truth—were their members sure of salvation? Some Evangelicals now resist interreligious dialogue and openness endorsed by Vatican II. Eric Sharpe faults some Catholics for not crediting distinct Protestant insight into Christ's fulfillment long before Vatican II. Rita Gross wonders why people cannot just receive and enhance religious diversity. Why not live together in peace rather than require the same teachings or debate which came first or is more relevant? "Why worry about whether or not [others] believe in Jesus Christ as the only savior, regard the Qur'an as the deity's final revelation to humanity, or meditate correctly on emptiness?"[59]

Paul Knitter's Mutuality model stresses God's universal love and presence in religions. It affirms difference and seeks common threads within faiths. It avoids absolute or final claims as well as relativism. ("That *many* religions are true does not mean that *all* are true.") Uniqueness is affirmed: "the unique truth of each religion is *really and universally* true, but not *solely and definitively* true."[60] Each tradition deserves honor.

For Shirley Guthrie, Christians with a *pluralist* view believe that Jesus is "the way, truth, and life" for them. With multiple paths to God, Jesus is one way, not the *only* way for people to know God. Knitter values John Cobb's dictum: "Christ is the Way that is open to other Ways. To follow Jesus is to be radically open to others."[61] Christians are saved through Jesus' name; other people of faith know other saving 'names,' other ways that give life meaning or answer their unique questions. Faith exists in *God*; believers credit God "at work saving in all" faithful groups.[62] The pluralist model expands ideas about God's Reign and terms like *truly*. With Knitter, I proclaim Jesus as a universal savior, not the world's only savior. While Christians confess that "Jesus *truly* embodies and expresses God's love," they avoid saying that he does so *solely* or *fully*. Not the whole of God, Jesus is wholly God. Other religious figures may also be wholly God.[63]

Wesley Ariarajah, a Sri Lankan who teaches at Drew Seminary, calls for a new review of theology of religions. Building on Wilfred Cantwell Smith's insight, Christians will see the limits of doctrines, creeds and theologies, all of which are 'human constructs.' Plurality of religions will be essential along with mutual respect for all religions. Further, religious language will be valued for what it is—*confessional* thought—rather than claiming literal interpretations of select texts as 'official.'[64]

> Krister Stendahl notes Harold Coward's insight: the Christian tendency toward exclusiveness is rooted in the fact that although Jesus preached [God's] kingdom, the church preached Jesus.[65] What results from those two messages is quite different, I believe. People of living faiths feel included in God's universal Kingdom. To emphasize the messenger Jesus alone—unique as his role is in God's redemptive work for Christians—can fail to faithfully convey Jesus' central message of God's inclusive Kingdom.[66]

Conclusion

With intent to know more than one religion, may we trust others' Truth, trust others' intent to be loyal and religious. The *how* of proceeding to know more than one religion is found in writers like Peter Phan and Paul Knitter who revise Max Mueller's insight into: "One must be religious interreligiously." Some guidelines to ponder:
- avoid superior language and attitudes;
- combine commitment or personal faith with genuine openness to the 'other';
- reorient certain biblical texts—how explained or lived out; pursue a better balance with Trinity;

- engage in dialogue – formal and informal – as intent to learn as to confess, to empower as be empowered;
- hold and express conviction with integrity and a lightness that invites the hearer to listen;
- be better informed of others – avoid ignorance that prompts arrogance;
- examine the concept of 'other'; expect and receive the other's strengths;
- encourage future generations to approach people of living faiths more wisely [than ours];
- call church agencies and education centers to re-vision, to be accountable to multifaiths;
- claim difference as a positive quality; own xenophobia (fear of difference);
- learn from other scriptures, prayers, meditation patterns, disciplines, and rituals;
- be committed to the journey, not content with brief encounters.

Endnotes:

[1] Israel Selvanayagam. "The Bible and Non-Christian Scriptures," *Epworth Review*, January 2002, 49.

[2] 1997, Western Theological Seminary, Holland, MI

[3] Retired from Xavier University, Professor Knitter mentored my one year, second DMin degree work (2004-05) at United Theological Seminary, Dayton, OH, a program titled "Spirituality, Sustainability and Inter-Religious Dialogue." Knitter now is Paul Tillich Professor of Theology, World Religions and Culture at Union Theological Seminary in New York City.

[4] Paul Knitter. "My God is Bigger than Your God!" *Studies in Interreligious Dialogue*, 17/1, 2007, 101-5.

[5] John B. Cobb. [Edited/Introduced by Paul F. Knitter]. *Transforming Christianity and the World A Way beyond Absolutism and Relativism*. Maryknoll, NY: Orbis, 1999, 60, 72.

[6] C. S. Song. *Tell Us Our Names Story Theology from an Asian Perspective*. Maryknoll, NY: Orbis, 1989, 143-44.

[7] *Alex Kronemer.* "White Hats and Black Hats," *Harvard Divinity Bulletin*, Autumn 2007, 63-64.

[8] Elisabeth J. Harris. "Double Belonging in Sri Lanka." She discusses Aloysius Pieris' view of the terms in Catherine Cornille *Many Mansions? Multiple Religious Belonging and Christian Identity*. Maryknoll, NY: Orbis, 2002, 88.

[9] Jeannine Hill Fletcher. "Shifting Identity—the Contribution of Feminist thought to Theologies of Religious Pluralism," *Journal of Feminist Studies in Religion,* 19/2, Fall 2003, 18.

[10] Claude Geffre. "Double Belonging and the Originality of Christianity as a Religion," in Catherine Cornille. *Many Mansions? Multiple Religious Belonging and Christian Identity*. Maryknoll, NY: Orbis, 2002, 100.

[11] Cobb, 50.

[12] *Ibid.*, 17, 63.

[13] Quoted from Kaufman's *The Theological Imagination: Constructing the Concept of God*. Phila: Westminster Pr, 199 in Paul Knitter. *One Earth Many Religions*, Maryknoll, NY: Orbis, 1995, 100.

[14] Paul Knitter. "Between a Rock and a Hard Place: Pluralistic Theology Faces the Ecclesial and Academic Communities," *Journal of Theology*, Summer 1997, 91.

[15] Harris discussing Pieris in Cornille, 86.

[16] Jeannine Hill Fletcher. *Monopoly on Salvation? A Feminist Approach to Religious Pluralism*. NY: Continuum, 2005, 9-10.

[17] Diana L. Eck. "Honest to God: The Universe of Faith," in *God at 2000*, Marcus Borg and Ross Mackenzie, eds., Harrisburg, PA: Morehouse Pub, 2000, 21-41.

[18] Diana L. Eck. *Encountering God A Spiritual Journey from Bozeman to Banaras*. Boston: Beacon Pr, 1993, 60.

[19] Diana L. Eck. *Darsan Seeing the Divine Image in India*. Chambersburg, PA: Anima Pub., 1981, 1985, 25.
   Point of view shapes insight into Ultimate Reality. Point of view, known by the term *darshan,* also means beholding or seeing, as in a temple. That means seeing truth perhaps more than seeing a deity. On entering a Hindu temple in Nashville or Cleveland, numerous deity forms vie for a non-Hindu's attention while adherents select god or goddess forms before which to bow, see truth, or kneel in silence. Temples themselves envelop rich meaning, notably where Hindu tradition began.

[20] Eck, *Encountering*, 61-66.

[21] Lao Tzu. *Tao Te Ching*. Translation and Commentary by Jonathan Star, NY: Penguin Group, 2001, 1:1, 14.

[22] Micah 6:8.

[23] Knitter, "Rock," 96-100.

[24] Dorothy Yoder Nyce. "Sharing God's Gift of Wholeness with Living Faiths: Biblical Examples," *Mission Focus: Annual Review*, vol. 15, 2007, 60-61. [Lecture to Association of Anabaptist Missiologists, Oct 2007, Winnipeg.]

[25] Knitter, "Bigger," 110, 111.

[26] *Ibid.*, 113-14.

[27] Dharam Singh. "Sikhism and Religious Pluralism" in *The Myth of Religious Superiority,* Paul Knitter, ed., Maryknoll, NY: Orbis, 2005, quoting Harold Coward from *Pluralism in the World Religions: A Short Introduction*. Oxford: Oneworld Pub.s, 2000, note # 8, 64.

[28] Knitter, *Myth . . . Superiority*, 33.

[29] Rita M. Gross and Rosemary Radford Ruether. *Religious Feminism and the Future of the Planet A Buddhist-Christian Conversation.* NY: Continuum, 2001.

[30] Robert Wuthnow. "How Pluralistic Should We Be?" in *America and the Challenges of Religious Diversity.* Princeton: Princeton Univ Pr, 2005, 287.

[31] Raimundo Panikkar. "The Myth of Pluralism: The Tower of Babel—A Meditation on Non-violence," *CrossCurrents* 29: 197-230 quoted in Paul F. Knitter. "Toward a Liberative Interreligious Dialogue," *CrossCurrents,* Winter 1995,   456,   retrieved   12/1/2005   ATLA   Serials http://63.136.1.23/pls/eli/pshow?1cookie=&pid=544606&1jk9de=A&1popts=S F&1size=95.

[32] Wuthnow, 290-2.

[33] Dorothy Yoder Nyce, "Wisdom or Folly: Thoughts of Religious Superiority," [Review Essay of *The Myth of Religious Superiority,* Paul F. Knitter, ed. Gross, 82-87], *Mission Focus: Annual Review*, vol. 14, 2006, 218.

[34] Victoria Lee Erickson. "We Have the Faith to Make Life Our Own," in *Still Believing Jewish, Christian, and Muslim Women Affirm Their Faith,* Victoria Lee Erickson & Susan A. Farrell, eds., Maryknoll, NY: Orbis, 2005, 98-99.

[35] Maura O'Neill. *Mending A Torn World Women in Interreligious Dialogue.* Maryknoll, NY: Orbis, 2007, 10, 46-47, 57.

[36] M. A. Muqtedar Khan. "American Muslims and the Rediscovery of America's Sacred Ground," in *Taking Religious Pluralism Seriously Spiritual Politics on America's Sacred Ground.* Barbara A. McGraw & Jo Renee Formicola, eds., Waco, TX: Baylor Univ Pr, 2005, 142.

[37] O'Neill, 80.
    'Dhamma' can mean the religion taught by Buddha or virtue, to realize law. "Pada" refers to the path or way. The Four Noble Truths: truth of suffering, truth of origin of suffering, truth of cessation of suffering, and truth of path that leads to the end of suffering. Jaroslav Pelikan. *On Searching the Scriptures— Your Own or Someone Else's.* NY: Quality Paperback Book Club, 1992, 43.
    Buddha traveled for 40 years, teaching the Dharma/oneness of all; this came to be known as "turning the wheel of the dharma" therefore the wheel symbol of Buddhism. While the Theravadin school (home, Sri Lanka) or Way of Elders focuses on monastic life, the counter movement (Mahayana or Greater Vehicle) opened up enlightenment (Nirvana or salvation) more broadly, giving lay people access to Buddha's teachings.
    Bodhisattvas, having met the goal, choose to help others do likewise before they fully realize their own. O'Neill, 81, 85.

[38] Pashaura Singh. *The Guru Granth Sahib Canon, Meaning and Authority.* New Delhi: Oxford Univ Pr, 2000, 265, 271-78.

[39] Mary C. Boys. *Has God Only One Blessing? Judaism as a Source of Christian Self-Understanding.* NY: Paulist Pr, 2000, 153.

[40] John Howard Yoder. *The Jewish-Christian Schism Revisited*, Michael G. Cartwright & Peter Ochs, eds. Grand Rapids, MI: Eerdmans Pub., 2003, 43, 60, 69, 140.

[41] Cobb, 19.

[42] Peter C. Phan. "If Jews are Saved by Their Eternal Covenant, How are Christians to Understand Jesus as Universal Savior?" A Roman Catholic Perspective. 1, retrieved 11/25/2007, 7pp. http://www.bc.edu/research/cjl/meta-elements/sites/partners/ccjr/phan0.

[43] Boys, 33.

[44] *Ibid.,* 266.

[45] Nyce, "Sharing. . .," 62-67. [See Appendix for more on this text.]

[46] Veli-Matti Karkainen. *Introduction to the Theology of Religions.* Downers Grove, IL: InterVarsity Pr, 2003.

[47] William C. Platcher, "What about Them? Christians and Non-Christians," in *Essentials of Christian Theology*, William C. Platcher, ed., Louisville: Westminster John Knox Pr, 2003, 297-327, notes 407-10, 300.

[48] Knitter, "Liberative," 457.

[49] Cobb, 48, 133.

[50] S. Wesley Ariarajah. "Power, Politics, and Plurality, The Struggles of the World Council of Churches to Deal with Religious Plurality" in Knitter, *The Myth of Religious Superiority*, Maryknoll, NY: Orbis, 2005, 189.

[51] Boys, 210-14.

[52] Hill Fletcher, *Monopoly*, 126-28.

[53] Hill/Knitter/Madges. "Religions—Why So Many?" and "Understanding Theology," in *Faith, Religion, and Theology A Contemporary Introduction*. Brennan R. Hill, Paul F. Knitter, and William Madges. Mystic, CT: Twenty-third Pub., 1997, 211 and Platcher 300.

Some Roman Catholics stress that a milestone came with Vatican II when *Nostra Aetate* (Declaration of the Relations of the Church to Non-Christian Religions), called the Catholic Church to "reject nothing true and holy in religions."

[54] Knitter, *Introducing Theologies of Religions*, 105; affirmed by Dorothy Yoder Nyce, "Faithful and Pluralistic," *CrossCurrents*, Summer 2003, 219.

[55] Platcher, 301.

[56] Hill/Knitter/Madges, 212-13.

[57] K. P. Aleaz. *Theology of Religions Birmingham Papers and other Essays*. Calcutta: Moumita Pub.s & Distrib.s, 1998, 181-92.

[58] Shirley Guthrie. "The Way, the Truth, and the Life in the Religions of the World," *The Princeton Seminary Bulletin*, 7/1, 1996, 45-57.

[59] Rita M. Gross. "Excuse Me, but What's the Question? Isn't Religious Diversity Normal?" in Knitter, *The Myth of Religious Superiority*, 77-82.

[60] DMin class handout, Oct 13-15, 2004, 3-4.

[61] Cobb, 7.

[62] Nyce, "Faithful," 216.
[63] Knitter, *Theologies* . . . 122-23.
[64] Ariarajah, 191-92.

Some of us resist being confined to a 'box,' a label, even a typology. When my seminary professor with Clinical Pastoral Education (CPE) could not define me as of one counseling 'type,' I was delighted. Willingly a Mennonite, I at times resist being described as an 'evangelical' because of how that term can be narrowly defined. All of us move within and between categories. Hence, I value William A Graham's caution ("The Importance of Transcending Typologies of Difference," address to Harvard Divinity School's Class of 2008, *Andover Journal*, 7-8).

While typologies help make sense of the world, they can be too simplistic unless ever refined. Ever scrutinized anew, their flexible and provisional nature needs space. Rather than demean diverse groups or the varied individuals within them by classes or categories, to credit diversity and note the 'always more' that each displays matters. Sensitive to the unique, varied scope of every 'other,' Graham nudges to both use and transcend types.

[65] Harold Coward. "The Modern Christian Encounter," in *Pluralism Challenge to World Religions.* Maryknoll, NY: Orbis, 1985, 34.
[66] Nyce, "Faithful," 228.

I value increased reference to God's kin-dom rather than God's kingdom. Not only does this suggest inclusion and close relationship among all mutually committed with One God, it avoids the male/king/power over/rulership imagery that can distort Divine welcome and human solidarity. Ada Maria Isasi-Diaz, Mujerista theologian, used the concept fifteen years ago in discussion of Latina salvation and the coming of the kin-dom of God. Paul Knitter uses the term in *Without Buddha I could not be a Christian.*

4

Living Faiths
'Tread' Life-giving Water

Upon arrival in India in 1962, I soon learned the Hindi word for water—
pani. Not concerned only about water generally, an Indian taught me
peena ka pani, which means boiled water. For physical survival, a person
needs water that is safe to drink. For spiritual well being, the imagery of
water recurs in varied religions.

During a memorable trip out of Kashmir's stark beauty, in a
dilapidated, crowded bus, I thought I might not live to tell about it.
Crammed into space not intended for a seat, my legs bent near the hot,
metal, motor cover. As the driver's 'helper ji' funneled a paltry jet of
water into a near-by black hose, steam hissed. My own thermos (called
flask) had little left of the sacred element, certainly none to spare. As my
mouth went dry from the blasts of heat spewed with each hill's climb,
mind-over-matter shifted into gear. 'Don't even think about drinking, not
even sipping.' A juicy orange then came to mind. But I had savored the
last one from my shoulder bag along with a final krackel Cadbury bar
with biscuits. Those biscuits had gone stale during a recent night in a tent
when conversation gave way to pouring rain. Already behind schedule,
the wheels rotated forward.

But water for quenching thirst will not be the focus of this
exchange. Here, water's religious meaning receives attention: symbolic
depth, properties of mobility and formlessness, purifying power.
Speakers in the dialogue segments know that the world's supply has
limits. They also know that religions value its qualities. Wesley Ariarajah
says, "Water has a very special place in all religious traditions."[1] Logic
suggests that just distribution of water will benefit all. Faith implies that
religious loyalty includes insight into and respect for another's ritual use

of the element. Rejoicing through common insight, people need not 'battle' over variables inherent in Truth about sacred water.

Excerpts from an imagined, longer dialogue follow. Readers might note where internal work complements interreligious exchange, where speakers affirm personal tradition, where they build trust, affirm hope, alter prejudice, or miss opportunity to learn more. If speakers were neighbors, might they be moved to relieve common, survival problems with water, having had such exchange? Dialogue takes place in India. Gauri, an educated Indian Hindu, and Carol, a Christian seminary student who recently arrived from North America, converse about sacred experience with holy water.

Carol: Good Morning! Thanks for agreeing to meet with me.

Gauri: A great morning it is, and welcome to India. I understand that you'd like to talk about water. Could I offer you a glass of it?

Carol: Thanks. Even the mornings start out hot here.

Gauri: Keep drinking, and know that it is sacred.

Carol: Sacred water. . . While riding over here, I noticed people gathered at several "taps," as you call them. One young boy enjoyed his bath, right there on the edge of the street.

Gauri: Perhaps he has no running water at home.

Carol: Might his family store some in the house?

Gauri: Sure, in large clay or brass pots. But it can't be stored for long, lest it lose its vitality.

Carol: Vitality?

Gauri: We understand that part of the energy in sacred rivers is in the water's constant flow. Only flowing water purifies—absorbs and carries away pollution. . . .

Carol: I've never experienced drought.

Gauri: If you had, might you revere water? We experience a monsoon as a Deliverer. The brown of barrenness transforms into fertile green. The wetness of water brings life. The flow from a tap, compared to a teasing sequence of drips, restores the soul. Whereas neighbors bicker, standing in long lines to fill their buckets during weeks of drought, a renewed aura of harmony settles over people during the early days of drenching rains.

Carol: Your image of being drenched suggests that monsoons can also destroy.

Gauri: Depending on the "verdict of the gods." Even so, the rains are "rupees from heaven." A monsoon can either terrorize or prompt survival. It can paralyze life patterns or leave a layer of silt needed for the next rice crop. Rainfall can sustain or be relentless.

Carol: How does that paradox affect emotions?

Gauri: I'm not skilled to analyze. I receive what comes. We understand both mercy and fate.

Carol: And that shapes your point of view. How do people respond when they feel desperate?

Gauri: You're a Christian, so I'll mention Goa, a state over on the southwest coast. When the rains were late, Christians carried "loads of rocks up steep mountain slopes in penance." Did that act "shape their point of view"? Or, Goans, praying to St. Anthony for rain, also lowered his statue into a well during drought.

Carol: They prayed to a saint for rain?

Gauri: Have you never felt desperate? . . . *[Silence]*

Carol: Explain why the river Ganga's water at Varanasi holds such an aura.

Gauri: Far too briefly. Thought to be eternal, the city also is remarkable. It's been inhabited for three thousand years. Fifteen hundred temples fill the spaces between milling worshipers. The riverbank, entirely lined with stone, provides many *ghats*, or landing places. "Crowds, like the river itself, never cease to flow."[2] And, central to life flows a rich symbol— water. What contradicts converges too—purity and pollution; sin and salvation; birth, death, and birth again.

Carol: Let's discuss the phrase "sacred rivers." My Bible is sacred, but rivers?

Gauri: Why not? We believe that they come down from heaven. Didn't Jews value the sacredness of water in biblical rivers?

Carol: Of course. I don't often recall the abundance of water in paradise or the four rivers that spread out from the Garden of Eden.[3] But, early Israelites saw water as a symbol of life and an agent of fertility. They turned to springs or sacred trees to receive revelations of God. They had purifying rituals on the last day of the Feast of Tabernacles.

Gauri: Guess you just needed prodding to recall your heritage.

Carol: And there's Ezekiel 47. The prophet describes the trickle that runs out from under the temple's threshold; it was first empowered in the innermost sanctum. From the temple, where God's eternal presence made all things holy, the miracle of a stream transpired. A guide led the prophet along the rising water, to behold the river ready to heal the wilderness or plateau, whatever was ill. It first covered his ankles. Then, his knees were submerged, before he paused waist-deep.

Gauri: That's a dramatic portrayal of Divine control through water. I understand the power of the temple's inner sanctum too.

Carol: Furthermore, trees grew on either side of the bank. Ever-bearing fruit and leaves offered food and healing. . . .

Gauri: Don't you Christians sing hymns with the river image?

Carol: Perhaps it's not really a hymn, but there's "Old Man River. . . It just keeps rolling along."

Gauri: I connect with the imagery of constant rolling, but did you say "man" river? We think of rivers as feminine, as nurturer, as Mother—like goddess Ganga, our most sacred Ganges. Rivers feed us; they supply energy; they touch our ordinary time or place. And we feel the divine light. . . . Are you with me?

Carol: Interesting. Excuse me; I was remembering hymns. "Shall we gather at the river?" is one. ". . . Gather with the saints at the river that flows by the throne of God," the refrain concludes. One verse states: "Soon we'll reach the shining river, soon our pilgrimage will cease."

Gauri: You share with Hindus the figurative miracle of "crossing over" a river at death.

Carol: Perhaps crossing over a river is a motif for other religions too.

Gauri: I'm reminded of the seven Indian cities where people near death long to go. To be released from sin for generations. To be cremated at the water's edge. To have one's ashes glow silver in the river at dusk.

Carol: You remind me: "O healing river" is the title of another hymn.

Gauri: There you are. You too personify the river when you think of it as a healer. Do you recall more?

Carol: "O healing river, send down your waters, send down your waters upon this land." The last line ends, "O healing river, from out of the skies." But my first reaction to your Hindu idea of rivers coming from heaven was, 'How strange!'

Gauri: Ah-hah! Perhaps you can recall other hymns. [Pause]

Carol: Would you believe, I have. There's an African-American spiritual called "Wade in the water." It includes a phrase, "God's gonna trouble the water" and has verses about people dressed in different colors. It ends, "There ain't but one God made them all."

Gauri: That last phrase has a wonderful link to my experience! When Hindus wade in the water, we become so focused on the rituals we're doing. To rhythmically lift water expresses deep gratitude to the sun. We totally overlook barriers. Caste difference has no bearing when we immerse ourselves in sacred water.

Carol: Remarkable! I hear that Muslims also overcome barriers, when, all dressed in white in procession at Mecca. May I mention one more hymn? "Oh, have you not heard of that beautiful stream?" From the refrain, I recall: "O seek that beautiful stream. . . Its waters, so free, are flowing for thee." Other phrases: ". . . Its fountains are deep and its waters are pure. . . A balm for each wound in its water is found; O sinner, it flows for thee!"

Gauri: There again I resonate—with reference to purity and sin. To bathe in a sacred river purifies one from amassed wrongdoing. Effort to visit sacred places itself is a form of penance. Pilgrimage is a key form of popular piety here, like to Varanasi. Leaving attachments behind, pilgrims might pursue the discipline of *sannyasa*.

Carol: I know a little about Varanasi, the sacred city also called Benares. Explain the term *sannyasa*.

Gauri: A *sannyasi* renounces this world, is an ascetic intent on the spiritual. Dependent on daily charity, a sole *sannyasi* walks between holy places. Also called *sadhus* and known for two thousand years, they take vows of poverty and chastity, like Christian monks. Thousands gather for the Maha Kumbh Mela that takes place at Allahabad every twelfth year.

Carol: Why at Allahabad? The name sounds Islamic.

Gauri: Wherever rivers come together, that place is especially sacred. Near Varanasi on the famous Grand Trunk Road, the Ganga and Yamuna rivers converge. Such a confluence is called a *Sangam*. There, the "mythical river of enlightenment called Saraswati" once flowed.

Carol: *Sangam* and Saraswati, hmm. . . Hindus stream to the Maha Kumbh Mela?

Gauri: Crowd estimates of fifteen to twenty-five million make this the largest human gathering anywhere in the world. Tent cities with shopkeepers fill the dried riverbed sections. Plays depict Hindu stories. Astrologers determine auspicious times for bathing or for dipping images. 'Dressed' in ash, sadhus or holy men merge with the thronging pilgrims in immersion rituals. All who worship believe that their sins of past lives are washed away. . . .The location draws tourists the rest of the year too. . . .

Carol: Perhaps we could note several biblical texts that highlight water.

Gauri: Good suggestion. The element must shape your view of creation.

Carol: Yes, in the Bible's first book called Genesis and the final book titled Revelation, reference to water recurs. "The Spirit of God was moving over the face of the waters" or "over the deep" suggests God's plan for water and wind, the two shapeless elements.

Gauri: God the Creator that is, or Brahma.

Carol: And God said, "Let there be a firmament in the midst of the waters, and let it separate the waters from the waters." That text reflects the ancient view of the cosmos. Out of, or superimposed upon the chaos of primeval waters, the formless began to know shape. It's known in Hebrew as *tohuwabohu,*

Gauri: What a melodic, energizing term—*tohuwabohu*. So too, in my myths, Vishnu removes the earth from watery chaos. Or Prajapati invades the special properties of primal waters in the form of wind.

Carol: As God set boundaries for the waters, created goodness took place. Some water formed above the firmament, from which rain falls to the earth. And some formed below it, as the earth's dry ground emerged distinct from seas.

Gauri: What appears in the Christian Revelation about water?

Carol: Your question puts me in a bind. I had hoped to talk about water from texts in the Gospel of John. . . .

Gauri: Let's turn to Sister Vandana's book, *Waters of Fire*, with stories from the biblical writer John. Your messenger left it here yesterday, so I read several chapters.

Carol: Good. We won't explore all the texts. Was Sister Vandana's insight into Hindu thought appropriate?

Gauri: Authentically Indian. I especially valued her knowledge of and numerous references to the *Upanishad* writings.

Carol: Sister Vandana's reference to "God's Spirit's hovering over the water," both at creation and Jesus' baptism event, seemed right to me.

Gauri: So was her naming of *Shakti* as the power of God hovering over the waters.

Carol: Water, when used with Christian baptism, symbolizes the Spirit's washing sin away. It corresponds with the Hindu tradition of being purified through the power of rivers.

Gauri: How purification happens is less important to us than that it does. The greater the sin recalled, the greater the river's glory to overcome it. While Hindus have fewer texts about sin than Christians, one from the *Rig Veda*[4] states: "O waters, carry off everything that is sinful in me, the wrong I have done, or the false oath I have sworn."

Carol: How do waters carry off sin?

Gauri: We understand that water removes sin and carries it away. An idea from the book *Water & Womanhood* comes to mind. Like a woman who at a stream swings wet laundry high above her head and then slams it down onto a rock to remove dirt, so the waters carry off sin.

Carol: Even the rhythm of that action rings true. The other day I watched a family of laundry workers in their open-air work room. Their dependence on water might have symbolic merit.

Gauri: Sure. Which chapters impressed you from Vandana's writing?

Carol: Her discussion of God's words spoken at Jesus' baptism. "Thou art my Beloved Son" relates to a guru's word to a *sannyasin* when he's initiated—*Tat- tvam-asi* / "That Thou Art." Each awakes to Self-consciousness. By the Jordan, Jesus awoke to his life's mission.

Gauri: As the *sannyasi* descends into a holy river to begin his fourth stage of life, he renounces his lower self to find his true Self—*Atman*, or Spirit within.

Carol: Even difference has integrity. Whereas adult baptism cleans the participant's conscience to move <u>into</u> the world with new commitment, the *sannyasi* leaves the water to <u>renounce</u> the world, commitment bold.

Gauri: Further, symbolism in the story of Jesus' turning water into wine resonates. Large water pots stacked at the door where a wedding occurs symbolize new life, for Jews then and for Indians today. Water symbolizes God's abundant love. Also, the servants who tasted the new supply truly knew the fine quality of the changed water.

Carol: Jesus also took radical action with water when he met the Samaritan woman at Jacob's well. A Bible professor explained, "Every river and every well was a symbol of the woman, was a symbol of God." Jesus requested water from her and drank from her vessel; orthodox Jews rarely did that.

Gauri: For a brahmin (high caste) to interact with a dalit (underclass) might correspond.

Carol: A final water scene to mention involves washing feet.

Gauri: At some Hindu *ashrams,* disciples wash the *guru's* feet in a weekly ceremony called "Guru's Pad-Puja."

Carol: From Jesus' pattern of washing the disciples' feet on the night of his betrayal, some Christian ashrams, I read, practice "Christ's Pad-Puja" each week. Residents wash each other's feet. Vandana suggests that "foot washing portrays a complete bath."

Gauri: We Hindus find that a ritual bath cleans thought as well as body. Special merit goes with doing the ritual in the Ganga. To purify the mind involves certain steps: naming Ganga while bathing, hand postures, and casting water. For example, "water poured out over the tips of the fingers is for the gods, while water poured out between the thumb and the forefinger is for the ancestors."[5] Other ritual steps include repeating verbal mantras, offering water mixed with flowers or grains of rice, and bowing to the sun while circling a lotus.

Carol: My own experience of water with worship is less ritualized. You referred again to Ganga, the Hindu's most holy Ganges River.

Gauri: We also call her the River of Heaven. We believe that God's three major forms—Brahma, Vishnu, and Shiva—took part in the descent, when she agreed to flow upon the earth. She came down for the sake of humanity—to elevate the human to the divine. To show "the interconnection and harmony among all facets of heaven and earth," Lina Gupta suggests.[6]

Carol: We've only begun to talk. But I've learned so much from you and your religion. My practice with sacred water will deepen; I'll avoid casual thought of it. Thanks so much.

Reflection:

Find a container, anything that holds liquid, and fill it with water.
Hold it gently. Look at it with love. Smell it. Listen to it splash.
Drink it—slowly.
And by all means touch it; feel the wetness. Play with it.
Dab the middle of your forehead and your tongue—and then again.
Talk with God or let God talk in the near-silence of holy water.
Imagine a Hindu's ecstasy on stepping into the Ganga.
Reflect on Jesus' water lessons.
Ponder baptism—yours or another's.
Further directions not needed, be creative with the Creator of water.

Endnotes:

[1] Wesley Ariarajah. "The Water of Life," *The Ecumenical Review*, 34/3, July 1982, 271.

[2] T. D. Allman. "The Eternal City of Benares," *Asia*, Jul/Aug, 1981, 54.

[3] Genesis 2:10-14.

[4] *Rig Veda* 10.9.8.

[5] Diana L. Eck. *Banaras City of Light*. Princeton: Princeton Univ Pr., 1982, 390.

[6] Lina Gupta. "Ganga, Purity, Pollution, and Hinduism," in *Ecofeminism and the Sacred*, Carol J. Adams, ed., NY: Continuum Pub Co., 1994, 100.

5

Crossing Cultures in Sacred Arts: Drama, Dance and Temples

People often cross cultures, at times resulting in severe shock, on other occasions without notice. Crowds might gather for a local Diversity Day. An event to celebrate distinctions of culture, Diversity Day in Goshen, Indiana, provides opportunity to try a new game or dish. It affords time to look more closely at what might at first appear to be strange. It bridges difference. It attempts to diminish prejudice. It enables people to reach out, to invite others to reveal their treasured arts or point-of-view. Whether through face painting, cultural dances, or drinking mango shakes, people increase trust. Activities offer occasions to ask questions and learn. They prompt smiles, if not words, when language divides. Planners hope for positive vibrations, for new appreciation to avoid future, careless judgments of the less familiar. But, critique can also surface, as toward a World Religions display. Christians who fear crediting symbols of Hindu, Muslim, Buddhist, or Sikh strength find fault; a Wiccan devotee complains when her group is not represented.

A person need not leave northern Indiana to meet ethnic Indians of South Asia. They attend or teach at local schools. Hundreds gather at Hindu religious or cultural festivals in South Bend or Ft. Wayne. They buy houses and groceries, find employment, and celebrate marriage events. Their skin color may resemble that of the more populous Latinos. Most Indians in the States have spoken English since childhood, along with one or two of India's sixteen major languages. In India, cultural exposure may vary due to location, rapport between governments, features of climate, or friendships made with new neighbors. Questions of "Who am I" and "Who are you" toss each other cross-court, realigning borders.

How then, does living in a country other than one's own open cross-cultural eyes? One avenue is through the interplay of arts and religion; India is noted for both. There in the early 1960s, I was drawn to prevalent, diverse living faiths. Complex Hindu thought and worship both confused and attracted me. Openness to difference stretched awareness. Deep linkage between art and religion could surprise. Whether in the Himalayan foothills—with artistic shadows, rising mist, and sacred lore—or Chennai (formerly Madras)—southeast coastal city with millions who express pride in classical Indian temples or dance— religion pervades.

This chapter contains three segments. They reflect experience for a family from Chicago that is spending a year in Madarai, south India. The father has received a Fulbright Scholarship to study temple lore. The first excerpt depicts a children's book being read by the family's elementary age child. An uncle and child converse within book content. The second segment finds the mother of the family reflecting (in prose) on several artistic events that she has attended. The third segment involves the family's high school senior (Hank) in exchange with a private tutor (Mr. Sharma) about Indian art, giving some attention to Hindu temples.

. . . **Uncle Vishal**: Let's recall Indian classical dance and music's three basic parts. First the *raga*—the repeating melodies that merge within a person's being.

Anand: Are there really seventy thousand?

Uncle Vishal: Who could use them all, in order to know? Second, the *tala*, or rhythm, whether clapped or played on drums.

Anand: Then, there's the drone, that constant tone played by the stringed *tanpura*.

Uncle Vishal: Earlier we mentioned dance.

Anand: Have you watched some famous artists?

Uncle Vishal: Think first of Shiva, "Lord of the dance." Devotees see the great Cosmic Dance in Shiva.

Anand: Dancers' facial expressions and hand gestures attract me.

Uncle Vishal: They convey a profound language in classical dance. Have you watched for the thirteen ways to move the head? There are fewer, distinct moves for the eyes, feet, and waist.

Anand: How about the ears?

Uncle Vishal: They mostly listen. Physical strength and sacred depth intersect in dance.

Anand: A group that I saw in Jaipur had a woman dance atop double tumblers until they broke. She kept dancing, crushing the glass. What was sacred about that?

Uncle Vishal: Did you ask her? Jean Filliozat says that people who have not studied dance forms and ritual cannot expect to understand the art.[1] Two key classical styles still practiced are the *Bharatanatya* and

Manipuri. Dance poses suggest distinct feelings. Rooted in sacred rituals, dancers may impersonate gods and goddesses. Good and evil may compete; the former often wins.

Anand: Ankle bells thumping rhythmic footwork amaze me. By the way, have you seen mask dancers?

Uncle Vishal: They perform during festivals and often become ecstatic. Before an ascetic devotee dons the wooden mask to represent a deity, he gives the mask to a priest. The priest performs a rite to bring life into the mask. After the blessing, the god's voice speaks.[2] The audience understands that the mask either shields inner being from the outer world, or links the superhuman with those who need it when it 'speaks.'
. . .

The Mother prepares a report for international club members and a dancers' guild in her hometown in the States, to be given a week after the family returns.

Chennai, noted for classical concerts, includes a main festival season. Beginning dates and duration of events differ, depending on the concert hall. The fete began in 1927 at the historic hall called The Music Academy. For more than two weeks of December, five slots of daily events may pack the Academy's schedule. At least twenty venues offer programs in this city, proud of its festivals and recitals.

This array of events built on earlier events that I attended: a "flamboyant flautist" with a bamboo flute and a concert of fifty violins to mark India's Golden Jubilee of Independence. Chennai welcomes and honors native or visiting artists. A consulate or organization often sponsors events; free tickets are available on request. Hear some details of cultural events that I recall.

Appearing in the Museum Theatre's fine concert hall, Galina Heifetz, Russian-born but later of the United States, stood to perform. She exuded senior vigor near her youthful accompanist. Feet firmly planted, Heifetz offered a stage presence of exceptional power and boundless technique. With the violin's rounded base tucked near her chin, her left fingering arm extended away from and to the left of her face. By contrast, Indian violinists most often position the violin in front of them. Seated on the floor, players extend the instrument from the chin down, its narrow neck shielded near bare feet.

Fewer Indians resonate with the sound and scales from the instrument that we westerners call 'grand.' Indians long for intimacy, like warmth conveyed when an artist nestles the *tabla* or *mridangam* (drums) near his knees. Although a stringed instrument, the piano fails to offer the plucked, haunting sound of a *sitar*'s seasoned gourd or the stringed *sarangi* played with a bow. No pedal provides the constancy of drone like that from the stringed *tanpura*. For many Hindus, those sacred vibrations of the gods add verve to inner being. We who choose to cross cultures strive to discern those deeper quivers.

With an invitation in hand to "Search for my Tongue," we waited with the growing crowd packed onto the outer, circular walkway of the Museum Theatre. Sujata Bhatt's poem stood at the heart of the production—focusing the quandary of a bilingual background. The stage set included short, stark trees with mounds and scattered clumps of autumn leaves. The dance scene opened with puffs of early morning, gray smoke. Dancers gracefully swept dry leaves together. Suddenly, an arm followed by its stealthy body stretched and danced out from the largest pile of leaves.

Daksha Sheth's 'chorus' of six performers combined abstract images with silent, 'spoken' messages. The syncretism of roles and patterns made by dancers gliding across the stage drew audience attention. Indians saw the noises of their Motherland and heard its color. Memories of torrential rains zoomed in as Rajasthan's parched, northwestern desert blew off stage. Even foreigners could imagine the vim of childhood games, could 'hear' the hawkers on cornered streets plus the incessant, barking, nighttime hounds. Dancers gracefully conveyed energy. Leaps seemed barely to touch ground before rising again, to higher heights. "The mood of the moment in movement." As South Indian classical dance speaks ancient wisdom, so this event expressed modernity. Each conveys its tempered beauty.

A bilingual dilemma also faces Asian youth raised in the west and caught between two cultures. Their search for identity includes the search for a mother tongue left dormant. Or, for resident Indians the search may grapple with culture in transition. Feeling dislocated, people can neither return to nor be freed from the "womb of the past." Bhatt's poem pleads:

> . . . I ask you, What would you do
> if you had two tongues in your mouth,
> and lost the first one, the mother tongue,
> and could not really know the other,
> the foreign tongue? . . .

The plea can haunt an audience alert to crossing cultures, in Chennai or Chicago. The dilemma occurs in diverse art forms, as with the book and later movie titled *The Namesake*. Recall when our group reviewed that story several years ago? In that novel Jhumpa Lahiri portrays diverse ways that characters—parents with Calcutta roots and their two children born in the States—struggle with living in or belonging to America. Features of identity like name or traditional holidays can cause a child to rebel, a mother to relish memories.

Many loyal Hindus know the god Shiva as "lord of the dance." One verse (of five) of a Christian hymn with Chorus, by Sydney Carter, states:

> I danced in the morning when the world was begun,
> And I danced in the moon and the stars and the sun,
> And I came down from heaven
>   and I danced on the earth,
> At Bethlehem I had my birth…
> Dance then wherever you may be.
> I am the Lord of the Dance said He….

The reference to Jesus as the Lord of the Dance parallels the imagery of Shiva as "lord of the dance." Noting common features helps people cross cultures with honor.

During the third century BCE, a Brahmin sage named Bharata Muni wrote a book of treatises from scriptures (called *Natya Sastra*). It details techniques of theatre and dance performance. Hindus believe that the god Shiva taught Bharata to dance. Part of that teaching, the sacred Bharatanatyam (or Bharata Natyam) dance is often performed at South Indian temples. I saw multiple segments of this dance performed in Chicago before we left and again at a Hindu temple.

Watching, I failed to absorb much that a trained Hindu does. For example, the *Rasa* theory failed on me. In that theory, a spectator becomes momentarily identified with the character or theme being danced. Something about the Indian genius—their range of emotions, their being spellbound by what they see—triggers their mental capacity for aesthetic enjoyment. For a dancer, not how many hours she dances but how much "she puts herself into her work" matters. Each rehearsal serves as a performance. Her assurance—through leaps or glides, via gestures or intensity—determines her ability to project essential ideas.

More obvious features come to mind. Dancers' eyes pose with fierce attention or plead with calm compassion. They roll and flit and yearn. Other features of the head might appear: a tight headband, decked with multiple layers of white and orange flowers; facial expressions ever-engaged; and prominent jewelry that shimmers at the neck, nose, and below the ears. A braid of black hair may snake down the dancer's erect back, tied at the end with a strip of cloth. A dozen to fifteen bangles grace each arm. Red henna paint on the thumb and fingertips make dramatic, elongated motions, or on occasion circle the face left exposed.

Larger motions also express cultural details. Sweeping arm movements or conscious bending at the elbow grace formal bends at the knees, as sari pleats spread to squat or horizontal stripes stretch out.

Painted slippers on the lower edge of bare feet contrast with four rows of constantly jingling, metal, ankle bracelets. Marked by occasional thumping, the bottom of a foot rarely comes into full view.

Arthi Devarajan explains such details.[3] Movements are of three types: *nritta* (technical, non-emotive, structured body movements), *nritya* (movements of hands, eyes, and feet to express certain ideas or emotions), and *natya* (dramatic gestures that enact stories). Different types of music are choreographed with these: percussion compliments the first, instrumental interludes grace the second, and verbal songs express messages with the third. Dance students learn such details of the classical art from an able guru. Imagine what you an informed observer might recollect or recognize, as the story gets handed down through generations.

The precision and speed with which motions change require fleeting observations, a sense of being teased. A pause could precede a sustained position hold or almost martial gait. For spectators, like photographers with a speed-driven lens, quick reflexes help. An informed Indian knows that length of religious exposure causes a person to overlook, take for granted, or penetrate the mystery of sacred dance. More than gestures, scripture, rhythm, or costume, the medley performed engages a Hindu's mental, emotional, and spiritual being.

A second dance segment, the *Shiva Shabdam*, had a strong communicative aspect (*Nritya*). The dancer, acting as devotee, displays devoted love for the powerful Shiva. She divulges to her confidante (her *sakhi*) her deep yearning to achieve union with Shiva, the beloved. Describing "the unfathomable power of his cosmic dance," she laments how overwhelmed she feels because separated from Shiva. Then dreaming that she is wedded to her Lord, she asks the *sakhi* to bring her Lord Shiva near. Not that the dancer becomes the channel for imagined connection, the ambience she creates makes connection more or less tangible. But, not all depends on the artist. An observer's state of being enhances or hinders spiritual ecstasy.

The first dance segment invoked five deities or forms of the One God—named Ganesh, Kartikeya, Shiva, Devi, and Krishna. Devotional love for elusive Krishna found expression in complex, rhythmic footwork and elaborate movements in the thirty-minute *Varnam* dance. Again in the *Padam* piece, Krishna took center stage, as a child and as one who conquers. Krishna the child pleads with his mother for freshly churned butter, and his divine strength unwinds as he kills the snake that had poisoned a lake. Inviting Krishna to come in "tiny, tiny steps"— whose feet astonish, inspire, and bring tears of joy—the dancer portrays both the devotee and the mother. To know basic story details, like when Devi Maheshwar slays a demon figure, helps a North American understand this major work of art. Then, why the goddess is praised for her energy, or how she combines compassion with power over evil, become clear. Learning to cross cultures takes time and merits respect.

The intensity of the prescribed final segment, the *Thillana*, almost annoyed me. Perhaps because solo dancers had performed all but the opening piece, I felt confused by the return of two. Uncertain which dancer to follow, I lost concentration. Then too, the intense drumming of the *mridrangist* produced a fierce quality. With his double-faced drum lying flat and directly in front of a microphone, he executed wizardry with rhythms. Through technical skill, he holds an audience engrossed or spellbound, enhanced by his interplay with the tonal quality of a vocalist. Uncomfortable with the loudness of sound or the perpetual pressure, I succumbed. Yielding to the surrounding powers, I nevertheless admired the synchronized movements, with dancers either side-by-side or one slightly ahead of the other. Unable to comprehend the depth of spiritual pleasure in the dance, I still valued the exposure to an art form that is central to Hindu culture.

Felicitations earmark Indian dance events. First, the guest of honor, noted violinist Dr. L. Subramaniam, was gifted. Called "Emperor among Violinists," his unpretentious tone and precise control of the violin are unmatched, I'm told. Also a composer, his score appears in the film *Mississippi Masala* [which most of you saw]. The dancers then bowed to their *guru* (teacher), also one of the four musicians. To revere the Shiva form surrounded by lighted candles near the front of the stage concluded an event gifted by the gods.

Whether in Chennai or Chicago, the boundaries of artistic and religious cultures intersect as people receive each other's rhythms, costumes, and stories, as performance links with the Divine.

A teenager and tutor exchange.

Mr. Sharma: Today's lesson on Indian arts reinforces the sacred quality of Hindu tradition.

Hank: The holy seems to pervade life here.

Mr. Sharma: Perhaps especially the arts. Art "not only depicts gods and goddesses and their stories, but also participates in sacred cosmic mystery."[4] Not only reflecting beauty, Hindu art expresses the endless forms of universal harmony.

Hank: How do we comprehend the holy? It's more than pure emotion.

Mr. Sharma: The Holy refers to the morally good; Rudolf Otto calls it the "numinous," a state of mind.

Hank: Expressions of cosmic force, inspired by an artist, awaken another's being?

Mr. Sharma: Standing before certain objects or beholding a distinct sunset or through the vibration of sound in music, observers can be overwhelmed by their own nothingness. "I am naught; Thou art all" they breathe. Inspired by the Mystery beyond, a sweeping sense pervades. In part hidden or fleeting or because not expressible, the holy causes a person to shudder or tremor in awe, Otto explains.

Hank: Is there a term for that quality?

Mr. Sharma: Otto calls it *"mysterium tremendum"*—the awe-full, majestic, vital energy that compels a worshiper. Noted Indian poet Rabindranath Tagore said about the arts, "In poetry, as in all creation, there is opposition of forces."[5] Resolving discord requires breath similar to playing a flute. Being creative happens when divergence moves into harmony.

Hank: Must discord always be part of creating?

Mr. Sharma: Ponder your question. Many Indians believe that both music and dance are gifts from the gods. Occasions of worship transpire as performers consecrate their music to the gods. As divinities preside, Hindu music basically expresses "vac" or cosmic sound. David Scott suggests: "sound either invokes or symbolically represents the power of the universe."[6]

Hank: Does that explain the Hindu *mantra* AUM or OM?

Mr. Sharma: Yes. That most mysterious *mantra* is "the Supreme Being in the form of sound."[7]

Hank: Any artist engages the spirit realm?

Mr. Sharma: Yes, but religions differ in how people comprehend or convey sacred encounters. An "opposition of forces" inherent with the creative lingers. Rather than comment on differences, we might contemplate several statements in silence; we'll pause between each:

Reflection
- *The One-Creator-God designed the human body to create and respond to beauty.*
- *Melody, rhythm, movement, and design are divinely inspired.*
- *Discipline, repetition, and multi-focus combine within art.*
- Dar'sana *(vision, or taking in all that an object depicts) enters a person's consciousness when visiting a temple or house of God.*

Mr. Sharma: Let's continue, keeping that exercise in mind.

Hank: Fine.

Mr. Sharma: Consider now, too briefly, the Indian temple.

Hank: Will we reflect on how Indian, Hindu temples differ from other countries or religions?

Mr. Sharma: You'll see, either today or later. Every large, Indian city surrounds its temples with special meaning; the temple dominates what surrounds it. Temple location and its lore also mark rural villages.

Hank: Once, on leaving a countryside train station, I saw a Hindu temple and Muslim mosque side by side.

Mr. Sharma: That closeness reminds worshipers of their neighbors, of perhaps the One God known in diverse ways. It counters "opposition of forces."

Hank: It shows tolerance. Christian places of worship are called churches or cathedrals.

Mr. Sharma: But, temple is also used. You sing a hymn titled "To Thy Temple I Repair." The first verse states: "Lord, I love to worship there, When, within the veil, I meet Christ before the mercy seat."

Hank: Whatever meeting Christ "within a veil" means, teach me more about my heritage.

Mr. Sharma: Of interest too, the melody appears for women with lower voices, while higher voiced women provide an extended, ascending tone, somewhat like an Indian drone. Other verses express faith, as singers identify Jesus as God's representative at the Temple:

> While the prayers of saints ascend,
> God of love, to mine attend;
> Hear me, for Thy Spirit pleads; Hear, for Jesus intercedes.
> From Thy house when I return, May my heart within me burn,
> And at evening let me say, "I have walked with God today."

Hank: The central effect seems simple.

Mr. Sharma: Good point. Most major Indian temples, as well as Christian cathedrals in Europe, were built between 900 and 1600 CE. In that Age of Faith, people expressed religious fervor through architecture—an art in itself.[8] While an Indian temple opens to Buddhist, Hindu, Jain, or Sikh followers, Hindus more often use them for worship.

Hank: They seem as central to India as pyramids are to Egypt.

Mr. Sharma: Or the Parthenon to Athens. With the idea of a personal God, the temple offers a setting for the deity to receive prayers and gifts from devotees.

Hank: That's true of the altar in a home too.

Mr. Sharma: "More than a place of worship, it's a beautiful monument fit for the gods."[9] Each temple is a microcosm. Above the dark, small, *sanctum sanctorum*—also called the womb or *garbha griha*—where a replica of the main deity is located, the main tower rises. The doorway of the sanctum, facing eastward, opens into the vestibule or passage where worshipers circle around. Beyond this is the pillared hall where devotees gather. Varied figures, stories, or themes are depicted on the wall; they "picture before the faithful the righteous ways of the gods and the sins of evil-doers."[10]

Hank: Not all of India's temples tower above ground though. I recall seeing the Elephanta Caves from the third century, located near Mumbai and dedicated to Shiva.

Mr. Sharma: And there's the row of Buddhist caves at Ajunta, built out of solid rock. Wherever they are located, temples symbolize God's house. A temple with its thick walls enshrines some symbol for God. The image located at the center is known as the *jiva*, or life, of the temple. The symbol may be the Shaivite *linga* stone that symbolizes cosmic energy, a god's consort, one of Vishnu's twenty-four forms, or one of his ten earthly descents (*avataras*). This central room is to the temple "what the principle of life, the vital breath, the soul [or *nephesh*, in Hebrew] is to a human person." To look at the temple, to absorb its meaning and power through sculptures on its walls, helps a person experience part of the whole of religious meaning.[11]

Hank: Perhaps we could visit several temples together? You could teach me further on site.

Mr. Sharma: Let's plan for that.

Hank: Beauty and the arts surround me when I appreciate them.

Mr. Sharma: When you daily communicate with God through them. I truly believe that the wisdom of India is passed on through oral and visual means more than through written words. Words can either enhance or detract from silence. To learn the difference is part of Divine art.

Hank: Hopefully, we visitors to India value the power of image, or the symbolic, for Indians. To cross into your culture truly involves attention to your sacred arts.

Mr. Sharma: Listen to Swami Rama's quote: "God is within you and that which is within you is subject to self-realization. No one can show God to anyone else. One has to independently realize [one's] real Self; thereby [one] realizes the Self of all, which is called God."[12]

Hank: Swami's thought is deep. May I copy it before I leave in silence?

Mr. Sharma: Of course. Go well; I'll see you next week.

Endnotes:

[1] Jean Filliozat. *India The Country and its Traditions*. Englewood Cliffs, NY: Prentice-Hall, 1961, 154.

[2] Barbara Stoler Miller. *Exploring India's Sacred Art*. Philadelphia: Univ of Pennsylvania Pr, 1983, 102-03.

[3] Arthi Devarajan. "Embodying Text and Dancing the Word: Reflective Opportunities through the Non-Discursive Text of Classical Indian Dance," in *Hermeneutical Explorations in Dialogue: Essays in Honour of Hans Ucko*. Anantanand Rambachan, A. Rashied Omar & M. Thomas Thangaraj, eds. Delhi: ISPCK, 2007, 91, 95, 99.

[4] David C. Scott, Personal Correspondence.

[5] Rabindranath Tagore. *My Reminiscences*, Calcutta: Rupa & Co, 1991, 151.

[6] Scott, Correspondence.

[7] Klaus Klostermaier. *A Survey of Hinduism*, Albany, NY: SUNY Pr, 1989, 71.

[8] (Department of Tourism). *The Temples of India*. Delhi: Publications Division, 1964, 7.

[9] Bobbie Kalman. *India, the Culture*. NY: Crabtree Pub., 1990, 12.

[10] *Temples*, 8.

[11] Stoler Miller, 118, 241, 253.

[12] Swami Ajaya., ed. *Living with the Himalayan Masters Spiritual Experiences of Swami Rama*. Honesdale, PA: Himalayan International Institute of Yoga Science & Philosophy, 1978, 69.

6

"Splitting Differences":
A One-act Play

Characters: Arvind, Raffat, Tom, Bailey, Harris (pronounced Ha-rish'), Shaku, Ellen

Setting: Arvind, Raffat, Tom, and Bailey have settled into their space in a university dormitory suite in the United States. Arvind, a Hindu from south India, and Raffat, a Muslim from New Delhi, each unpacked two suitcases, including some reminders of their homeland. They arrived in the States when the fall semester began, each transferring after two years in Indian universities. Bailey and Tom, each with a car in the parking lot, found enough hookups in the suite for all of their equipment. They model Christianity's hybrid quality. Exchange reflects how current issues emerge out of history and tradition.

With Tom and Bailey off to the football game and Raffat gone to the library, Arvind takes up his Saturday ritual (what would be a daily ritual for his father in India). Having showered and donned the dhoti, *with his sacred thread draped over his bare, right shoulder, he picks up his polished, brass water pot, red strip of cloth, and an artificial garland of marigolds. He chants prayers while circling clockwise, three times, around a small flowerpot. (He' borrowed' this substitute for the* tulasi *[sacred basil] plant from the quad garden outside his window.) He sprinkles water onto the plant and verbalizes characteristics of the god Krishna before draping the garland on a framed print of another Hindu God form. He lights a cube of camphor in a small, flat tray and circles it in front of the image (three times: at head, center portion and feet); he then rings a small brass bell with his right hand. Setting the tray down before him, he moves his hands through the cool flame and then touches his eyelids. Expecting to meet God and to be seen by God, he eats a portion of puffed rice, sweetened with molasses and duly blessed. Seated erectly on the floor while drinking a cup of* chai*, he reflects on his religious heritage—the spirits of home and family. He appears centered and conveys a feeling of wellbeing. Then snuffing out the incense, he returns items to their stored places, finds a campus sweatshirt, and relaxes with the latest issue of the journal* India Today.

Raffat: *[Enters]* I've just had a couple good hours in the computer lab, searching the Net. Should we leave before long to buy groceries?

Arvind: Why not? Hope this sweatshirt is enough for that strong wind. But, I'll warm up from walking and carrying our supplies. Could we take time to pick out an Indian DVD?

Raffat: Okay, as long as we're back by 2:30; I'm expecting a call from my dad.

Arvind: I'll need to study a few hours before we watch the video. *[R & A leave. On returning, they put supplies in the kitchen and settle down, Arvind at Bailey's computer. Indian classical music fills the space.]*

Tom: *[Entering]* What a great game! Didn't you guys go?

Raffat: I'm expecting a call from my dad. My whole family is together because dad's father is quite ill.

Tom: Was he ill when you left home? Tell me what develops. I was with my grandma last summer when she died—a meaningful family time.

Bailey: *[Bouncing in]* How was that for a comeback! At halftime, I feared we couldn't win. But then Dave found his passing targets. And of course that one call went in our favor. Maybe the rain worked for us too. Wow! Wasn't it great to have so many scoring occasions to toss students into the air, Arvind?

Arvind: What do you mean, toss students? Will you want to use your computer now?

Bailey: On a Saturday afternoon? No way! Weren't you there? Don't tell me you were stuck in this stuffy room. Man, let's open a window! Did you forget how they work? *[Opening window]* Oh, the rain's from this direction. We may need to flick on the a.c.

Raffat: Then I'll get my jacket. Looks like you're soaked.

Bailey: Barb offered me a plastic trash bag, but that's not for me—after what you said the other day about a "bag wallah."

Tom: But you're chilling. . . I see the goose bumps from here.

Arvind: Goose bumps? What goose do you see that I don't?

Tom: It's an expression; he's shivering.

Bailey: Guess I'd better have a warm shower. I'm to meet Barb in twenty minutes. We're going bowling with the youth from church. Hey, Raffat, get out of the books; have a life! *[B exits into his room]*

Arvind: *[To Tom]* Raffat and I went to the football game last week. But it's so different from what we call football. We left part way through.

Tom: I didn't know that. We could watch part of a game on TV. I'll explain details and you can ask questions. Then two weeks from now, Jim and I can sit with each of you for play-by-play comments.

Raffat: Sounds good. But students don't even sit!

Tom: Right. Those benches are for standing. Do you sit for cricket matches? *[Phone rings]*

Raffat; Oh, that call might be dad. "Hello. It's good to hear your voice! How's *Dada*?" *[Walks to kitchen with cell phone, talking]*

Arvind: I was reading from *The Hindu* on the Internet about India's match with Pakistan.

Tom: *The Hindu*? Something to do with religion?

Arvind: That's the name of a major, secular, Indian newspaper. We're having elections soon, so I want to know the latest about the opposition candidates too. *[Knock on door]*

Tom: *[Calling]* Yes. Oh, it's you, Gene. Excuse me *[to Arvind]*; we're meeting friends at a Pizza hangout. . . . Or, d'you want to come along?

Arvind: Thanks. We walked to the store and bought stuff for making curries. The *bhindi*, or ladyfingers, looked fresh this time, and I'd like to try a new recipe that Mama sent. See you later. *[T & G exit; R returns]* So, what's the news?

Raffat: My cousin called to say that they've taken *Dada* to the hospital. They'll call again when they know more from the doctor.

Arvind: Guess we're bound to miss some important family times while over here. Tell me when you hear more. . . . I'm getting hungry. Guess I'll start making the veg curry.

Bailey: *[Out from bedroom]* "See you later. *[Exits main door]*

Raffat: Good. I'll join you in a little, Arvind. Then, while we eat, we can plan for political science 101.

[A. exits to kitchen. R. unrolls his prayer rug. Bowing toward Mecca, he prays for a few minutes. A. returns to the doorway. About to ask a question, he notices R's posture, and retreats. Finished with prayers, R. replaces his rug under the bunk bed. R. and A. cook as time lapses. Finished cooking, A. and R. hear a knock as they enter the main room, their plates full. A. finds space for the pot of vegetable curry.]

Arvind: Come in.

Raffat: Oh, Harris. We're just ready to eat. Have you had *khanna*?

Harris: I just made a great shrimp curry and thought why eat alone if you two are here. I'll be right back with my *tali*. *[H. Exits]*

Raffat: We can still plan, even with Harris here.

Arvind: That means that I'd be a minority Hindu. Perhaps Shaku is in; I'll check with her. *[Dials cell phone]*

Shaku, want a break from your studies? Raffat and I are about to eat and Harris is bringing his *tali*….Sure. Bring your *dal bhat,* and I'll share something hot, like decent food is meant to be.

Raffat: Guess we'd better clear off a couple chairs. If Bailey didn't have so much stuff, this place could be neater.

Arvind: He's always so busy, especially with church events.

Raffat: Are we to be impressed or feel guilty? Living with Christians is so different.

Arvind: No kidding. They likely say the same about living with us. I wonder what Bailey's essay reported.

Raffat: Oh, I've got an English lit assignment to finish. *[Knock]* Aiya! *[S. & H. enter]*

Shaku: Thanks for calling; I needed a break from statistics. This place can get dreadfully dead after a game. Hey, what's that spice I smell in your curry? Hope you like dill in your *dal*.

Arvind: Anything beats the bland cafeteria mess on Saturdays.

Raffat: Indeed. By the way, Arvind and I are to speak about the Muslim-Hindu conflict in India, in political science class this week.

Shaku: So, that's why you called me?

Arvind: Knowing that Harris was coming, I knew I'd be a lone Hindu.

Harris: Hey, it's great to have an equal number! Muslims are only about eleven percent of India's billion plus.

Shaku: Say more about your class. This *bhindi* is super, by the way.

Arvind: When Raffat and I first knew that we'd share a suite . . .

Raffat: Don't call us "suite-mates."

Shaku: Reminders of sticky *goor*?

Arvind: Anyway, on meeting, we knew from our last names which religion each honored.

Raffat: Then, when the prof named religious conflict as a key to politics, we decided that we might as well be the ones to talk about it, from lived experience.

Harris: You can't avoid political-religious overlap. *[Eating with his right hand, he gently slurps the sauce and grabs another* papad.*]*

Arvind: But too complex to explain in twenty minutes.

Shaku: Students can't help but learn from you though.

Arvind: Mostly North Americans, they've lived mainly in a single religious environment—Christian.

Harris: How that can limit outlook!

Arvind: Where do you suggest we begin?

Raffat: Perhaps we could name main features of Muslim-Hindu conflict now, and refine the outline later.

Arvind: Sounds good. Did you see the five-hour serial *Tamas*?

Harris: Filmed more than ten years ago, and based on the dark weeks before Partition?

Shaku: My parents weren't sure if we kids should see it. I'm glad I did, though it wasn't pleasant. *[Gets more curry from the pot and a* papad*]*

Arvind: Do we need to explain Partition, from the Indian context?

[Writes notes]

Harris: You probably should. Some students have lived so insulated from global events.

Raffat: Remember the portrayal of Nathu?

Harris: An innocent *chamar,* he followed orders to kill a pig. Then it was dumped at a mosque, to defile our sacred space. *[Pausing, glances at A. & S.]*

Shaku: Then, Muslims took revenge by setting the market on fire.

Raffat: That communal carnage and flames led to Partition, forming a Muslim Pakistan.

Shaku: Our religions couldn't tolerate each other.

Arvind: Yet, here we are. We'd better explain the word 'communal.' *[More note-taking]*

Raffat: Communal riots, fueled by on-going tension, need only one rash incident. They result when we project negative feelings onto an enemy.

Arvind: Sudir Kakar, an Indian psychoanalyst, describes a communal person as: "one whose exclusive attachment to his or her community is combined with an active hostility against other communities which share its geographical and political space."

Harris: So many died that communal death. And the trauma left hundreds who had lived in villages for decades with no option but to run. *[Shifts from sitting next to Arvind, to being across from him]*

Raffat: But praying.

Arvind: We still pray. . . for light, to see through sectarian strife.

Shaku: Yet, *Tamas* means darkness.

Arvind: An appropriate term for scenes from "the winter of communal discontent," as an *India Today* article called it.

Harris: By the way, have you seen the latest issue of *IT*? Coverage of the cricket match with Pakistan really compliments India. *[Heads toward the kitchenette]* Got a clean glass here?

Arvind: Stick to the subject, Harris. Back to *Tamas.* I'd compliment Govind Nihalani for a terrific, calm job as producer, with volatile content

Raffat: I liked the fact that the gentle, elderly Sikh was played by Bhisham Sahni, the author of the book on which the movie is based.

Shaku: What a way to see India's history unfold, especially for people who were children in '47.

Raffat: They must have grown numb to the awful suffering—among Sikhs, Muslims, and Hindus.

Arvind: With religion so central to it all, so pervasive, where was Ultimate Reality? . . . I guess that's a major point of conflict.

Harris: *[Returning with water for himself]* So often my people cried out *"Allah-o-Akbar,"* God is Great or Unity of God—with each dead body.

Raffat: A quarter of a million people died. Prayers and hate crossed in the same breath.

Shaku: Such intense emotions.

Raffat: How incongruent, to think "Allah will provide.". . . .*[Reflective]* Yet, I still pray it.

Arvind: I know; I saw you this afternoon, on your prayer mat. We Hindus also pray.

Raffat: I know; I smelled your incense when I came back from the lab.

Arvind: At least you and I can honor our differences. But, Islam's exclusive claim to truth can't credit our Hindu beliefs.

Raffat: At times, I too struggle with the judgment that people are either "believers or infidels."

Arvind: Oh, yeah? For us to talk so casually about Partition seems blasphemous too. *[Tom opens the door, with Ellen not far behind.]*

Tom: Hey, looks like a heavy discussion.

Raffat: Right. Arvind and I are to speak in political science 301 about Muslim-Hindu conflict in India. So, we're tossing around some ideas.

Tom: Mind if we listen in? This is Ellen.

Ellen: Hi. I wish I remembered your names.

Shaku: I'm Shaku. Raffat and Arvind live here, and Harris lives upstairs.

Harris: You'll discover who is a Hindu and who Muslim. *[Moves to another chair]*

Ellen: Fair enough. *[E.& T. find cushions and join the circle]* Just carry on.

Harris: I read an article about the Hindu pattern of teaching children, especially sons, to "wield the lathi."

Raffat: Recall the question in *Tamas*: How can a youth who can't kill a hen deal with an enemy?

Arvind: *[Reflective]* Enemy. . . .Kill a hen. . . .Face an enemy.

Harris: A fair number of youths dealt with one in the Ayodhya debacle.

Arvind: We'd better explain that event. *[A. writes notes; Tom brings a pan of brownies from kitchenette and offers it around]*

Raffat: Go ahead. . . . I'd be interested in your account.

Shaku: That sounds like a religious challenge, with near-political threat! By the way, Harris, thanks for bringing water for yourself. *[Tom distributes glasses and water to others.]*

Arvind: I'll start. On December 6, 1992, in five hours, a mob of three hundred thousand *kar sevaks* demolished the famous Babri Mosque, built in 1528.

Harris: Explain *kar sevaks;* they're volunteers for a movement. At Ayodhya they were "foot soldiers of militant Hinduism."

Shaku: The *kar sevaks* also built a makeshift temple on the same grounds, ground that Hindus believe was the birthplace of Ram(a), an important God.

Harris: Communal riots mushroomed. If figures are correct, seventeen hundred to two thousand people died, and fifty-five hundred others were injured.

Shaku: Savagery in Mumbai [formerly Bombay] boiled over a month later.

Arvind: Prof Ramesh Thakur wrote that, "Muslims were the main victims of violence."

Raffat: Our minority posed a threat to your Hindu mainstream.

Harris: But the conflict didn't happen just overnight. *[Shows signs of anxiety: rubbing hands, looking often at his watch]*

Raffat: Communal tensions had grown during the eighties. "More than 7,000 people were killed in some 4,500 communal incidents," Thakur reports.

Harris: Recall the brutality in Bhagalpur in 1989? Ninety percent of the deaths were Muslims.

Arvind: I regret the Hindu VHP group's violent slogans.

Shaku: Didn't a smaller number of volunteers, perhaps a third as many, threaten to destroy the Ayodhya mosque already in 1990?

Arvind: Despite that forewarning, our government didn't "have the courage to enforce the law of the land." That's what the editor of *India Today* said.

Raffat: Let's mention the rumor mill, how seemingly innocent yet lethal it is.

Harris: Often baseless, rumors reflect deep distrust. After the Ayodhya debacle, I heard about a girl who ran through a Muslim ghetto carrying a can. Neighbors ran indoors shouting that they'd be attacked. No one stopped to think that perhaps she needed to get some cooking oil for her family when curfew was 'off.'

Shaku: Why weren't TV shows interrupted to plead with people not to panic?

Arvind: Or politicians could have given police megaphones—to hit the streets, to counter rumors, to calm scared people huddled or hiding.

Harris: *[Shifts to another position: on the floor, leaning against a chair]* It seems like leaders wanted divisions to simmer.

Shaku: Large-scale outbreaks always prolong divisions.

Raffat: Is that just human instinct, to let religious scorn whet enmity between groups?

Harris: Religious or political fervor quickly incites trouble. *[Looks with fear toward A.. & S.]*

Arvind: Rationally, I know that a secular democracy is the only way to survive, with a minority as large as yours—a-hundred-and-ten-million and growing—but . . .

Raffat: And we know the fallout when Rajiv took political action to gain votes, as in the Shah Bano case.

Arvind: If a question surfaces, we'll explain the Shah Bano case. *[Writes notes]* But I wonder whether Muslims and Christians comprehend how much your invasions and domination caused us Hindus to feel insecure.

Shaku: Muslims controlled from 1200-1750 and the arrogant British for two more centuries.

Arvind: Most ancient and original to "Mother India," we the majority faith suffer from fear of your power.

Raffat: Therefore?

Arvind: We feel inferior, even though the majority.

Harris: *[In disbelief]* How can you? *[Standing behind the couch, he clips his fingernails.]*

Raffat: When a dominant group feels threatened, it attacks the other group's self-worth?

Arvind: I'd say that having felt bullied, we decide to be timid no longer.

Shaku: Rage simmers and piles up and then spills from both groups, I guess.

Arvind: Then, we resent when the government grants *any* further privilege to you minorities.

Shaku: Our government claims to be secular or impartial, but…

Arvind: We insist that, within the emerging India, Hinduism be prominent. *[H. shakes head, No]*

Shaku: With our new pride in being Hindu and Indian, we experience you as imports.

Arvind: You Muslims seem to be more loyal to Middle East Islam, at the expense of strong national loyalty.

Raffat: You Hindus often make that charge. Your rhetoric of nationalism can get pretty demanding.

Harris: *[Moving to a more central position, remains standing]* And the dissension that follows causes mutual distrust.

Raffat: From 'my side,' think of the pain you cause, *[pointing to A. & S.]* when you perceive us as not really Indian.

Harris: Muslims have lived in India for generations. To deprive us of an important part of who we are makes us angry.

Raffat: The more you Hindus doubt our patriotism, the more we turn to our religion for refuge.

Shaku: So, politics becomes the criminal of sectarian pain.

Arvind: Perhaps if we express emotional ideas like this in class, students will see the interplay of political and religious realities.

Ellen: Please do! It's coming through.

Tom: Definitely. I'm impressed by your honesty, yet controlled anger.

Raffat: We're raising so many issues and mixing different time periods.

Shaku: Will North American students know about Ayodhya? Or Partition?

Ellen: More will know about Partition.

Shaku: In a distant way—like the English sipping gin, I suppose.

Harris: Repeating what *communal* means won't hurt. Even *lathi*. Will they know that it's a strong stick, a couple feet long, used by police instead of guns?

Arvind: We can't explain every detail.

Tom: Could I ask a question? How have you worked at hatred—as a religious group or as individuals?

Harris: *[Finding a place to sit]* Yes, explain. Don't give Americans excuse to see us Indians with more contempt than they already do.

Raffat: Christians frequently denigrate our faiths.

Shaku: We're told to expect Christians to have peaceful solutions. But we know better.

Ellen: I see the mirror pointing my way.

Arvind: I'd add a comment from the *Tamas* serial, even though it too has nationalistic strains. The very *awful* violence that I saw acted out turned me against being violent. It convinced me of how inhumane religious groups can be.

Tom: So, seeing the outcome tempers your instinctive urge? *[He sets up the ironing board]*

Shaku: The aftermath of deep compassion and profound risks that some people of faith took struck me.

Raffat: I recall an incident after Ayodhya, early '93. In Calcutta, a Muslim rushed into a temple when bombs were tossed into it. He rescued a Hindu priest and a family of eight and protected them inside his own home. He even rescued the Hanuman deity.

Arvind: And the majority Hindus of Bhopal went door-to-door to gather food for five hundred families—Hindu and Muslim—who fled their homes during that city's riot.

Tom: Such actions by people of your faith must instill some pride.

Harris: Two weeks after mobs destroyed temples in Calcutta, a Muslim raised rupees among his community to rebuild the structures, so that Hindus could again offer prayers.

Shaku: The image that sticks with me is of a human chain in Mumbai. Not long after the place burst into flames, people of diverse faiths joined hands to call for peace, to promote mutual, secular beliefs. One chain of people grew to fifty-five kilometers.

Harris: You could report lots of such incidents, in Kanpur and Ahmedabad, Patna and Delhi.

Ellen: How do you explain that? Christians serve because of Christ.

Raffat: Such actions reflect universal, human good will. It's not confined to one faith. It may at times even express political action.

Arvind: People take risks to condemn wrong. Rage against political leaders, who instill hatred based on religious ties, enters those human chains.

Shaku: Poisoned minds find relief.

Raffat: And secularists come to the fore—those who expect the government to maintain composure with each living faith.

Harris: If Christians could outgrow narrow views, you'd likely face your internal injustices.

Arvind: Did you hear about Bhiwandi—a city of twelve lakh (12 x 100,000) people, two-thirds Muslim, not far from Mumbai?

Shaku: A documentary's to be produced about it.

Raffat: Known for major, communal riots in 1970 and '84, the city now offers a counter model.

Tom: What caused the 1970 riots?

Harris: Some say it was economics mixed with religion. Asghar Ali Engineer notes Bhiwandi's power-loom industry. It was owned by and supported many Muslim workers. Because of heavy traffic through Bhiwandi, and the revenue gained through road tolls, Muslims began to challenge fixed Hindu leaders.

Ellen: *[Bringing more water, checks for needed refills]* Shifts in power can affect justice—whether related to sex, faith, or class.

Arvind: But, communal tension doesn't stem from economics alone. Our secular system remains flawed. And our hope for nationalism plus our heritage of nonviolence fail at strategic times.

Raffat: True. But recall the police officer who formed a political scheme of seventy committees in Bhiwandi in the late eighties.

Harris: Or, consider the current police chief who chairs a major Peace Committee. Having worked to solve problems, by the time of Ayodhya's aftermath, some people chose peaceful efforts, not riots.

Ellen: They had done their homework, rather than just react at the time of an incident?

Arvind: That's what justice making is. With vision and cooperation, Indians can live with our religious pluralism, pluralism that offers profound benefits.

Shaku: Yet, tolerance fails when intolerant acts show their dreadful head.

Raffat: Ellen or Tom, do you know of the Henry Martyn Institute of Islamic Studies, in Hyderabad?

Tom: Never heard of it.

Raffat: There, Christians, Muslims and Hindus try to prevent clashes.

Harris: In Hyderabad, where toward seventy percent of the population is Muslim, less rioting followed Ayodhya than you might expect. But deep feelings flared up more recently, I heard.

Shaku: In India, we know that Mother Teresa doesn't have a corner on "loving the neighbor." *[Sets dirty dishes from all four on table]*

Arvind: Strife in India plunges millions into working toward harmony.

Raffat: Nor should Christians point-the-finger at Muslim-Hindu conflict.

Ellen: We know. Although Irish differences might heal, we recall the Crusades, the massacre of Jews, and more recent atrocities.

Tom: Or, we continue to destroy through prejudice of class, race, and sexual orientation.

Arvind: Most of our class members are active or nominal Christian; we'll recall such admissions.

Tom: How do Christians in India respond to multifaith conflict?

Shaku: They're a small minority—less than three percent—compared to Muslims.

Arvind: With eleven percent, Muslims have always threatened us more.

Raffat: No doubt Indian Christians 'feel closer' to Muslims; our history is partly shared.

Harris: *[Standing, looking at his watch]* My uncle has Christian neighbors in Calcutta. After Ayodhya riots, those friends stored my relatives' valuables. They could have hid with them too.

Arvind: In *Tamas*, Sahni says, "Neighbors quarrel, but...a neighbor is like one's right hand."

Raffat: Well . . . history leads me to qualify that ideal. Some Christians regret being smug about strife between other faiths in India.

Shaku: They often avoid strong support of either Hindus or Muslims in the thick of conflict.

Arvind: I know a Catholic Father Bhatt who defied curfew in Allahabad during the Ayodhya aftermath to gather supplies for riot victims and bring together leaders of seven faiths to pray.

Raffat: But, Christians can't risk majority Hindu disapproval. They fear being your next target.

Harris: Acts of violence over recent years justify that fear. *[H. stands up to stretch]*

Shaku: Hey, Harris, we soon have a planning meeting for International Students Club.

Harris: Oh, right. I'll take my *tali* to my room and meet you at the front door.

Shaku: Thanks for the curry, Arvind and Raffat.

Arvind: And you for the ideas. *[S. and H. exit as Tom waves. He finishes a pair of trousers and puts the ironing board away.]*. I guess we have plenty to discuss in class.

Raffat: Perhaps we could start with issues of fear.

Arvind: Both religious and political fears . . . But let's watch the video now.

Ellen: Thanks for letting us listen. I'll see you later. *[E exits]*

Tom: *[Picking up the glasses]* Hope your presentation goes well, guys. I have a media conference this coming week, so won't be around much. *[T. exits to the kitchenette and into his bedroom as A. flicks on the DVD.]*
[Lights/End]

7

Biblical Texts and Multifaith Issues

Imagine this exchange between two seminary students as it takes place in Bangalore, India. Ranjith, student at United Theological College, welcomes Rachel from The School of Theology in Toronto, Ontario in Canada. Rachel has just arrived at UTC for a new semester. An Insider-to-Insider exchange, this reveals two Christians as they cross cultures with each other and with an ancient (also Jewish) text.

Ranjith: Hello. My name is Ranjith. I noticed you in my Religions of India class. Welcome to UTC.

Rachel: Thanks. Are you a theology major?

Ranjith: No, I'm focused on biblical studies. What interfaith ties have you made in Toronto?

Rachel: Not enough, though quite a few Muslims live in the city and the number of Asians increases each year. I lived in south India during three years of high school and always wanted to return. My degree area is New Testament, with a focus in Cross-Culture and Faith Studies.

Ranjith: That's a good combination. You've no doubt had Early Church courses at Toronto?

Rachel: In fact, the Peter-Cornelius story supports my interest in interreligious questions.

Ranjith: Of course. Both religious and cultural settings shape how we interpret.

Rachel: You just expect to combine features from multifaiths over here, right?

Ranjith: Well, we value resources beyond the Bible, like the experience of people around us. We draw from both our Judeo-Christian heritage and Hindu scriptures, with their four-thousand-year history.

Rachel: Say more.

Ranjith: Our history intersects with our present—classical language and religious insight with socio-economic realities and actions.

Rachel: God's action being part of both.

Ranjith: Wesley Ariarajah rightly said, "Christians have come to claim or see God as tribal." But that view counters the biblical message that all people and the whole creation belong to God.

Rachel: And within that universal framework appear many cross-cultural options. Consider the Hebrew Esther. That she and Mordecai kept their being Jewish a secret from the Persian king and court reflects a burden. Their identity was incongruent.

Ranjith: Incongruent? Because they knew dual loyalty? Didn't features from both faiths enrich their total experience?

Rachel: Valid question. Western Christians praise her Jewish loyalty (though married to a Persian) but might fault people with Hindu heritage who retain rituals or strong family bonds after choosing to follow Christ.

Ranjith: Might we all be more respectful if we held our personal faith "lightly"? Not without conviction, mind you, but without aggression toward other faiths. Not to endorse truth from only one group. Peter's decision not to baptize Cornelius' household—not to form "Petrine Christians"—may have helped people be more tolerant.

Rachel: That text in Acts has more 'lessons.' Cornelius was a God-fearing, non-Jew who was known for piety—prayers, almsgiving, devotion, and service to the synagogue.

Ranjith: At the time, many Jewish Christians believed that Gentile men had to be circumcised, to observe Moses' law, in order to be one of them.

Rachel: We know about Peter's vision while praying. He resists the invitation to eat what he thought was unclean. After a voice warns him not to judge so bluntly what is or isn't clean, he discovers guests at his door. They ask him to return with them to Cornelius' household.

Ranjith: Trusting the vision, he goes. And he enters, to share space and food with Gentiles. Such sharing meant that he trusted Cornelius' faith in God, his way of dealing justly with others.

Rachel: I value William Willimon's comments on the text. He calls this the turning point of the entire book: Will "insiders" invite "outsiders," and with what outcomes? Knowing Peter's Jewish sense of identity, God needed to re-focus Peter's perception of clean and unclean, about both food and people. And God needed to help Peter admit that Jewish people of faith, newly Christian, had twisted the universal into the particular.

Ranjith: To limit God's inclusion of all into "only" language—'only we know who belongs'—distorts the breadth of God's family, or kin-dom. To insist that only Jesus reveals God's Way always limits insight. And Peter had to learn the tough lesson that God is <u>im</u>partial.

Rachel: For Christians today not to insist that Jesus is the only Way to comprehend God is probably no more radical than for first century Jewish Christians to accept uncircumcised men as full believers.

Ranjith: The choice is ours, and it's tough. Do we believe that God is impartial? Ariarajah says that no community is closer or more important to God than another. Will we humbly "see the sheets" (like Peter) heavy with people of all nations who fear God?

Rachel: Peter's profound learning has yet to sink in.

Ranjith: If Christianity were to become a universal religion, how the Church would need conversion! I sometimes wonder if, similar to Peter or Jonah, we are called to "Arise and Go."

Rachel: What's your view of Jonah . . . or Daniel?

Ranjith: I value Ariarajah's outline of Jonah's annoyance. He didn't expect the people of Nineveh to repent. Nor did he expect God to respond once he (Jonah) invited the Ninevites to change. God could embarrass an already-isolated prophet. Jonah simply doubted whether God would carry out the threat.

Rachel: Jonah resented God's mercy toward non-Israelites.

Ranjith: When people of one faith resent another, they get jealous of God's favored actions toward that 'other.' They need to re-view the limits that they impose on God's universal concern.

Rachel: Daniel expressed a different type of resistance, right? He persisted in praying, when told to quit.

Ranjith: What intrigues me about Daniel reflects Gandhi's comments. Gandhi thought of Daniel as one of the greatest passive resistors. Gandhi knew quite a bit about the Bible. The minimal study by Christians of the *Upanishads*, the *Brahmasutras*, or even the *Gita* shames me.

Rachel: I know none of them. However, I read an article about Gandhi's influence on the study of Daniel. It stressed how a reader's cultural context influences interpretation.

Ranjith: Cultures determine how we perceive any event. You know the elephant story. People, if blindfolded and given one part of an elephant to touch, like the tail, will imagine a quite different object from one who holds the ear. Perceptions vary, depending on experience too. How Muslim men genuflect might shape their view of Jains at prayer. But . . . your comment about Gandhi and Daniel?

Rachel: Because Gandhi, an active resistor, noted Daniel's passive resistance to a foreign ruler, scholars ask new questions when studying Daniel. Gandhi also compared Mirabai, the noted Hindu *bhakti* saint, with Daniel. She defied social expectations for a woman by countering marriage and traveling alone. Her utter devotion to Krishna mattered; to submit to domestic or political pressures did not.

Ranjith: Gandhi valued common traits across faith lines even as he blessed kindred spirits.

Rachel: Might we, for contrast, mention some exclusive Hebrew trends?

From early on, many felt that they had a monopoly with God.

Ranjith: That attitude suggests communal identity here in India. Christians may explain Hebrew vision as: Our Hebrew God is superior to your god. Our way of salvation surpasses yours.

Rachel: Israel has tried to learn that they were "chosen" to tell others about God's universal light. Being "chosen" required being "agents of [God's] blessings upon all the families of the earth." Rather than be set apart from, being 'light' to others meant to include them.

Ranjith: God truly yearns for equity and dignity for all. Prophets like Amos, Micah, and Hosea stressed God's global condition for justice. "... let justice roll down like waters." Or, ". . . what does God require? Do justice, love kindness, and walk humbly with your God."

Rachel: Also, "I desire steadfast love and not sacrifice." Yet, western Christians who see justice primarily as a call to do charity may neglect the more radical work of systemic or structural change. We could work harder to find God's long-term solutions to oppression.

Ranjith: Have you seen S. J. Anthonysamy's word about religious arrogance? Thinking of God as absolute, early Israelites denied other peoples' valid views of the Divine.

Rachel: Yet, Isaiah the prophet declared that God blessed Egypt and Assyria, as surely as Israel. Seeing Christian resistance to God's presence and actions among other faiths today helps me believe that the task for Israel was tough.

Ranjith: Anthonysamy sees God's mission as bringing "justice to the nations" and naming all nations as part of God's Kin-dom. It makes total sense for my land of multifaiths.

Rachel: Even Jesus had to learn that lesson. Think of the Syrophoenician woman's meeting.

Ranjith: A good example.

Rachel: In order to rest, Jesus went into a house in the 'outer' region of Tyre. But, a Greek-speaking (Gentile) woman sought him out on behalf of her distressed daughter. Jesus' reply to her plea that he heal her child expressed priority: Jews get such ministry or 'bread' first. To give to Gentiles, called "dogs," what was meant for Jews would not be fair ('kosher'). Noting the imagery, she countered: even dogs eat children's crumbs that fall. Because so wise, she was assured that her daughter's health was restored.

Ranjith: That sounds like Mark's account.

Rachel: Elizabeth Schussler Fiorenza, whose work with biblical texts renews my faith, states that the Syrophoenician woman "represents the [repressed] biblical-theological voice of women." The patient, undaunted pillar attacked Jesus' use of common attitude and lingo—dogs.

Ranjith: How can religion justify such 'dogged' disrespect of another? To denigrate another's faith is not even a cheap way to commend one's own. The history of disdain toward those who differ judges people of faith to the core!

Rachel: What amazes me is Jesus' revolution—his own attitudes and practice. He then had to prod the Twelve, also long-biased. To watch as some Gentiles caught his message—his Way too radical for many Jews who thought of themselves as "chosen"—convinces me of Jesus' humanity. He turned around. He understood in a new way God's inclusion of all people of faith.

Ranjith: The woman rebuffed Jesus. Thought of as second class, as worthy to eat only after "first place or world" people had their fill, she balked. She won the argument while extending his metaphor. Her insight revealed that she and her daughter have a place in God's kin-dom.

Rachel: As David Rhoads suggests, "she bears God's word to [Jesus]." Because of the woman's faith, Jesus knows that Gentiles deserve to receive his ministry. He leaves for Decapolis to heal and feed four thousand Gentiles, a major change in strategy having transpired.

Ranjith: The story says a great deal about crossing borders. But our Christian heritage defines boundaries or seeks to guard and protect "the holy."

Rachel: Many western Christians tend to isolate ourselves from what differs.

Ranjith: Borders hinder wholeness for all. But, Jesus created bridges.

Rachel: We are challenged "not to set limits on the universality of the good news of the kingdom [kin-dom] of God," Rhoads said. Jonah needed to learn that lesson with the Ninevites. The disciples needed to learn it from Jesus more than once. Like when he perceived the theological depth of the oppressed woman at Jacob's well.

Ranjith: The Good Samaritan demonstrates the principle when serving a needy traveler left stranded by religious leaders. And the message applies to India's religious scene—due to barriers, to contempt for people who worship the One God in 'strange ways.' Ariarajah says that "Truth can only be shared. There is nothing to defend, nothing to thrust upon others."

Rachel: Distinct faith traditions, laws and borders often fail to encompass God's Ways for meeting or extending wholeness to people. So we learn through today's 'Syrophoenician and Samaritan women.'

Ranjith: We turn to 'Peter and Jonah' to renew us. . . . .

(calling) "Oh, Avinash and Fiona, wait up. I'd like you to meet Rachel. She's just come from Toronto. We're both taking Religions of India and already had a good exchange."

8

Hindu Scriptures Introduced

Two Hindu guests are imagined to have been invited to speak at a Christian function in Chennai (Madras), south India. The occasion was the fiftieth anniversary of the beginning in 1947 of the ecumenical CSI, Church of South India. All speakers raised important questions about next steps for interreligious respect and understanding within India. Prior to a report about a new interreligious ashram to be opened fifty kilometers away, participants hear this exchange about Hindu Scriptures. Meera and Sundar are welcomed, the convener draping flower garlands over their heads.

Meera: With this group's warm welcome, we're pleased to be here. Our time will be well spent.

Sundar: Yes, we're honored to join you on this occasion. And we welcome all of you to celebrate our Diwali festival next week.

Meera: During tea break, a woman said that our names reminded her of other saints.

Sundar: Oh, you reminded her of Mirabai, the esteemed sixteenth century *bhaktin*.

Meera: And your name reminded her of the notable Indian Christian mystic Sadhu Sundar Singh who died in 1929.

Sundar: We value the linkage but can't claim such honor. Being who we are, we're grateful to share our present task.

Meera: We agreed to review basic Hindu scriptures.

Sundar: While several of you are quite informed about Hindu scriptures, others need an overview, to place known texts in proper groupings or chronology.

Meera: Thanks for your interest in our religion. During our next presentation before dinner, we'll explain Hindu theism.

Sundar: The task of direct comparison with Christian scriptures we'll leave for non-Hindus. To deal with the spectrum of Hindu texts is task enough.

Meera: I'm always glad to learn more about my own religion. A central check for multifaith exchange is whether people of a religion can affirm what *others* say about *them*.

Sundar: That posture shows respect, but not all adherents of religions practice it.

Meera: Not all people who *dis*agree with another religion *mis*understand it either.

Sundar: Further, members of the same religion differ from each other when describing its history, practice, and beliefs, or the truth and piety that result from beliefs.

Meera: We can experience another's religion without believing it. But, to believe or disbelieve my own or another's does not in itself make it true or false. Any belief can be mistaken.

Sundar: Or, it can ring with Truth. Hindus also wish to learn about our faith from those who are not loyal to it.

Meera: We hope that you non-Hindus understand our content within this framework.

Sundar: And we invite you non-Hindus to ask questions, to re-examine and perhaps modify your understandings of our themes.

Meera: Our introductory words might alert non-Hindus to another factor. Calling you "non-Hindu" is not pejorative; we identify our Hindu heritage as normative, the norm from which we determine who is 'other.'

Sundar: Not a slip of the tongue, we prod Christians to accept your being a minority in India.

Meera: Christian literature refers to those not of that faith as "non-Christian." Here, we intentionally refer to people who are <u>non</u>-Hindu. Perhaps at the new ashram, an alternative to "non" language will be used, perhaps 'followers of religions.'

Sundar: People of *living* faiths might be the emphasis, or *essential* Hinduism. But, Meera, begin our mini-history of Hindu scriptures. (Many of the terms that we will use are on the blackboard.)

Texts		Terms		God names mentioned
Rig Veda	*Upanishads*	*bhaktin*	*dharma*	Varuna
Sama Veda	*Yogasutras*	*samhita*	*smriti*	Indra
Yaju Veda	*Dharmashastra*	*veda*	*Trimurti*	Agni
Atharva Veda	*Manusmriti*	*yajna*	*sruti*	Brahman
Samhitas	*Itihasa*	*mantra*	*Isvara*	Shiva
Brahmanas	*Ramayana*	*jnana*	*atman*	Vishnu
Aranyakas	*Mahabharata*	*karma*		Brahma
Vedangas	*Bhagavadgita*	*samsara*		Krishna
Purusasukta	*Puranas*	*varna*		

Meera: On occasion questioned, broad sweeps of time suggest that Aryan people moved from Central Asia to places such as Mohenjodaro and Harappa between 2000 and 1500 BCE (Before Common Era). They left no literature. The thousand-plus hymns or *mantras* of the *Rig Veda* collection (*samhita*) were composed and compiled between 1200 and 1000 BCE. Christian writer A. S. Appasamy Pillai suggests that the germ of concepts like *logos* or atonement might appear in the *Rig Veda*.

Sundar: Several categories of religious knowledge (*Veda* means revealed knowledge.) emerged between 1200 and 600 BCE. Vedic writings are known as revealed *(sruti)* texts. Hindus believe that ancient seers like Marichi or Atri perceived the words that were 'breathed' on them by a deity.

Meera: Having heard the words or sounds, they in turn passed on or recited the archaic Sanskrit through oral tradition.

Sundar: We hope that non-Hindus will honor our study pattern of extensive memorizing.

Meera: Sacrifice was central during the Vedic age. Christians also know of sacrifice through your ancient Jewish heritage. As everything comes down from above, all is symbolically returned to God. Through sacrifice (*yajna*), the offering is made sacred in return.

Sundar: Swami Prabhavananda includes parallel columns for the four major collections of *Vedas* and the stages that overlap or augment them.[1]

Meera: In general, we have four *Veda* types: *Rig Veda* or hymns, *Sama Veda* or musical chants, *Yaju Veda* or sacrifice details, and *Atharva Veda* or poetic charms and oracles.

Sundar: The categories Meera just noted then have stages within them more expressive of work (*karma*) or knowledge (*jnana*). Subdivisions of *Samhitas* and *Brahmanas* center on sacrifice, therefore action. But emphasis with *Aranyakas* and U*panishads* is on speculation or inner reality, rather than outward symbols.

Meera: Now we should briefly explain those parts. Non-Hindus are perhaps most familiar with the *Rig Veda* collection of hymns, used by priests to address the gods. After being transmitted orally by families of poet-priests for several centuries, these ten thousand verses (*rics*), or revelations of praise, were compiled.

Sundar: The *Rig Veda* is one of the world's oldest, intact religious texts. Its religious concerns and social values have been strictly memorized and recited for almost three thousand years. Toward the end of the *Rig Veda* period, the importance given to gods like Indra or Agni was transferred to new, functional deities.

Meera: Much earlier, Varuna, the sky god, had been known as the highest god. Then Varuna's theism shifted to a latent quality when replaced in importance by Indra, god of thunder.

Sundar: Whether thirty-three or three thousand and three, whichever particular god was worshiped, it "summed the power of the other gods and represented all."

Meera: We'll expand on that comment in our next session on Hindu theism. Just to say here that the more abstract Brahman (Absolute) of Hindu philosophy differs from *Isvara*.

Sundar: Today, *Isvara* means much the same to us that God does for non-Hindus. God is "supreme and benevolent."

Meera: For major Hindu religious movements that center in Vishnu and Siva, God is definite.

Sundar: As you alluded, Hindu thought includes both theism—the idea of Divine existence—and monism—the idea of a formless substance. You referred to Brahman, the abstract Absolute that controls all. The term Brahman, or Self, names or identifies Reality, that which exists behind all else.

Meera: Later, each person was thought to have one self, termed *atman*. For a person to worship the more abstract Brahman annuls any separation between Brahman and the person. The self, or *atman*, merges with Brahman. Naming Brahman with Atman or Atman with Brahman came to be the "central event" at the time of the *Upanishads*, a writer named Kulandran says.

Sundar: More on that theme later too. Shifts occurred in ancient religious sacrifice. For some generations its practice grew. It was perceived in part as a means to defeat demonic enemies or to "engender the order of cosmos and society."[2]

Meera: Specialists in the musical aspects of ritual chanting involved with sacrifice turn to the *Sama Vedas*. And those who serve worshipers about to make offerings learn formulas *(yajus)* of the *Yaju Vedas,* to enhance the power of ritual acts.

Sundar: A later, separate class of priests, the *atharvans*, compiled the poetic magic known as *Atharva Veda*. To detail the overlapping chronology becomes complex. But auxiliary texts like the *Vedangas* followed to deal with topics like grammar, mathematics or poetics. They stress exactness in the study of the *Vedas* through pronunciation, etymology of rare words, or the practice of verse meters. Hymns are never simply read; practitioners learn to recite each verse in multiple ways.

Meera: Non-Hindus might fail to comprehend our sense of discipline or respect for repetition. Even our concept of God as both One and Many can 'draw a blank.'

Perhaps we should explain the other Vedic divisions. Non-Hindus might be more familiar with particular mantras or hymns of the *samhitas*. Neither magic nor logic describes the objective and subjective aspects of reality that connect through *mantras*.

Sundar: I value Raimundo Panikkar's explanation of how faith, understanding, utterance and being continued (handed down by a master) come together in *mantras*. The *Veda's* first *mantra* links praise, meditation, sacrifice, engagement with divinity, and payment.[3]

> I magnify God, the Divine Fire,
> the Priest, Minister of the sacrifice,
> the Offerer of oblation, supreme Giver of treasure.
>   *RV* I.1.1

Meera: For us, the most sacred Vedic *mantra* is the Gayatri. Chanting it at dawn or evening, we feel released from sin.

> *Om Om Om.*
> Let us meditate on the glorious splendour
> of the divine light (Life-giver).
> May he illuminate our meditation (mind).
> *Shanti* (peace) *Shanti, Shanti.*   *RV* III.62.10

Sundar: *Brahmanas* offer detailed commentaries on everyday sacrifice or rules of conduct. Through rituals, we pay our debts to different categories of people or spirits.

Meera: Non Hindus might ask if Hindu practice of *karma*—action that produces fruit—or caste began here.

Sundar: Links are possible. Whereas sacrificial actions at first were thought to cause overall good, personal actions came to determine status within one's rebirth (*samsara*). Further, status evolved for the specialists (*brahmanas*, Anglicized as "brahman" or "brahmin"). They fashioned or recited the liturgical speech that conveyed power in sacrifice.

Meera: We know that the inherited, priestly *brahman* class, prominent in sacrificial ritual, did engage with the new ruling class. In turn, they gained political authority through increased sacrifice.

Sundar: To look into this development, see the *Purusasukta* hymn text. It first depicts what later became the fourfold *varna* scheme.[4] But we must hurry on.

Meera: Yes. Before focusing on the *Upanishads*, we might mention again the *Aranyakas*, also called forest treatises. They interpret truth through mystical mantras, not rites or ceremonies.

Sundar: Though they took shape over a thousand years, the classical Sanskrit *Upanishads* are dated from 600 BCE. Their mystic writers, who knew Vedic hymns, were intent to include intuitive experience. They pursued liberation from *samsara* through austerity or devoted "sitting near." The Way of Knowledge transpired as sacrifice declined or took a different direction.

Meera: As the ideal of complete self-denial surfaced, "nothing higher than Brahman" came to be a central teaching of the *Upanishads*. Some non-Hindus have no doubt read Bede Griffiths' *The Cosmic Revelation*. He explains how the *Upanishads* start from the immanence of Brahman (God's Power) within all creatures, to recognize God's transcendence.

By contrast, the Judeo-Christian approach begins from God's transcendence.[5]

Sundar: That comment moves us into our second session. But hearers should understand the transition spurred by the Upanishads, located at the end of the *Vedas*, therefore also called *Vedanta*.

Meera: Some non-Hindus know of the brahman teachers Aruni or Yajnavalkya. The *Upanishads* are known through stories used to explain philosophy.

Sundar: For example, Aruni questions his son Svetaketu, who had returned from twelve years' study with a guru. Through practical lessons, profound truth was reinforced—like repeatedly splitting a seed or adding salt to a bowl of water.[6]

Meera: Or, recall Yajnavalkya's account of multiple gods. The *Upanishads* record our first attempt at a systematic philosophy to accent spiritual knowledge.

Sundar: Consider Radhakrishnan's statement: "The aim of the *Upanishads* is not so much to reach philosophical truth as to bring peace and freedom to the anxious human spirit."

Meera: To attain a high state of consciousness, we combine hearing, through Vedic *sruti* or a *guru*, with reasoning and concentrated yoga. We meditate upon ultimate reality.

Sundar: We simply don't have time to explain Patanjali's second century BCE system that merged older practices into the *Yogasutras*.

Meera: Nor will we introduce the texts of the six major philosophical schools. In fact, we can only mention the body of literature called *Dharmashastra*. It obviously focuses on *dharma*—"that which upholds and supports order."

Sundar: It explains a person's or a group's sacred moral duties within the world. Rituals were no longer considered adequate.

Meera: *Manusmriti* is part of *dharmashastra*. Of human origin, the Law of Manu was more widely accepted than other codes.

In contrast to the *sruti* or revealed *Vedas*, the texts that we'll next introduce are known as *smriti* or remembered scripture.

Sundar: Most familiar is the *Itihasa*, the corpus of texts known through two major epics. We will only mention the *Ramayana* and attend more to the longest poem in the world, the *Mahabharata*.[7]

Meera: Non-Hindus likely know that it is much longer than the Bible.

Meant for all Hindus, the sweeping yet relevant epics were not to be passed on verbatim like the *Vedas*. Accounts expanded until the somewhat final form of the fourth century CE (Common Era).

Sundar: The *Mahabharata* story surrounds a great war between the sons or clans of Bharat, from perhaps 900 BCE. The human conflict depicts jealousy between Pandva's five sons and the one hundred sons of an egotistic King Dhratarastra. The epic teaches people to overcome the drive for earthly glory via truth, renunciation, peace, and salvation.

Meera: On another level, writers may see the epics as a new *theophany* (divine appearance). Whereas Vedic gods like Indra could not "contend with the demons and threatening chaos,"[8] the deity of the epics was capable. Not only transcendent Absolute, Vishnu "intervenes directly in human affairs." Through *avataras* or forms like Krishna, Vishnu descends to earth to restore righteousness. Vishnu is personalized through Krishna.

Sundar: That insight moves into the *Bhagavadgita* or "Song of God." Its eighteen cantos (seven hundred couplets) are part of the *Mahabharata's* Book VI called *Bhismaparvan*. Whereas the *Upanishads*, though true, were meant for the elite, the "*Gita* is meant for all."

Meera: Most Indians, non-Hindus included, know this second century CE story of the Pandva hero Arjuna. Although a small portion of the vast Hindu texts, it may be the most popular or influential. Bede Griffiths calls the *Gita* the "essential teaching and spirit of ancient Hindu scriptures."[9]

Sundar: Perhaps a summary paragraph will suffice. Disenchanted with social problems and hesitant to kill his kin, young Arjuna engages his charioteer who happens to be Krishna, Shiva's eighth avatar. Lord Krishna explains the disgrace of either fleeing from or expecting personal gain through duty. He advocates victory over desire and compassion for all creatures. He assures Arjuna that he cannot destroy his relatives' souls. Hopefully, Arjuna will combine *bhakti,* active love of the personal Absolute (Krishna), with earlier modes. With sacrifice, yoga, or becoming Brahman no longer adequate, the *Bhakti* movement stems from Brahmanism.

Meera: "Worthy of worship . . . the way of Devotion to Krishna is of all ways the best."[10] We'll address that personal aspect of Hindu theism, plus the views of Brahman endorsed by Sankara, Ramanuja, and Madhwa later. Finally, we mention the genre of texts called the *Puranas*.

Sundar: Although *Puranas* were composed during the thousand years after 500 CE, some may be as old as the *Vedas*. In addition to countless others, eighteen *Puranas* are called major (four hundred thousand verses) and eighteen sub-major. Long verse narratives, they explain Hindu mythology.

Meera: Not limited to the primary deities—Visnu, Siva, or Brahma the Creator of the Hindu Trimurti—*Purana* texts also present the complex picture of the Goddess.

Sundar: We regret having rushed this survey of Hindu scriptures. If you have questions or comments, please ask them now or at the end of our next session.

Meera: Thank you for listening so well. I hope that one of you will offer a survey of Biblical texts. The array of types of literature, stories, and characters confuse most Hindus.

Reflection: *Selections from Hindu scriptures to ponder:*

Lovely of form art thou, alike on every side;
Though far, thou shinest brightly as if close at hand.
O God, thou seest through even the dark of night.
Let us not in thy friendship, Agni, suffer harm.   (Rig Veda I.XCIV.7)

From unreality lead me to reality;
from darkness lead me to light;
from death lead me to immortality.
         (Brhadaranyaka Upanishad I.3.8)

Give me your whole heart,	*Who love you dearly,*
Love and adore me,	*Lay down all duties*
Worship me always,	*In me, your refuge.*
Bow to me only,	*Fear no longer,*
And you shall find me:	*For I will save you*
This is my promise.	*From sin and from bondage.*

(Gita XVIII 6306)

Endnotes:

[1] Swami Prabhavananda. *The Spiritual Heritage of India*, Garden City, NY: Doubleday & Co., 1963, 4.

[2] Richard H. Davis. "A Brief History of Religions in India, Introduction," in *Religions of India in Practice*. Donald S. Lopez, Jr., ed. Princeton, NJ: Princeton Univ Pr, 1995, 14.

[3] Raimundo Panikkar. *The Vedic Experience Mantramanjari*. Berkeley: Univ of California Pr., 1977, 39, 37.

[4] Davis. 11.

[5] Bede Griffiths. *The Cosmic Revelation: The Hindu Way to God*, Springfield, ILL: Templegate Pub., 1983, 83.

[6] Swami, 42 ff, or R. R. Diwakar and S. Ramakrishnan, eds. *Upanishads in Story and Dialogue*, Bombay: Bharatiya Vidya Bhavan, 1st ed. 1960, 1981, 123.

[7] The story of Rama's heroic battle with a giant king on behalf of his faithful wife Sita is explained in the dialogue about Hindu goddesses (chap. 10)

[8] Davis, 23.

[9] Griffiths, 12.

[10] Sabapathy Kulandran. "The Rise of Hindu Theism," in *Grace A Comparative Study of the Doctrine in Christianity and Hinduism*. London: Lutterworth Pr, 1964, 140-41.

9

Encounters: "spiritual beings having a human experience"

My respect for what is plural about religion spans five decades. I first lived in India from 1962-65; the diverse religious scene attracted and puzzled me. A poster now near my desk states in eighteen languages, "There will be peace on earth when there is peace among the world religions," noted by Roman Catholic theologian Hans Küng. Difference persists within religions too as with Suni, Shia, or Sufi loyalty within Islam or distinct features within countries, as with Islam in Egypt, India, or Malaysia, with Hinduism in India or Indonesia. To probe the meaning of religious conciliation or the strength of fragmented yet sacred expressions within society involves spiritual and human being.

In addition to multiple Asians (names like Aleaz, Ariarajah, Amaladoss, Samartha, Sharma, and Thangaraj), two Americans have distinctly shaped my interreligious being. Articles and books (like *A New Religious America)*, the CD-ROM *On Common Ground*, and taped lectures by Diana Eck provide data and a spirit of openness toward religious others. As director of the "Pluralism Project: World Religions in America," Eck inspires engagement with the sacred plural. Her insight into Hinduism within India's multi-religious landscape impresses too (in *Encountering God*). Paul Knitter's friendship, teaching and writing have further taught me. With global connections, he exudes faith commitment alongside readiness to receive spiritual difference. He presents western, Christian views (*Introducing Theologies of Religions*) and multifaith insight (*The Myth of Religious Superiority* and *Without Buddha I Could not be a Christian*). To practice Knitter's approach to terms like *only, truly* and *wholly* enables multifaith openness.[1]

Decades of friendship across religious borders provide depth of perspective. When John and I taught at Woodstock School in the '60s, in the foothills of the ever-changing, colossal Himalayas, I met world religions through books, students, and worship settings. Indian and South Asian students at Goshen College—Hindu, Sikh, Christian, Buddhist and Muslim—have taught me while sharing curry meals. Feminist thought also values human and spiritual being: openness to diversity and ambiguity, validation of experience, and connection rather than dualistic opposition. A Fulbright study tour ("Women, the Family, and Social Change in India") and six other short-term assignments in varied Indian locations (one on staff with a theological college) have deepened my spiritual and human being. During return visits to India, Hindu families often host us, confirming the Wisdom of *Just Hospitality* as Letty Russell's recent book promotes.

Encounters prompt musing and produce growth. Whether perched in a third-class-sleeper car of a train with a book of ancient temples in hand, conversing between class preparations, or pausing inside a mosque in Hyderabad or Mussoorie, I absorbed culture—and thereby religion. I read extensively about India's living faiths. Events held sacred meaning: meals begun with prayer to the One God in Muslim, Hindu, Sikh, or Parsi homes; newspaper features or regular columns; multifaith meetings on themes of light, ritual or holidays. Back in Goshen, I addressed issues at the local college: when no Islamic prayers or scriptures were included in a memorial service for a Muslim student who died; when Hindus wished to celebrate Diwali or Holi on campus.

How does "loving the neighbor as oneself" shape contexts where sacred difference abounds? Freed not to know the extent of God's Ways, as of salvation, I trust divine Wisdom rather than defend exclusive absolutes. My journey, from a small-town, Mennonite heritage, to understand God alongside people with unique names or forms for the Ultimate, lies open to the plural. For, "every religious tradition promises salvation in some form," theologian Gordon Kaufman says.

Rooted in Christian strengths, my interest in India shifted from curiosity with the exotic to deeper questions and insight into Hindu, Indian Islamic, or animist religions. From the local minaret in the bazaar, Muslim calls to prayer echoed across the valley. Hats worn by shopkeepers identified religious loyalty just as Hindu forehead markings distinguished Shaivites from followers drawn to Vishnu. Sikh women became more than those who wore two-pieced, Punjabi outfits, their turbaned men more than trusted taxi drivers.

When traveling, I slipped out of shoes to enter temples and mosques. Ambivalent about invading others' sacred space that I failed to fully discern, I both observed and respected people's rituals. Their trust in The One beyond themselves had integrity. However, when caught in a frenzied crowd at the Jagannath temple festival in Puri, I knew fear—for personal safety, not awe. At such times, Christians had best stay near the coast and enjoy fresh shrimp bargained for dinner. At Varanasi in 1963, I lacked knowledge for what seemed like "holy chaos." Although a Muslim guide sensitively explained the rituals and temples of that holiest of Hindu cities, both his and my 'outsider' status surfaced.

'Holy ground' gained new meaning. The quiet of near-by Sarnath—its *stupas* and the panorama depicting Buddha's sermons—appealed more. It stretched the unfamiliar less. To stand, later, under the bodh tree where Gautama received enlightenment prompted holy awe, not unlike years later when I stood near the presumed site of Jesus' tomb. To tour the Ajunta Caves further explained an era when Buddhism and the subcontinent's leader Ashoka influenced Indian life toward tolerance. To routinely greet an elderly Muslim vendor in Mussoorie—his basket of fruit on one side and open *Qur'an* on the other—brought together Word with deed. However, surface encounters always left me yearning for deeper Truth. Experiencing God, I longed to know more of what others engaged in sacred rites found meaningful.

Content in *Blossoms in the Dust*, by Kusum Nair, resonated with exposure during vacation months in the '60s to rural, village India. We walked by mini, animist poles leaned together in fields in the state of Bihar. We shared in the rite of Christian foot washing, bucket and bare feet complementing the simple room for worship, made of earth and dung. We heard the distinct tones of *bhajans* and observed deep friendship between eastern tribal folk and western missioners. And we crossed rutted terrain to join villagers (Christian and Hindu) for annual harvest events near Jagdeeshpur. A row of plodding ox carts silhouetted against the setting sun lent spiritual peace to agrarian life at end of day.

Although Hindu families or village groups worship different forms of the One God, they seem not to compete. Honoring several deities at the same time, they draw from each the divine Essence needed at a given moment. To decrease confusion of Protestant denominations, Indian groups formed CSI in 1947 followed later by CNI, Churches of South or North India. My ecumenical self grew when involved with them. Puzzled by Christian fear of compromise, I paused: Why not value the 'hybrid' nature of each denomination, religion and person—in order to move toward greater solidarity among all?[2]

In India for the summer of 1967, distinctions of living in the more central city of Jabalpur revealed depth. Among no Christians in an Institute of math and science teachers, John and I joined city Methodists for Sunday worship. In a country pulsing with sacred symbols, dance, and temples, we keenly yet naively absorbed the interplay of culture with religion. Hindu processions passed. Drivers of three-wheeled scooters kept colored pictures of god forms overhead. In light of congestion and "near-misses," I resonated with trust in a Greater One.

During weekly restaurant meals with Institute teaching staff, conversation often turned to religion as chunks of cheese melted in the warm minestrone soup. A Hindu math professor and I discussed how my faith in a personal relationship with God differed from his concept of "seeing and being seen by God"—*darshan.* We valued the difference and mutually learned from the other's integrity. At the final staff meeting, a Muslim professor gave me a gift: Muhammad Asad's *Islam at the Crossroads.* I felt honored. The book describes a Christian's shift of loyalty to Islam. Through that experience of being gently 'evangelized' by a person convinced of his 'better way,' I felt neither defensive nor offended. I trusted the One God to receive and engage both of us on our chosen spiritual journey. Sri Lankan Wesley Ariarajah states:

> To say that God is not present in the religious life of neighbours would amount to blasphemy. It is false witness against the Creator. It is an attempt by us humans to put limits on God and to dictate to God where God might and might not be active.[3]

Another experience taught openness. On entering a state emporium in Delhi to purchase a tablecloth, I paused. On prominent display were large symbols of three major religions. The multiple arms and legs of a brass, Hindu god form stood posed to 'offer' support for varied needs. A rotund Buddha form made of heavy metal sat poised in contemplation. And a wooden, inlaid portrayal of the Lord's Supper hung boldly—the Jesus figure linking a common meal with personal covenant. En route to choose a table cover—to see color and shape, to touch woven threads, to ponder an artist's craft—I stopped, there being no choice. In India where all of life exudes Spirit, where the spiritual and practical provide context for each other, this experience drew my attention. Intent to select a cloth to enjoy with spiced curries, I pondered faith. Spiritual and human being intersected. Not present to cast judgment, symbols affirmed Ultimate Reality. God cares for all peoples.

Worship with urban and rural Christians in India enlarges awareness of ecumenism. On a Palm Sunday in 1993, I was among thirty local people who walked or biked, passing people of other living faiths, to a Mennonite church in Ranchi, Bihar. Each child carried a palm frond shaped into a small cross. We greeted each other with "Jeshu sehai" before and after worship. We sat on back-less planks of wood. Then, in 1998, I was speaker for five sessions of the fifth All-India Mennonite Women's Conference. Singing and drama were spirited among the 170 women from five language groups gathered to ponder peace (*shanti*) themes. We shared communion—*chapati* pieces and juice—made special because blessed and served by women. Short on cups, women also washed the used ones in buckets just outside the brightly colored *shamiana* (tent), until all were served.

Less than three percent of India's population, Christians worship in varied settings. Whether near temples or mosques, all are rarely far removed from those who humanly suffer. A Delhi Fellowship met in the restaurant area of the top floor of the Taj Mahal Hotel. Looking out over the Indian capital's sandstone government buildings, we sang and heard a sermon: "We are not human beings having a spiritual experience; we are spiritual beings having a human experience." In Kolkata, outside a British-style, Baptist church hung a large sign marking two centuries since William Carey, British missionary, arrived. Inside, seated in armed chairs, we joined Indians to hear that day's guest preacher from Germany. We listened, despite airplanes taking off overhead and birds zooming through window openings, wooden shutters wide open.

In Chennai (formerly Madras) we also worshipped. With Methodists, we experienced an insightful service led by blind people. And with Baptists, who had gathered in one location for 150 years, we felt the joy of dedicating a new piano. An array of 'angel' children processed to begin the service, and the adult choir offered "Hallelujah" pieces new and old, composed by the pastor and G. F. Handel. Members were as delighted to hear Mozart's "Sonata in A Minor" on the piano as to donate major offerings for flood relief in India and El Salvador. Memories also linger of worship with Mar Thoma Christians, those thought to descend from preaching of Jesus' first-century disciple Thomas. Rituals included a lengthy liturgy recited by all from memory while standing in incense-filled space.

Also in Chennai, patterns of worship in Church of South India congregations vary. (Over fifty years ago CSI merged Anglicans, Presbyterians, Congregationalists, and Methodists.) Merging does not require identical views or rituals. At St. Mary's, blessed with an Anglican heritage since 1680, the priest serves weekly communion to worshipers kneeling at the altar. At St. Andrews, with Scottish Presbyterian roots, the Bible is carried in to begin and out to end each service. A brigade of lay elders passes the Eucharist elements through the pews to five hundred believers, once a month. With hymns sung— hymnals that include words, not music—and the Word proclaimed, worshippers leave sacred settings to acknowledge God's grace among neighbors. So, we might anticipate the End of Days when both Jews and non Jews will know God: as Jews fulfill their 613 commands, non-Jews follow their diverse practices.

Religious holidays further promote ecumenical wisdom. On Reformation Day, we staff and students (seated on the tile floor on braided mats) at a Lutheran seminary were challenged by a Roman Catholic priest to claim the One God. On Mission Sunday 1998, I, a Mennonite from the United States, spoke in two CSI churches about the

German Lutheran Bartholomaeus Ziegenbalg. The first Protestant missionary to India, he arrived in 1706. A skillful writer and translator loyal to the Good News, he learned the common people's language. He also learned from sermons and grammars written by Roman Catholics de Nobili (early 1600s) and Henriques, in India before him. He credited the living piety of those now called Hindu people, learned the complex nature of their *Bhakti* (devotional) religion, and credited their effort to reach God.

In 2003 I researched at the Henry Martyn Institute in Hyderabad. Like de Nobili and Ziegenbalg centuries before, Martyn (1806) inspires through multifaith exchange. Anglican chaplain for East India Company personnel, he struggled to gain rapport with his own countrymen due to his love for Muslims and the poor. His deep and broad knowledge of biblical languages reinforced his need to know Indian languages. He studied Bengali, Persian, and Arabic in addition to Urdu, the language of many Muslims. Assisted by language *pandits*, he then translated the New Testament into such languages, wrestling with meanings of words and idioms. Further, he founded schools and enjoyed children. "He extended equal worth to Indians and recognized Muslim culture and loyalties."[4]

Visits to worship places of other living faiths always enrich a person. Parents of Hindu and Sikh students at Goshen College attend to the spiritual 'back home.' A father explained goddess and god forms and stories to me in a major Delhi temple. Open to difference, we then climbed, shoeless, a hill with a Buddhist worship center on top before entering a large, white, lotus-shaped Bahai temple. There, hundreds quietly lined up to enter between small, clean pools and green grass. The history and philosophy of tolerant Bahai teaching, lining basement walls, further informed us.

Next, we entered a temple where most people prostrated before Lord Krishna or Rhadha forms. With a group prayer service set to begin, a lead chanter and drummer led the sacred event. Motions and chanting vigor increased along with a distinct shuffle. Participants moved hands through a camphor flame in an *arati* tray, circled by *saddhus*. Near the end, blessed water sprinkled out over all. As at the beginning, the leader blew several blasts on a conch shell. On leaving, people took a pinch of *prasad,* offered to digest. Whereas Hindu worship often centers in private acts, this group ritual conveyed the corporate, with welcome for all, whether regular or guest attenders.

My journal entries include other temple visits. One would hold distinct interest for any sculptor—100 pillars. Often, a nearby 'tank' makes ablutions possible. Symbols linked to a distinct God form appear, as the *linga* with Shiva temples. Near the southeastern shore stands the very ancient "temple by the sea." Others date to the ninth or eleventh century when elephants and shrines were carved of solid rock. This work matched the carvers' 'payment' in food during a famine. Another complex finds people in procession with forms of varied names that mark a particular day of the year. Through rituals and greetings, musicians assist people to say "Hello" or "Goodbye" to an aspect of the Divine—as to a house guest.

A guide rich with insight—Sunithi—introduced my tour group to Kanchipuram—town of a thousand temples dedicated to many aspects of the Divine. One structure, dedicated to Shiva, is thought to be the oldest temple constantly in use since the seventh century. A great sage resides there. With its high tower over the inner sanctum area, its sandstone structure lined with cells for meditation (a sign of later, Buddhist influence) surrounds a courtyard. Why might I a Christian value Sunithi, or how might temple activity enrich my faith? A religious person, she explains details clearly, with sensitivity and passion. She honors sacred views, traditions, and practice—hers and those of others. People worship Yahweh, Allah or whatever the Name in her presence. Personal belief systems might counter or modify, as with the term Trinity. Steven Huyler, noted photographer of Hindu devotion, also describes Sunithi's integrity—her "welcome of Lakshmi, the Goddess of Abundance and Prosperity, as a guest in her home."[5]

While Muslims resist any image of the One God, called Allah in Arabic, Sikhs honor with profound depth their scripture *Guru Granth Sahib*. That text now stands as personal Guru—in home, *gurdwara*, or wedding hall. It offers guidance for how to live and deep consolation in the event of a loved one's death. Having worshiped in a Sikh *gurdwara* repeatedly, I commune there with the Universal God. Although Muslims never honor a form of Muhammad, relics might bring worshipers or tourists together. Items fourteen centuries old—a hand-written scripture copy by the grandson of Muhammad or a presumed hair of the Prophet's stored at the Delhi Jama Masjid mosque—prompt people's respect.

Circles of discs gold in color glisten on the large dome of the Matri Mandir within the intentional Auroville community in south India. Circling hundreds of steps upward into that dome, that place of contemplation open to all, I sense the sincere effort of comrades engaged with silence. Ascended, prayer resonates on mats, in hearts, to The One. Not far away, ashrams or shops in coastal Pondicherry offer written materials to keep teachings of Sri Aurobindo and The Mother alive.

Pausing at the Isha Yoga Centre (near Coimbatore) which is also open to people of all religions, I but begin to comprehend union with existence. That the Body is the temple of the Spirit matters for those solemn in worship. And coming 'home' to a cappella singing or Jesus' clear call to justice, I rejoice, with both the familiar and memories of distinct holiness.

Memories indeed pervade this essay; may readers muse on the

sacred for them. With counsel from Mennonite theologian Gordon Kaufman, we share, learn, and adapt:

> Only as we find ways of stepping back from . . . features of our traditions (both religious and secular) that wall us off from others, can we hope to come into genuine understanding of and community with them. Building such community with others, it seems to me, is the most profound religious necessity of our time.[6]

Endnotes:

[1] Paul F. Knitter. *Introducing Theologies of Religions.* NY: Orbis, 2002. Also, his lectures in the DMin (Doctor of Ministry) Program, United Theological Seminary, Dayton, OH, 2004-05.

[2] Jeannine Hill Fletcher. "Shifting Identity – The Contribution of Feminist thought to Theologies of Religious Pluralism," *Journal of Feminist Studies in Religion,* 19/2, 2003, 5-24.

[3] Ariarajah discusses Wilfred Cantwell Smith's view of theology as "human construct" in "Asian Christian Theological Task in the Midst of Other Religious Traditions," *CTC Bulletin,* xviii/1, Apr 2002, 21.

[4] This quote appears in my article about the Henry Martyn Institute. "Seeing is Believing," *Studies in Interreligious Dialogue,* 14/2, 2004, 160-76.
      See also: *Henry Martyn Confessor of the Faith* by Constance E. Padwick, Jesse Page's *Henry Martyn of India and Persia* or Sarah J. Rhea's *Life of Henry Martyn.* The privilege was mine in September 2009 to spend several days in research at the Henry Martyn Centre in Cambridge, England; further writing using a portion of that primary material by him will follow.

[5] Steven Huyler. *Meeting God Elements of Hindu Devotion.* New Haven: Yale Univ Pr, 1999, 176-83. Huyler's earlier resource, *Painted Prayers,* also sensitively conveys Hindu religious practice.

[6] Gordon D. Kaufman. "Religious Diversity, Historical Consciousness, and Christian Theology," in *The Myth of Christian Uniqueness Toward a Pluralistic Theology of Religions.* John Hick and Paul F. Knitter, eds., NY: Orbis, 1987, 14.

10

The Hindu Goddess:
Stories that Evoke an Image

Ever since first living in India in 1962, I have pondered the social impact and wisdom of honoring god and goddess forms and pairs, stories and names within sacred experience. Christians have produced negative results, for people and God, I believe, from centuries of perceiving God as male. Resistance to naming God's breadth while preferring exclusive, language—king, lord, he/him—persists. The Ultimate Being is neither male nor female, but human beings relate to and image qualities of divine being and action.

Life in India—where a multitude of god and goddess reflections of the One God exist within Hinduism—has not meant social equality for women with men either. Not expecting direct correspondence, other complex features of Hindu thought matter. For example, *darshan*. Diana Eck's book—*Darshan: Seeing the Divine Image in India*—explains the art of seeing the divine in image, in a person, or in a set of ideas. She writes, "The central act of Hindu worship, from the point of view of the lay person, is to stand in the presence of the deity and to behold the image with one's own eyes, to see and be seen by the deity."[1] By contrast, so-called religions of the "Book" (Judaism, Christianity, and Islam) trust the Word to mediate divine truth, more than the Image.

How might western Christians better understand the sacred experience of seeing a goddess form? This exchange provides information and reflects respect. Two young women have greeted each other several times in the playground area of their apartment complex in Cleveland. Each has a two-year-old who needs to expend energy prior to naptime.

Nancy: Hello, I'm Nancy. I've seen you around here but never asked your name.

Kamala: Likewise. I'm Kamala and this is Gayatri.

Nancy: Hi, Gayatri. Would you and Nathan like to play together? Nathan, this is Gayatri; she also likes the playground.

Kamala: Perhaps you two could build with sand over there; it's moist and will pack well. (*Off they run.*)

Nancy: We'll be here on the swings. . . .Evidently, you live here in the Towers.

Kamala: In Tower B.

Nancy: We're there too, fifth floor.

Kamala: How old is Nathan?

Nancy: Last month he turned two.

Kamala: Gayatri's about a half-year older.

Nancy: I like the name Gayatri. Am I right to presume that you're from India?

As conversation continues, Nancy mentions that she lived in Jabalpur, in central India, on a yearlong Fulbright scholarship. They discover that each is currently an adjunct professor in different area universities, Kamala in Tamil literature and Nancy in anthropology. Each respectful toward religion, neither discloses her faith loyalty. But each knows. We listen to the exchange. . . .

Nancy: Review a couple stories from Hindu goddess mythology for me, please.

Kamala: Keep in mind that powerful male deities developed alongside male power gains.

Nancy: But, David Kinsley cautions: "Female power, creativity, and authority in the theological sphere do not necessarily imply high female status in the social sphere."[2]

Kamala: Although a powerful goddess predates the Vedic era, throughout Vedic history the idea of *shakti* was less developed than it is today. Sara Mitter's discussion of *shakti*—energy or the ability inherent in a cause to produce a needed effect—is good.[3]

Nancy: Goddesses activate that strength?

Kamala: A god's male, passive, potential aspect might also combine with the dynamism of *shakti*. For example, god of destruction Shiva is energized through Durga or Kali's *shakti*.

Nancy: Before details about those manifestations, explain the supreme goddess, the one in whom all others merge.

Kamala: You refer to Devi Mahatmya or Mahadevi. A new era took shape when the seven-hundred-verse *Devi Mahatmyam* was added to legends dated from 200-400 CE—called *Markandeya Purana*. Author unknown, *Devi Mahatmyam* was edited between 400 and 600. A key focus is the cosmic conflict between divine powers and evil spirits. Orthodox Hinduism recognized and synthesized the Great Goddess. Known as supreme energy, she is both mother and spouse of Brahma, Vishnu, and Shiva, the three main reflections of the Ultimate.

Nancy: So, her portrayal through Parvati, Durga, and Kali together depicts total womanhood.

Kamala: While Parvati reflects beauty or wifely devotion (duty), Durga the fighter gets rid of evil demons. And ambiguous Kali might destroy through frantic action or save on other occasions.

Nancy: Also, while Durga might become active force in Shiva, Kali could link with Shiva to symbolize the unity of opposites, I've heard. . . . Tell me about Mahadevi's battle with the demon Mahishasura, a water buffalo bull.

Kamala: Okay. The Creator god had told Mahisha that his foremost desire of being immortal was impossible: "All birth must be followed by death."[4] But when the gods could not destroy the formidable demon king, each gave up one of his qualities to the Great Goddess. In the form of Durga, with each of her many arms holding a 'weapon' and seated on a fierce lion, she set out to destroy the misguided Mahisha. Alone but through collective energy, Durga conquers each form that he presents.

Nancy: And each victory of the goddess vanquishes forces of darkness. The order of cosmos triumphs over discord, so to speak.

Kamala: After drinking a bowl of life force, she charged the final bull shape, spearing Shiva's trident through its neck, to decapitate the demon. Being gracious, she didn't destroy the rest of the body. In that choice, she absorbed something of the demonic alongside her *shakti*. Releasing him from doing further evil, she redeemed the universe or restored order.

Nancy: And thereafter, the Devi accepts with love all worship or sacrifice—cattle or flowers or food given to brahmins. But how do such stories affect ordinary people?

Kamala: Mitter states that in Hindu thought opposites interact "within a unified divine essence."[5] Females can be either devoted and chaste or destructive—"the Absolute embraces all divisions and dualities."

Nancy: Clear or puzzling, tales are thought to live or operate within a person's soul?

Kamala: Or, as Shobita Punja observes, the battlefield of the Mahisha myth is within each person's mind. When inclined to be stupid, a devotee is invited to be mind-full and to call on energetic Durga.[6] Unconquerable wisdom waits to be aroused. Good qualities exist in each person. Singly, or having shared burdens with others, the worshiper confronts internal enemies of desire, anger, delusion, or pride. S/he engages Durga's *shakti* through her varied weapons: "memory, steadfastness, intelligence, beauty, peace, mercy, forgiveness. . . "[7]

Nancy: A grand goddess like Durga has many names too. Her energies certainly counter the stereotyped image of a dependent Hindu woman.

Kamala: Names expand her diversity rather than limit her being, whether as Uma, Sati, Kali, or Parvati.

Nancy: The focus of a goddess also shifts through time.

Kamala: Recall Sarasvati. She first appeared as a river in Vedic literature. After going underground for some time, she became "personified as a goddess of wisdom, learning, the arts."[8]

Nancy: We really need to review the well-known goddess Sita.

Kamala: You might read Punja's explanation about Sita as daughter of the earth. I presume that you know that Sita honors Rama's welfare. She worships him as metaphor for devotion to God.

Nancy: I recall from the *Ramayana* story that she's banished, abducted, and recaptured.

Kamala: Yes, but much more. The childless king Janaka finds an infant girl while plowing. He eventually sets up a contest to decide who will marry his beautiful princess. Only Rama, eldest son of King Dasaratha, succeeds to lift and break the golden bow. When Dasaratha pledges with a second wife to let her son inherit the throne, Rama is exiled to the forest.

Nancy: And loyal Sita goes with him.

Kamala: Then a demon woman, sister of ten-headed Ravana the king of Lanka, tries to seduce Rama. She is avenged for his resistance when Ravana, as sign of human greed and lust, forcefully kidnaps Sita. They fly in his chariot to Lanka.

Nancy: Such a story could captivate an audience, I'd think.

Kamala: Knowing the penalty for possessing a woman by force, Ravana offers to remove his other wives and give his wealth to Sita. Not impressed, she refuses the temptation and remains loyal to Rama despite Ravana's abuse and threats.

Nancy: Some Indian women whom I've known waver between enduring abuse and remaining loyal to a husband.

Kamala: The same seems true for some American women.

Nancy: Excuse me for implying otherwise. Features of this epic live on, ingrained, I suppose.

Kamala: More imagery surfaces as Rama and his brother secure a monkey army and form a bridge to Lanka where Rama battles and kills Ravana. Having retrieved Sita, Rama then doubts whether she had remained faithful to him while in another's palace.

Nancy: Many who read or watch this story then must empathize with Sita's being rejected. Or, do they expect her to preserve her husband's honor, or to forgive Rama's jealous renunciation?

Kamala: Another option is to simply absorb the story as story. Sita orders that a fire be lighted. She walks around it, calling on Agni, god of fire, to intervene her plunge into the huge flame. Without hesitation, Agni endorses her purity.

Nancy: Making the forces of good prevail over evil.

Kamala: On returning to Ayodhya, Rama yields to what he imagines that people say as they gossip. Moved by public censure, or ready to blame others rather than pursue duty, he banishes his pregnant Sita to a forest. She bears twin sons who, at age fifteen, reunite with their father. Rama invites Sita to return, on condition that she again suffer an ordeal by fire.

Nancy: Do people, on hearing this epic, wonder if Rama remained faithful to Sita during their separations?

Kamala: Few; conditioning prevails. This time, even Sita's spirit resists. She draws the line, a line that women comprehend. Endless suffering has limits. One writer believes that Sita shows Rama that he doesn't deserve her virtue. Mitter suggests that Sita sets her own terms to prove her virtue. "If I have never dwelt on any but Rama, may the Goddess [Earth] receive me!"[9]

Nancy: Patient, she rebels.

Kamala: And the earth in which she was found receives her again, a bold sign.

Nancy: Yet, the tradition of long-suffering women devoted to their husbands continues to be glorified. Doesn't the ideal of utter loyalty persist, even as the struggle to survive pervades?

Kamala: Yes and no. For we comprehend Sita also as *Shakti*, as that energy that motivates women because of what she represents. Suffering can either increase or restrict a woman's religious being.

Nancy: From an account about goddess Kali, I recall *Shakti* being described as "the energizing force of all divinity, of every being and every thing."

Kamala: Yet, most living faiths ignore it, in part because of their patriarchal mindset.

Nancy: Religion often presents a disjunction with social spheres.

Kamala: More popular, fair religious options emerge then, as some followers oppose an in-grown, elite, patriarchal base.

Nancy: You likely know of the Brahma Kumari—Daughters of Brahma—a sect founded over fifty years ago. Disturbed by the Hindu ideal that a woman should consider her husband a deity, the Brahma Kumari founder stressed celibacy. Women should transform their homes into 'temples.'

Kamala: Doesn't Christianity include a popular tradition about women?

Nancy: From what I know, its ancient Jewish heritage likely stemmed from a matriarchal epoch. Then, as a male God-concept served by male priests prevailed, women's place within the cult diminished. At first not required to attend special religious events, women later, due in part to their sacred blood, were kept from involvement.

Kamala: And exceptions always lingered.

Nancy: But men with power can minimize or present women characters from a male perspective.

Kamala: Such patterns also exist between our religions.

Nancy: Fear of women and the desire to bless social hierarchy read male privilege back into the Bible, setting the tone for centuries.

Kamala: But change occurs?

Nancy: Too slowly or too rapidly, depending on a person's stance.

Kamala: Religions often correspond—where protest begins. How tradition becomes entrenched. And which outlasts the other.

Nancy: Back to Sita's example, have you read Savara and Thadani's *Reclaiming Female Energy*? A friend talked about their observation. In devi's many forms, she hardly ever appears as passive or obedient to father, husband or son.

Kamala: Fascinating, isn't it? Women conditioned to practice dependence overlook the chance to "reclaim female energy." But, driven by survival instinct, change may follow.

Nancy: What effect on women do you see from increased religious fundamentalism, among Hindus or Christians?

Kamala: Vrinda Nabar sees any form of fundamentalism as inherently hostile to women. Women become its first victims.

Nancy: So also, folk religions, being more woman-centered, threaten orthodoxy.

Kamala: Right . . . Oh, look—Nathan and Gayatri are playing so well.

Nancy: While their capering lasts, I'm delighted to talk about things Indian.

Kamala: You were in India just long enough to whet your interest, right?

Nancy: Highlight for me the ten-day festival called Durga Puja.

Kamala: Details vary about any myth. The September-October festival, also known as Navaratri ("nine nights"), honors several goddesses and Rama. On the final day, called Dassehra, devotees celebrate the triumph of good over evil. Tall effigies of the demon Ravana might burn in the north, while in southern Mysore a large procession of elephants and fireworks takes place near the royal palace. And in Bengal, Durga's defeat of Mahisha is re-presented in clay at scattered structures.

Nancy: I visited friends in Kolkata last year during Durga Puja. Both Sikh and Christian friends explained the Hindu celebration. Scenes of the story appeared in about a thousand Pandals, structures hastily built, often with elaborate towers and a painted facade. Citywide contests were held. Crowds of several million people 'toured' the displays and 'shopped' the impromptu booths that offered food and wares.

Kamala: Snarled traffic teems with millions on foot who gawk at flickering lights as they might stumble into rain-filled potholes, as I recall.

Nancy: Artists have free-reign during the festival, creating with materials from sugarcane to straw. On the final day, images are carried to the water's edge to be immersed. And soul-stirring, morning or evening devotional songs echo beyond the gala event.

Kamala: You describe it well. Do you also know of Laksmi—consort of Vishnu whom she serves?

Nancy: She's linked to wealth and wellbeing.

Kamala: Devotees strive to perfect their duty, or love. Symbolized by the elephant or lotus, Laksmi represents royal authority and fertility. The lighted clay lamps of the festival Diwali honor her. Later versions of the myth link her to several male deities.

Nancy: And how do you, briefly, explain Kali? I've read Lina Gupta's idea that Kali may be a projection of hostile, male fear of the female.

Kamala: Gupta's source is good. She ponders whether Kali is the mythic Great Mother. Although she manifests Durga, Durga at times calls on Kali for help. Gupta believes that Kali embodies conflicts common to women's struggle for social rights.

Nancy: So, women value Kali because she shows how to face and overcome limits?

Kamala: Her striking features encourage devotees to confront who they are, to squarely face their fears. She combines dripping blood with an invitation: "Come/Fear not." She personifies *shakti*, what Gupta calls "the female principle of creation."[10]

Nancy: Is Kali known as the consort of a male god?

Kamala: Compared to others, she is barren and rarely seen with Shiva. Less attached, she mostly lives outdoors or haunts cremation sites. Her creative power will not be reduced.

Nancy: I struggle to absorb the paradox of this goddess—benevolent and malevolent, dominant and gentle.

Kamala: Consider the cremation ground that Kali haunts. It too suggests yet overcomes contrast. Both a place of erotic ritual and "where all desires are burnt away with the body,"[11] it suggests Hindu absorption with God.

Nancy: Profound.

Kamala: Are you aware of goddess Sati's lore, source for the unity of "Mother India"?

Nancy: Say more.

Kamala: For a special sacrifice, her father Daksha bypassed her husband (Shiva) and her. When he invited and dispersed shares of the world to other gods, great sages, and nymphs, Sati was ignored. She was most offended.

Nancy: Why were they ostracized?

Kamala: Daksha thought that Shiva was impure since he represents all species and sustains the good, bad, and indifferent. Devoid of noble lineage and having countered social conventions of exclusion, Shiva's approach addressed all systems that segregate or fail to value difference.

Nancy: So, Sati stands for equality and totality. Since she refused to compromise truth, the pair retaliated and turned the sacrifice into a cremation ground where Sati committed suicide.

Kamala: Versions vary. One suggests that her father's act of exclusion drove Sati to enter a yogic trance, the fire of which "consumed her body and reduced it to ashes."

Nancy: And ash has distinct symbolism.

Kamala: Ash symbolizes "matter that has ceased to be, from which the spirit has been released to freedom."[12]

Nancy: How did Shiva respond?

Kamala: Enraged by Sati's death, Shiva gathered an army to destroy Daksha and his sacrifice. With a measure of mercy, Shiva later restored the sacrifice. Deeply grieved, he is thought to have wandered throughout India, dropping segments of Sati's body. At those points, 51 or 108, worship of the Great Goddess continues. Local village people bow to her image saying, "Oh, Mother."[13] Pilgrims linked by the network of her *pithas* receive her benediction; each sacred place calls them to love.

Nancy: How do you reconcile the truth of Sati's acceptance of diversity and the term *sati,* the new widow who joins her recently-deceased husband on his funeral pyre?

Kamala: Punja suggests that ancient myths offer diverse meanings and interpretation. Sensitive people who address the injustice of discrimination might call on the goddess within to start afresh, "to rebuild the world from ash."[14]

Nancy: But through time, *suttee*, the act of a wife immolation, came to reflect "an extreme form of women's subjugation."[15] It redefines freedom. It involves fear of a woman's sexuality and denies her worth without a husband.

Kamala: It can either glorify the sati by identifying her as a goddess, as with Roop Kanwar in Deorala as recently as 1987, or it can activate justice-seeking groups to condemn the rite.

Nancy: Mention one other goddess.

Kamala: There's Gouri, another consort of Shiva's. Women and children celebrate her annual festival with cone-shaped creations of flowers. On the eighth day of ceremonies, artistic offerings are taken to a lake or temple pond. Before throwing them into the water, women form small groups, light oil lamps, burn incense, and sway gently while clapping and singing.

Nancy: Quite a sight.

Kamala: Even more, a sense of cleansing the spirit or baring the soul results. A woman combines praise to the deity with wishes for long life for her husband.[16]

Nancy: Thanks for reviewing the multi-layers of meaning with Hindu goddesses. What I have noticed superficially provides only part of the whole. A part of my Christian being nudges me to learn about your stories as I ponder the ancient stories of my heritage.

Kamala: I enjoyed the conversation. And our children did a good job of ignoring us!

Nancy: We'll meet again. Stop by 520 sometime.

Reflection:

One form of Ultimate Being,
Guide our inward and outward journeys
  to heights and depths;
   to views and vistas this world craves.
       You who honor Divine forms,
         claim your *shakti* and release sacred desires.
          May your energy ignite your dreams.
          May your being, when absorbed in the Ultimate, know Peace.
One form of Ultimate Being,
Receive our cleansed spirits and soul made bare,
  through multi-orange flowers,
   through those who share the silent pain.
       You who honor Divine forms,
         Rebel against injustice and absorb offense.
          Cling with courage to sisterhood, and
          fling the patriarchal stone far out-to-sea.
One form of Ultimate Being,
Accept our bridal yoke with You, committed
  in loyalty and praise and trust, our
   inner experience a relentless quest for Rest.
       You who honor Divine forms,
         confront within the real you; face squarely your fears.
          Rock boats as oft' as cradles, and un-
          lock your Soul to self-discovery.
One form of Ultimate Being,
Validate our Truth, another's need to know
  that motive clear makes reaching out in love Sustained;
   that arm of strength most surely circles round.
       You who honor Divine forms,
         Your sister's feet behold, and washing them
          stand tall to greet, then dot between the eye.
          Brandish the flame, no threat to friendship find.
One form of Ultimate Being,
Believe our myths; unloose our tethered tales—

a story meant to lead us on the Way;
a promise kept, to You who will prevail through Time.
>   You who honor Divine forms,
>   Bring change into the "ordered lives; tradition
>   long expose, and like your mentors bold, Lead;
>   long-sprouted, a banyan bent for neighbor's Good.
One form of Ultimate Being,
Hide not from us who call you many names.
>   Be foremost in our grief, our joy;
>   Be Fortitude, plus Normative and Just.   So be it.

Endnotes:

[1] Diana L. Eck. *Darsan Seeing the Divine Image in India*. Chambersburg, PA: Amina Bks, 1981, 1985, 3.

[2] David Kinsley. "Introduction," in *The Goddesses' Mirror Visions of the Divine from East and West*, NY: SUNY, 1989, xvii.

[3] Sara S. Mitter. *Dharma's Daughters*. New Brunswick, NJ: Rutgers Univ Pr., 1991, 74. [Also, as *Dharma's Daughters Contemporary Indian Women and Hindu Culture*. New Delhi: Penguin Bks., 1991.]

[4] Shobita Punja. *Daughters of the Ocean Discovering the Goddess Within*. New Delhi: Viking, 1996, 93.

[5] Mitter, 78.

[6] Punja, 100-01.

[7] *Ibid.*, 129-30.

[8] *Ibid.*, 16.

[9] Mitter, 90.

[10] Lina Gupta. "Kali, the Savior," in *After Patriarchy Feminist Transformations of the World Religions*. Paula M. Cooey, William R. Eakin, Jay B. McDaniel, eds. Maryknoll, NY: Orbis, 1991, 26.

[11] Jeffrey J. Kripal. "Kali's Tongue and Ramakrishna: 'Biting the Tongue' of the Tantric Tradition," *History of Religions*, 34/2, Nov. 1994, 164.

[12] Punja, 181.

[13] Diana L. Eck. "Myth, Image, and Pilgrimage," Lecture # 8 of Video "Hindu, Buddhist, Muslim, Sikh: The Religions of India," *Great World Religions: Beliefs, Practices, Histories*. The Teaching Company Limited Partnership, 1994, 45 min.

[14] Punja, 196.

[15] Divya Pandey (RCWS) Research Centre for Women's Studies "News Letter," vol. 8, no. 3 & 4, Dec 1987, p 1, in Dorothy Yoder Nyce. *Strength, Struggle & Solidarity: India's Women*. Goshen, IN: Pinch Penny Pr, 1989, 45.

[16] Ramchander Pentuker. "Saying It With Flowers," *Discover India*. June 1988, 12.

11

Asherah of the Hebrew Bible: Story of a Divine Pair Revoked

Christians rarely discuss Asherah. The dialogue that follows may, therefore, warrant a longer introduction. Insight into a possible deity pair within the Israelite heritage enriches efforts to name and understand the One God. Jews, Muslims, and Christians strongly endorse monotheism, each with distinct emphases and results. Hindus also believe in one God, though they are more imaginative, through varied forms and names, about the Final One. Diana Eck, Harvard University professor who studied Hindu thought and expression for multiple years in India, notes Hindu comfort with plurality. They value the Many-ness of God's One-ness. Perhaps Jews and Christians might own the 'plurality of a pair,' with Asherah in their heritage?

Interreligious exchange pays attention to God-concept. While Hindus call on God via many names, Buddhists may by-pass God-talk. Yet, people loyal to those traditions experience the Ultimate God's love and grace, as surely as do Christians or Muslims. David Krieger draws from the notable Indian Raimundo Panikkar to discuss method and cross-cultural encounter in doing theology. He explains how interreligious understanding corresponds with a "founding event" in which something taken-for-granted gains a "new horizon." Such an event occurred for me during my study of Asherah. Only after seeing the importance of "Yahweh and his Asherah" for many ancient Israelites, did I address what I had taken for granted about the biblical Yahweh.

Earlier, my concept of Yahweh concluded that Yahweh was in fact *the* One God, a concept central to my monotheism. Believing in a single God led me to name that God YHWH/Yahweh. I identified with the biblical I AM, the One who Causes all to Be. At one level, I affirmed that belief in monotheism meant that all people in essence claim the same One. For, there can be but one of One, though different names or forms will express the One. Not until I accepted the fact of the "Yahweh and his Asherah" pair did I see that my concept of Yahweh was in fact a name, among other options, for the actual concept or Being. As with the name Allah, Yahweh identifies that Other Being behind or surrounding or penetrating all that is—the ultimately Un-namable. That insight offered a "new horizon" to shape my multifaith openness. A further "new horizon" might emerge from engaging with theologian Gordon Kaufman's work with "God as Creativity" (*In the Beginning—Creativity*). But, the present study remains with "Yahweh and his Asherah."

Musing can become statements on paper:

1. In order to better understand the One God, religious people refer to or call on the Divine by name—names such as Yahweh, El Shaddai, Allah, or Rama.

2. Both biblical texts and archaeological findings verify that the Christian heritage includes "Yahweh and his Asherah." First Testament leaders eventually curtailed support for a Divine consort.

3. Each attempt to understand the Divine through human experience (as through paired love, God as Friend, or Mother/Father) can enhance perception but remains partial.

4. Convincing, sexual justice in social experience has not followed from naming and knowing the One God in metaphors of primarily one sex or a combination of both.

5. Conflict about God-concept existed in Israel and persists in Christian circles.

6. Effective multifaith exchange depends in part on openness to options about matters of faith like God-concept.

What is the biblical evidence for "Yahweh and his Asherah"? Most of the near-forty textual references to Asherah or her symbol occur in Kings and Chronicles; others appear in Exodus, Deuteronomy, Judges, Isaiah, Jeremiah, and Micah. These may be grouped according to word endings: asherim, asherah, and asheroth. Asherah is singular while the other two forms are plural. While Asherim and Asherah each occur eighteen times, Asheroth appears three times. References to Asherim appear in I or II Kings four times and in II Chronicles seven times whereas Asherah appears in I or II Kings twelve times and once in II Chronicles. Whether consulting a 1912 entry on "Astarte and Asherah" in *A Concise Cyclopedia of Religious Knowledge*[1] or Claudia V. Camp's 1992 discussion of "Worship of the goddess" in *The Women's Bible Commentary,* insight into her part within the Yahweh cult grows.

Details of translation follow for two examples. Time periods may affect word choice. The King James Version first printed in 1611 includes reprints in 1881, 1901, and 1946. While the Revised Standard Version first appeared in 1952, the New International Version came in

1973, and the New Revised Standard Version in 1991. The text from Deuteronomy 16:21 states:

NRSV – You shall not plant any tree as a sacred pole (Asherah).
NIV – Do not set up any wooden Asherah pole
("tree dedicated to Asherah" in the note).
RSV – You shall not plant any tree as an Asherah.
KJV – Thou shalt not plant thee a grove of any trees near the altar.

Variables for I Kings 15:13 state:

NRSV – she had made an abominable image for Asherah
NIV – she had made a repulsive Asherah pole
RSV – she had an abominable image made for Asherah
KJV – she had made an idol in a grove

Several observations: NRSV capitalizes Asherah in parenthetical notes for <u>pole</u> suggesting a direct correspondence of the cult object with the goddess. Ancient and contemporary people realize that "what has no name has no existence." Did KJV writers perceive in the early 1600s that to name Asherah would allow her to compete with the LORD God for identity? (And did their use of LORD credit it as the Jewish alternate designation for the sacred name YHWH/Yahweh?) Does a translation that uses "groves" or "poles" presume that the goddess is literally thereby diminished? Or, does that shift reveal how Israelite worship of Asherah evolved over several centuries into a cultic pole, as editors tried to be rid of evidence of her former worship? In turn, what attitudes evolve today toward living faiths with diverse options for God-concept?

Mark S. Smith suggests that readers can learn about Yahwism in ancient Israel from inscriptions discovered through archaeological digging. He writes about a spectrum of views:

> All Yahwists were presumably committed to the centrality of Yahweh. Beyond this essential feature, there was a diversity of views. Some Israelites believed that Yahwism was compatible with devotion to Baal. Other Yahwists held a more restricted view that Yahweh was the only god and Asherah was his consort. Finally, the Deuteronomistic Historian's view of matters was even more restricted, not allowing even for devotion to Asherah or to her symbol, the asherah. Yahwism existed in a complexity of forms, which is one way of remembering that God is God the mystery. Whether in the form of asherah or Wisdom or the Jewish Shekinah-Matronit, femaleness has been fundamental to Yahwism.[2]

Four discoveries will be noted: those at Kuntillet Ajrud and Khirbet el-Qom, the Lachish Ewer, and Ta'anach cult stand. Ruth Hestrin writes about the Lachish Ewer, an ewer being a pitcher or large vase. The drawing on this particular one carries the inscription "An offering to my Lady 'Elat." 'Elat or Athirat-'Elat refers to the goddess or consort of El in Ugarit, and to Asherah in biblical Hebrew. Hestrin also identifies the following biblical depictions of Asherah: image (statue or figurine), a green tree, and a tree trunk (Asherim, eighteen times).[3]

A tenth century BCE (Before Common Era) representation of Yahweh and Asherah appears on the Ta'anach cult stand. From nearly thirty centuries ago, this is the earliest known depiction of Yahweh. Found in 1968 by Paul Lapp, the hollow piece measures about twenty-one inches tall. It was perhaps used for incense, offerings, or libations. In an article titled "Was Yahweh Worshiped as the Sun?" J. Glen Taylor describes cultic scenes in each of the four tiers, two each for Asherah and Yahweh, the one "in person" and the other symbolized. While a nude female figure represents the mother goddess on the bottom (tier 4), tier 2 depicts Asherah as the sacred tree.

Similar to the 'Ajrud jar side A (to be discussed shortly), the tree on this piece is also flanked by ibex. But this stand is 150 years older than the 'Ajrud jar. Tiers 1 and 3 portray Yahweh in abstract ways. Tier 3 depicts the invisible deity through empty space between two cherubim. Represented in Tier 1 by symbols of sun disk and horse, freestanding pillars flank either side. To make clear that Baal is not being signified, a horse rather than bull is shown. Also known as "Yahweh of hosts," here is the most important star—the sun. This stand recalls II Kings 23:11: "He [Josiah] removed the horses that the kings of Judah had dedicated to the sun."

A poorly formed text carved on a pillar, between tombs in a burial cave, appears near Khirbet el-Qom (identified with the biblical place Makkedah, eight miles east of Hebron). Originating between 750-700 BCE, the inscription contains four main lines and two fragmentary lines. The latter may have been, according to Judith M. Hadley, an afterthought of the writer or chiseled later by another person. Hadley translates the lines: Uriyahu the rich wrote it.

> Blessed be Uriyahu by Yahweh
> For from his enemies by his (YHWH's) asherah
>   he (YHWH) has saved him.*
>   by Oniyahu
> and by his asherah
> his a[she]rah.

*Alternatively, . . . this line reads "(and) by his asherah, for from his enemies he has saved him."[4]

Seemingly at the end of his life, Uriyahu thanks Yahweh and his asherah for protection, blessing, and salvation from enemies. Perhaps the writer prayed to Yahweh before the asherah in a shrine. Psalm-like material closely scrutinized by Hadley, this statement credits God for life and offspring and requests deliverance.[5] A fairly large hand, incised below the four lines, may suggest supplication to a deity. Scholars decide whether script and drawings found near each other in fact relate to each other.

Differences between translations of Ancient Near East inscriptions recur, raising questions for disciplined students. While one may see syncretism in the Khirbet el-Qom piece, others translate its blessing as:

- " . . . May Uriyahu be blessed by Yahweh my guardian and by his Asherah. Save him (save) Uriyahu." (Joseph Naveh)
- "Blessed be Uriyahu by Yahweh. And cursed shall be the hand of whoever (defaces it)." (William Dever)
- "Blessed is Uriahu by Yahweh, and from distress he praised the El of his cultus who saves him." (Siegfried Mittmann)
- "Blessed be Uryahu by Yahweh his light by Ashera, she who holds her hand over him . . ." (Tilde Binger)

Untrained in archaeology, others of us 'hear' interpreters. We depend on them to be open to discover or ready to reshape previous understandings in light of new finds. Or, we discern who might be threatened by discovery but unwilling to admit steps taken to deny the same. Such diverse responses might describe people involved in or hesitant toward interreligious dialogue too.

The significant jars found at Kuntillet 'Ajrud become part here of an imagined exchange. At a Kolkata university, two graduate students meet regularly. The Indian Hindu fellow and the American Christian woman, a yearlong Fulbright scholar, are researching aspects of their religions. Loyal to particular religions, each trusts the other's insight and rituals to enlarge personal views of the Divine. The Hindu had already explained goddess Kali's inherent power, within Hindu thought. He then asked the woman about the Christian heritage of a God-consort pair. Picking up the exchange . . .

Utpal: The ancient parallel of our two religions fascinates me. Consider our important cities.
Marie: You refer to Varanasi and Jerusalem? I've never been to Jerusalem.
Utpal: Since you don't live where your religious ancestors started, your religious being isn't rooted in your homeland.

Marie: But my concept of God is not tied to a place. God is universal, the God of all nations.

Utpal: Okay. But are you therefore less linked to centuries of ritual?

Marie: Likely so. My worship rituals are quite different from First Testament occasions of sacrifice. Even Jerusalem is not ancient in the sense that Varanasi, formerly called Banaras, is.

Utpal: Hindus also call our holy city, which borders the sacred Ganga River for three miles, Kashi, the Luminous, or the City of Light.

Marie: How ancient is it?

Utpal: Thought to be eternal, it has been inhabited for three thousand years.

Marie: It was contemporary with Babylon and Nineveh.

Utpal: Right. But distinct from them, it has continued to thrive.

Marie: That's amazing!

Utpal: Fifteen hundred temples, some very old, fill the spaces between intent worshipers.

Marie: So, when inscriptions about Yahweh and his Asherah were scratched into stone or marked on sacred jars, ancestors of those today called Hindus had already converged on Varanasi's riverbank with its *ghats*, or landing places.

Utpal: That juncture is useful. I presume that archaeologists dig for remnants of ancient Israel.

Marie: The 'finds' are quite revealing—especially related to Yahweh God's having a consort.

Utpal: Western Christians who come to India often belittle Hindu respect for the goddess.

Marie: Many would resist knowing about Asherah.

Utpal: I don't wish to be gleeful—'See there, your heritage honored a consort too.' But I do wonder, could universal Truth be involved here? Could we all, with more humility, grant to earnest believers of any faith the desire to know the One God, whatever the diverse forms that each finds meaningful?

Marie: I hear you. Today's western Christians might weigh our options, in light of increased, direct exposure to religious plurality. Further, archeological results augment the 'weighing' process.

Utpal: Give an example.

Marie: Two large *pithoi*, or storage jars, from a ninth or eighth century BCE site at Kuntillet 'Ajrud, contain etched inscriptions and items. Hebrew blessing formulas and cultic scenes appear on the jars.

Utpal: Where's Kuntillet 'Ajrud?

Marie: Southwest of the Dead Sea. At the inner courtyard entrance to what was likely a place for loading caravans, travelers read this, ". . . I bless you by Yahweh, Shomeron (of Samaria) his Asherah."

Utpal: So, in Samaria, the official cult of Yahweh included the worship of his consort Asherah?

Marie: That's what David Noel Freedman concludes from that side of jar A.[6]

Utpal: Have diggers found a shrine there?

Marie: Scholars wonder if it was a sanctuary, or perhaps just a school or an inn. A crew with Ze'ev Meshel excavated there in 1975-76. He translates the *Pithos* A inscription as: "X says: Say to Y and Yauasah and [to Z]: I bless you by Yahweh, our guardian, and by his Asherah."

Utpal: You mentioned cultic scenes or symbols, as well as text.

Marie: Near the front left are two characters, one slightly behind the other. And at a little distance to the right appears a lyre player seated on a throne-like chair.

Utpal: How is that explained?

Marie: For a scholar by the name of William Dever, the 'Ajrud motifs primarily suggest syncretism. He thinks the lyre player is the goddess Asherah and the standing figure Yahweh. He argues that their being worshipped together was fully suppressed by the eighth to sixth centuries. Worship of the fertility goddess of Canaan was such a threat.

Utpal: Any different views?

Marie: Yes. Judith Hadley thinks the male lyre player, perhaps a young prince, may have no link to the standing figures. She contends that a major goddess like Asherah would never be portrayed smaller than an Egyptian dwarf god is (a Bes figure known as patron of music and dancing).[7] Instead, she locates Asherah's image on the reverse side, in the form of the tree of life.

Utpal: That idea makes sense. I think of the sacred tulsi, mango, and peepal trees, often found near Indian temples. Or perhaps the goddess is shown as the trunk of a tree, who feeds others?

Marie: Flanked by two ibexes, the tree of life image would have prompted the traveling herdsmen to see other fertility motifs, like a cow licking a suckling calf, or gazelles.

Utpal: How about the second jar?

Marie: On one side of *Pithos* B appears: "Amaryau says: Say to my Lord [X]: I bless you by Yahweh [our guardian] and by his Asherah."

Utpal: The recurring blessing formula.

Marie: This reverse side is of more interest. Five worshipers appear in procession, their hands raised. The inscription alongside suggests: "I bless you by Yahweh of Teman (a region) and by his asherah. May he bless you and keep you and be with (you) my lord."

Utpal: That's a profound blessing, from both agents.

Marie: Yes. What's more, it states the blessing form that Christians now call the "Doxology." We might conclude worship services with it!

Utpal: And you'd never heard that the same blessing sent your religious ancestors on their way, grateful for Yahweh and his Asherah!

Marie: Precisely. To learn that a remnant of loyalty to Asherah persists in my heritage prods me to pause, when encountering the Hindu goddess form today.

Utpal: We can all recall visual and tangible symbols that connect people of faith with the One God. Most people who revere an object before them know that it's not actually divine. It reminds them that the Ultimate constantly enters human experience.

Marie: Christians include paintings of Jesus in homes and churches—perhaps a head of Jesus painted by Salmon or Rembrandt, or a scene of Jesus as the shepherd or overlooking Jerusalem. We don't worship those paintings. The art reminds us of Jesus' life; it arouses faith.

Utpal: Symbols in a Hindu temple mysteriously concur with the reality to which they point, however.

Marie: Maybe the small, clay figurines, later found over what was ancient Palestine did too. They 'spoke' assurance for women who held them in faith. Whether shown as a pillar (tree trunk) with heavy breasts or a head, the nude form symbolized a member of the cult—a mother or goddess figure in whom women could trust. Held in a hand while giving birth or when desperate to survive harmful natural events, the symbol expressed the holy, beyond words. In a posture of sacred surrender, the supplicant held on to hope—to Yahweh and Asherah.

Utpal: Hindus thrive on symbols. Don't all people of faith use symbols, names, rituals, and forms to bring Ultimate Reality closer, or to express gratitude?

Marie: I'll give more background, some recently learned. For perhaps six centuries, many Israelites worshiped Asherah and associated a consort with their God Yahweh. El, the chief god of the region of Canaan that surrounded Israel, had a consort named Asherah. She was also known as the Great Mother Goddess. Known for fertility, she was thought to be mother of seventy gods. For a period of time, both the names El (or Elohim in the plural) and Asherah were accepted as names within Israel's God-talk.

Utpal: Anything evolve from that?

Marie: A story familiar to Jews and Christians is the Mount Carmel contest (I Kings 18). The intent of the contest was to determine whether Baal or Yahweh was the "real god."

Utpal: Sounds like a strong over-against posture.

Marie: Biblical hostility toward Baal always surfaced. The ever-popular, storm-god Hadad was seen as Yahweh's main competitor. The stage was set by King Ahab (married to a Canaanite named Jezebel) to discover which god was responsible for rains, fertility, and agricultural productivity.

In Canaanite myth, Asherah, as consort of the chief god El, had four hundred prophets and Baal had four hundred fifty. When the rain fell, the people were convinced that "Yahweh is God!" Spurred by Elijah, they ruthlessly slaughtered Baal's prophets. And, thanks to the army general Jehu's trickery, worshippers of Baal also gathered and were slaughtered. (II Kings 10:18-28) The prophets of Asherah, the queen of the gods, however, were seemingly allowed to continue. She and Yahweh replaced El among the Israelites.

Utpal: Sounds like they decided which God to worship in Israel.

Marie: Interpreters prolong another point of confusion from early biblical writers when they link Baal with Asherah. In fact, Baal's consort/wife/sister was Anat, not Asherah. Asherah's bond, begun with El, continued with Yahweh, the Israelite replacement for El.

Utpal: And ancient inscriptions verify the biblical evidence of the supernal pair, Yahweh and his Asherah.

Marie: Since neither prophet Amos nor Hosea denounced the asherah object, some scholars presume that asherim were accepted as part of the cult of Yahweh, at Bethel. Others 'fault' Hosea for replacing yhwh w'srth with a **new** theology for Israel. He established Israel, the people, as Yahweh's 'wife.' That action, along with having a male priesthood, skewed later knowledge. And a patriarchal emphasis on Jesus' maleness (rather than humanity) still later 'blessed' the Christian view of God as male. That Asherah *was* in the end censored indicates that she and her wooden symbol had in fact been established and popular. She had been sensually valued with Yahweh, for a time.

Utpal: All most fascinating. Does honor toward them as a pair augment your understanding of Divine love? Certainly, Radha and Krishna's love inspired the great medieval Sanskrit poet Jayadeva to write *Gitagovinda*.

Marie: Stories surrounding the two pairs differ, of course, but the option of attributing deity to male-female lovers could add scope to God-talk.

Utpal: Radha and Krishna's celestial love guides love between women and men on the personal level. Moods expressed in songs convey desire and craving, restless tenderness, and dread of being separated. We know about the pair through yearly enactment of their story.

Marie: Perhaps Hindus are more alert to the sensuality of the tribal world as it existed for ancient Israel. Through time, and with a traditional, male concept of God, Christians diminished the divine expression of passion between lovers.

Utpal: Passion is valid, but not in the *eros* sense of love?

Marie: While Christians might validate the com-passion of God or of Jesus' suffering love, we may skirt around sexual passion as good. We tend to separate sexuality from spirituality. But a present-day feminist theologian like Sallie McFague has re-awakened a sense of God as Lover, or God as Friend.

Utpal: You're re-claiming how passion expresses deep feeling for reunion. Isn't that inherent with salvation?

Marie: McFague, who perceives the world as God's body, suggests that, "the model of God as Lover implies that God needs us to help save the world." We could talk at length about how the Christian view of sin engages this theme, but I'd prefer now to focus on Yahweh and Asherah.

Utpal: Do you have any concept of fertility with deity?

Marie: I think of an allusion rarely explained. The phrase "sons of God" corresponds with "the host of heaven." That host would have been known as Asherah's offspring. (2 Kings 17:16, 21:3, 23:4) Remember, however, that the historians eventually curtailed loyalty to "Yahweh and his Asherah."

Utpal: Texts report the strife among Israelites to keep her form and link to Yahweh God alive, right?

Marie: Opponents sought to keep her memory alive or to destroy it. Do Hindus not battle among each other to get rid of gods or goddesses, or to emphasize some more than others?

Utpal: Our approach is less conflicted. Different households will be more loyal to one expression of the Ultimate, like Vishnu or Shiva, or to one of the *avataras* (which means to descend) of a god, like Krishna.

Marie: But you have little history of one god or group trying to supplant another?

Utpal: As people are diverse, so interest in the divine will vary, but not compete. We will choose one divine form or one way to worship God or one religious path, whether through knowledge, devotion, or action. An important *Rig Veda* text guides us: "The Real is one; the wise speak of it by many names."

Marie: That reminds me of tribal Israel's different names for God—Elohim, El Shaddai, or Jehovah. Later, the tribe of Judah likely persuaded the others to join it in claiming the name *Yahweh*, perhaps as if that were better or supreme.

Utpal: Why or when?

Marie: Exodus 3:14 reports that Moses ended a significant encounter with God by asking what name he should use, to identify God for the children of Israel. God told him: "Y-H-W-H" which means "I AM or I Cause to Be."

Utpal: And yet, I don't often hear that name today from Christians. Back to your mention of a prophet named Hosea. Did thinking of the whole people as God's wife diminish value for women?

Marie: I might first respond: Are Hindu women valued more on the social level because of your worship of Kali or a mother goddess alongside forms with male names? Clearly some resisted the First Testament shift—for centuries. For women, valued in part because linked to Yahweh as consort, to be replaced by the collective people distorts a sense of balance. To think of God in male but not female terms deprives women of comparable worth. And it tends to credit men with being more god-like, a doubly false result.

Utpal: Anything else about the male Jesus, even though that's not directly about Asherah?

Marie: Only that Jesus the Christ also came to have a "bride"—the church—another collective.

Utpal: Interesting. People were again to submit to a male figure. I think of Manu, the lawmaker who lived seven centuries before Jesus. His law, and therefore Hindu law, expects a woman to always be dependent on man. It defines an 'ideal' wife as one who perceives of her husband as lord.

Marie: I think of a striking parallel in a well-known hymn: "The church's one foundation is Jesus Christ her Lord"!

Utpal: Remarkable. But, returning to Asherah, in the couple minutes before I must leave. We always live and express the sacred within a cultural context. You spoke of charge and counter-charge with<u>in</u> one faith, among the ancient Israelites.

Marie: So today, along with intra-Christian conflict, Christians often charge, or negate, the faith of other cultures. In part to validate our own religion, I fear.

Utpal: Your comment prompts a couple questions. Might Christians discredit Hindu experience of multi-god forms because Christians wish to celebrate God only through Jesus and his cross? Might the Israelites have accepted Yahweh and his Asherah as *one* expression, among others? Could diverse names and forms not witness more fully to the One God who creates, sustains and tenderly loves all of life?

Marie: Sounds like our next exchange has just begun. For now, I'll state a couple general conclusions: the True God behind all names and forms is beyond sexual identity. Yahweh is one name for the Ultimate, rather than the only or the 'best' one. And those of us who call God *Yahweh* do well to welcome names like *Allah* or *Shiva*, from sincere people like you.

Utpal: And so, we learn—from Krishna and Radha, from "Yahweh and his Asherah."

Marie: As ancient Yahwism existed in complex forms, Mystery surrounds our ever-Present and Passionate One.

Utpal: May the hand or vibration of God fill the sacred space of our experience. Go well.

Before leaving, Marie created the following Reflection:

Yahweh God,
who with Asherah
knew those who knew her through clasped figurines,
hold those who cry out.

Yahweh God,
who with Asherah
appeared at Taanach in ancient stone tiers,
stand next to those who waver.
Yahweh God,
who with Asherah
came to be known through sacred tree, sundisk, and horse,
be symbol for those with imagination keen.
Yahweh God,
who with Asherah
fill space between the cherubim,
assure those faithful to real kith and kin.
Yahweh God,
who with Asherah
received incense and offerings,
let oil spill to sooth those trampled underfoot.
Yahweh God,
who with Asherah
brought forth the "host of heaven,"
conceive in mind for those who wish they could.
Yahweh God,
who with Asherah
link the human with Divine,
bond those left isolated by default or disdain.
Yahweh God,
who with Asherah
caused enmity within the remnant,
struggle with those who displace or feel displaced.
Yahweh God,
who with Asherah
empowered the Sea or Sky through cloud,
endow all those who fear the "foreign" elements.
Yahweh God,
who with Asherah
stirred prophets, kings, and priests,
prompt those who think the sacred does not matter.
Yahweh God,
who with Asherah
found centers in Bethel, Dan, and Samaria,
create sacred places for those excluded by the "righteous."
Yahweh God
who with Asherah
stood present in Solomon's Temple for 236 years,
instill the sacredness of time for those who wait.

Yahweh God
who with Asherah
birthed imagery of Wisdom, Spirit—Sophia too,
emerge in those who seek the One Divine anew.
So be it, Evermore and Evermore!

Endnotes:

[1] Elias Benjamin Sanford, ed. *A Concise Cyclopedia of Religious Knowledge*. Hartford, CN: S. S. Scranton Co., 1912, 65. and Claudia V. Clamp. "1 and 2 Kings," in *The Women's Bible Commentary*. Carol A. Newsom and Sharon H. Ringe, eds., Louisville, KY: Westminster/John Knox Pr., 1992, 97.

[2] Mark S. Smith. "God Male and Female in the Old Testament: Yahweh and His 'Asherah,'" *Theological Studies*, 48, 1987, 338-39.

[3] Ruth Hestrin. "Understanding Asherah, Exploring Semitic Iconography," *Biblical Archaeology Review*, xvii/5, Sept/Oct 1991, 50.

[4] Judith M. Hadley. "The Khirbet El-Qom Inscription," *Vetus Testamentum* xxxvii/1, 1987, 51.

[5] *Ibid.*, 57.

[6] David Noel Freedman. "Yahweh of Samaria and his Asherah," *Biblical Archaeologist*, 50/4, Dec 1987, 246.

[7] Judith M. Hadley. "Some Drawings and Inscriptions on Two Pithoi from Kuntillet 'Ajrud," *Vetus Testamentum* xxxvii/2, 1987, 195.

Resources:

This dialogue lifts ideas from a larger study. Those included in the Resources Part II listing that follows are a sampling of the fifty articles/books that I read (plus scripture commentaries).

Judith Hadley's fine, more recent book, adds depth to the discussion; it includes content from the two articles noted here. She traces the goddess Asherah from Syria (as Asratum) to Ugarit where she was the head goddess. Prior to its years of monarchy, Israel encountered Asherah's cult. An ewer at Lachish from the thirteenth century BCE illustrates this fact. By the tenth century, Israelite worship included goddess worship—"Yahweh and his Asherah." By the eighth (and perhaps into the seventh) century BCE, her cultic tree or wooden pole had replaced her name. Yahweh would have needed to take on aspects of fertility earlier credited to her; the pole or asherah came to symbolize that attribute. Biblical editors (Deuteronomic historians) likely wished to destroy evidence that the Israelites had worshipped her. Whether Christians will destroy evidence of a male God-concept—that impairs views of both God and humanity—invites one to muse yet more.

12

Paradox of World Religions— Conflict and Peace-building

Introduction

What prompts conflict or peace within religions? Clearly, people, views and attitudes determine one or the other rather than the fact of religion *per se*. Religions may be involved in intensifying either kind of circumstance. Causes for *conflict* might be extremist groups, nationalism, or fundamentalism. Judgmental truth claims, negation like anti-Judaism or anti-Islam, or thinking of war as God-driven can also stir up strife. Refusal to critique personal faith might add to interfaith struggles. Increased *peace* might follow social activism, hospitality, or nonviolent action. It grows through deepened empathy for diverse beliefs or rituals, through increased openness, compassion, or mindfulness. To value members of other faiths—discuss their key concepts, learn from their scriptures, or credit their integrity—matters.

We look at conflict and then peace-building through paradigms (models) of five religions. Those to examine, from the most ancient, are Hinduism, Judaism, Buddhism, Christianity, and Islam. Some receive more attention than others. Themes covered differ. Sikhism or Taoism would have been strong complements, but . . . for another essay.

I. Conflict - First Word

At a Glance: "Does religion cause violence?"

If readers wonder whether this question is being explored, recent book titles make clear. *Religions in Conflict. Terror in the Mind of God. When Religion Becomes Evil. The Islamic Threat. The Buddha and the Terrorist. Religion and Violence in a Secular World.* Articles abound too, like: "The Cult of Violence in the Name of Religion: A Panorama."[1] The plethora of related content can stagger a reader.

To presume to be a peace-builder but not know about diverse religions—their fear, texts, or wisdom—limits perspective. To think of Christian–Muslim conflict through only Christian views suggests bias. It implies that Christians alone know essentials. Not wishing to be dogmatic, I believe that as Christians grow in knowledge of and trust for other religions, we enlarge our peace-building effort. This stance builds on good theory and decades of worthy experience before us. It draws from other religions' concerns and strengths. It credits Buddhist' views of suffering or emptiness, Hindu history with *ahimsa*, or Muslim leaders like Badshah or Ayoub. To consider myself a peacemaker, I must honor, understand and be open to learn from other living faiths; in other words, diverse religions are needed for peace-building.[2]

Conflict through Paradigms:
Hinduism, Judaism, Buddhism, Christianity, and Islam
   A. <u>Hinduism</u> – Fundamentalism, Direct clashes

We begin with Hinduism, the most ancient and complex of religions to examine here. Worship and rituals permeate Hindu culture; social order blesses or limits millions in India. Although many Hindus perceive of their religion as tolerant, open to and expressive of great diversity, some adherents also cause major conflict. Other groups have broken from its core—forming Jain, Sikh, and Buddhist groups. Hindu dependence on caste turned these break-off groups to alternate ways of being social.

Fundamentalism appears in varied expressions within most major faiths. It encourages a return to some form of religious authority. Martin Marty and Scott Appleby produced five volumes about fundamentalism between 1993 and 2004. We look at its influence on political and religious matters in more recent Hindu expression. In India, a minority, militant Hindu group—not the majority of either Hindus or Indians—promotes fundamentalism as nationalism.

The first organization, Hindu Great Council (Hindu Mahasabha) formed in 1915; it set the tone for Hindu doctrine through V. D. Savarka's publishing of *Hindutva*. *Hindutva* means "Hinduness." Its exaggerated rhetoric justifies violence through "blame displacement and fear mongering." In 1925 the RSS (Rashtriya Svayamsevak Sangh) brotherhood of believers was formed. This National Union of Volunteers train in martial arts; they master discipline.

By 1964 some RSS leaders founded the VHP cultural organization. This World Hindu Society is intent to maintain Hindu identity and teachings; it may stage large processions in order to revive religious zeal or to threaten minorities like Islam. Formed around a central, 'religious assembly' of committees (within thirty years it had 300 district units, 3,000 branches, and 100,000 members), the RSS ideal promotes Hinduism as the national religion of India. That stance conflicts with the country's commitment to pluralism, a fact since Independence in 1947.

A third Hindu fundamentalist party called the BJP (Bharatiya Janat Party) emerged in 1980. Some leaders of this Indian People's Party, while trained with the RSS, wished for broader support. In 1998 its Prime Minister Vajpayee formed a coalition government. Some members opposed nationalism that ranks the Hindu religion as supreme or that supports basic *Hindutva.* For, *Hindutva* expects a "true Hindu" to exchange the secular written law, formed in pluralism, with an order loyal to *Hindutva.*[3]

Direct conflicts between Hindus and Muslims recur in India. Majority Hindus resent century-old tales of Muslim rule. Muslims resent being thought second-class. These two groups, with markedly diverse views of the Divine, still celebrate each other's sacred holidays. But, memories and feelings of revenge for prior riots, Partition, or deep fear linger. Ayodhya, the city, holds history for both religions. But far more Muslims died and had property destroyed during the late 1992-93 debacle when a famous mosque there was destroyed by *kar sevaks* (Hindu fighters).

Noted author Arundhati Roy reports[4] on the aftermath of the "Godhra outrage" of 2002 when Hindu nationalists killed at least 2,000 Muslims and left 100,000 homeless in the state of Gujarat. She calls the "meticulously planned pogrom" fascist (meaning to rely on terror to achieve ends). Another writer, who fears physical injury from extremist *Hindutva* promoters, publishes under a pseudonym. S/he notes how a speaker for the Bajrang Dal (*Hindutva's* youth wing) distorts Islam when describing it as intolerant and intent to "convert or conquer all of India" in contrast to harmonious Hinduism. Some minority *Hindutva* organizers blame terrorism on Gandhi's pattern of nonviolence as they spread hatred for non-Hindus. Therein, fundamentalism gets 'out-of-hand.'

B. <u>Judaism</u> – Hebrew Scriptures, Holy War.

Great religions can have harsh texts and sources for kinship and empathy. Walter Dietrich[5] names six kinds of violence in the Hebrew Bible—between individuals, nations, or religions; between divine and human; within society; and against nature. Raymond Schwager gathers stark stats: six hundred passages of explicit violence occur in the Hebrew Bible; God's punishment appears in a thousand verses; Yahweh either tries or kills or commands others to kill in one hundred passages.[6] The Hebrew Bible also invites readers to reject, prevent, and remove causes for violence. Central laws of the Hebrew Bible remain: "Do not kill" and "Love your neighbor as yourself." While prophet Isaiah notes future "beating swords into ploughshares," several Psalms call people to rely on God, rather than an army. (20:7-8, 33:16-18)[7]

To call on the Divine in order to use force is how 'holy war' might be explained. Israel clearly invoked God to destroy or protect. Some Jews credit greater peace when war enlarges Yahweh's rule. Other writers discuss 'holy war' in which divine authority justifies use of force. Charles Selengut thinks that key ideas of covenant, land promised, and chosen people caused Israel to believe that God ordained violence and war.[8] Peter Macky's study of Hebrew violence notes where Yahweh or Israel directly violates or where Mosaic Law justifies violent retribution.[9]

Susan Niditch names seven Hebrew models for waging war. To destroy as sacrifice to God; to destroy condemned sinners; to gain honor for courage shown; to get rid of an unclean enemy; to show that an underdog can defeat someone superior; to justify a given purpose; and to give God the glory while the loyal watch the battle.[10] Clearly, ancient Israel's holy war tradition, with Yahweh as warrior or defender, led the people to see *their* role or weapon as trust in God's protection.[11]

Other religions call war 'holy.' But, Charles Kimball (former Middle East Director of the National Council of Churches) says that calling war 'holy' distorts the very core of defense. It corrupts religion. He believes that both Christians and Muslims have seriously wronged their faiths. Not direct war, conflict occurred also in 1492 when Spain's king and queen decreed that all Jews must either leave Spain or become Christians, within four months. Forty thousand fled; the same number converted.[12]

Addendum

Who could discuss religious conflict without mention of the destruction of millions of Jews during WWII? No doubt, readers are informed about that religious scourge. If not, the profound, Holocaust museum in Washington D.C. deserves a visit. Finally, more Christians seem to awaken to the anti-Judaism that prevails within their heritage, signs of which start in the Gospel of John. One writer to commend is Susannah Heschel, daughter of the noted Jewish thinker Abraham and pianist Sylvia (Straus) Heschel. Her book *Abraham Geiger and the Jewish Jesus*[13] explains that first Jew's analysis of Christian texts. Writing in the mid-1800s, he makes clear Jesus' Jewishness and the need for Christian faith to be seen as derived through Jesus' Judaism. In Jesus, Geiger found nothing unique or original, his teachings being "typical liberal Pharisaic teachings of his day." Christian religion then became dogma about Jesus, departing from that humble leader's teachings.[14]

C. Buddhism - Sri Lanka, Countering conflict

Buddhism is known more for nonviolence and peace-building endeavor than for conflict. A teaching from the *Dhammapada*, popular Buddhist text, reflects a strong stance:

Hatreds are never ended or calmed by hate,

Hatreds are only calmed by non-hate.

This is an everlasting principle.[15]

But some adherents also have been destructive, as on the Asian island of Sri Lanka. Although the Buddha received enlightenment and carried out forty years of preaching along the Ganges in India, Sri Lanka claims to be the world's oldest Buddhist society, the "homeland of pure Buddhism." As usual, religion and politics mix. Tensions over land, education, employment rights, and national language have persisted since 1948 between Buddhist Sinhalese and Hindu Tamils. Tamils invade from the southern state of India called Tamil Nadu. An upsurge of Buddhism came in the mid-1950s with the desire for state Buddhism. Then, starting in 1976, extremist 'Tigers' of Tamil Eleem (LTTE) hoped to form a separate Tamil state.[16]

Amos Yong explains how the *Sangha*, the self-governing order of monks and nuns, became a distinct force in Sri Lankan politics. It caused tension with local rulers, countered Christian education, and helped a new Prime Minister (Bandaranaike) make Sinhala the official language. Riots caused hundreds of Hindu Tamilian deaths; thousands were displaced. Strong dispute among Buddhist communities about traditions or meanings of texts added to conflict, not compassion.[17]

Eva Neumaier[18] explains how to counter conflict using the Buddhist Four Noble Truths.

1. Dissatisfaction is part of experience; that means that suffering (*dukkha*) occurs.

2. Such suffering results from being too ideal with hopes, from clinging to or thirsting after pleasure.

3. *Nirvana*—being beyond birth and death—transpires when a person is free from suffering.

4. Wisdom, intense mental discipline, and release from attachment bring *nirvana*, a state of otherness, to fruition.[19]

Whereas a dictionary might contrast conflict with: the end of war, freedom from civil discord, or quiet composure, Buddhist meaning for *shanti* centers more on inner calm. True peace, the Dalai Lama says, shapes mental quality. Not an ethical response, it arrives through meditation.[20]

D. Christianity – Just War, Crusades

After centuries of nonviolence, Christianity became the Roman Empire's 'official' religion. With questions of how to reconcile a clear conscience and acts of war, Ambrose and Augustine, in the 4th century, proposed a basis for 'just war.' They hoped to maintain justice and order, avoid undue harm, and restore just peace. Standards for declaring war <u>just</u> were: declared by a lawful leader, as a 'last resort,' with a sane chance for success, with moderate violence or more good than evil likely to occur, and intent for peace as a result.[21] By the thirteenth century, Thomas Aquinas declared "war as always sinful . . . even if waged for a just cause." Writers like Wesley Ariarajah state that by the twentieth century, some Christians doubt if any war can be called "just." Modern methods and nuclear weapons lead ecumenical people to call for just peace, not just war.[22] "Waging holy war is easy. Waging holy peace is painstaking," says Rabbi Justus Baird.[23]

Relations between Islam and Christianity around 1050 shaped the Crusades. By the end of the eighth century, Islam already posed a broad threat. As Islam questioned Christian culture, Christians could not tolerate such a 'demonic, counterfeit' religion controlling the Holy Land. Issues of power—commerce, land grabbing, glory—drove the Crusades.[24] Like drives to suppress heresy, Crusade plunder promised blessing for those who joined; booty followed plunder.[25]

Centered in mistrust, the two religions saw each other as harmful competitors. While Christians thought theirs was the only valid religion, Muslims felt that Islam corrected Christian corruption.[26] The only major, post-Christian religion, Islam presumed to supersede it in ways like Christians had presumed to replace Judaism. Such supersessionist views never bring accord; they fail to admit the good of difference. Further, Eugene March and others believe that "Muslim rule was far more tolerant toward other religions than the Christian intent to replace."[27] In the name of God, Christian Crusaders 'went on pilgrimage' to kill those of the house of Islam in its effort to regain Jerusalem and Holy Places.

From the eleventh to thirteenth centuries, devoted Christians destroyed Jews and Muslims. First impelled by Pope Urban's 1095 sermon, religion supplied the 'just cause' for holy massacre. A recital of battles followed.[28] Capture of Jerusalem in 1099 led to Islamic counterattacks. A second Crusade from 1147-49 failed to repossess Muslim Edessa. Sunni Saladin ended Egypt's Fatimid caliphate in 1171 and then re-conquered Jerusalem in 1187. The third Crusade soon after (1190-92) failed to take Jerusalem back despite new strategy. Fourth and fifth Crusades tried again, but in vain. They did not end there, theologian John Howard Yoder reminds us. Spain's conquest of Algeria occurred during the sixteenth century; a mindset persists about fighting for God or martyrdom.[29]

While these battles took place centuries ago, views gained then linger. For Muslims and Jews, Crusades echoed by "God wills it" suggest "ugly, human zeal to 'please' God."[30] Yoder says that "for the average Muslim, the Crusades define what it means to be Christian." Perhaps those who today point a finger at the Taliban or Al Quada might first look squarely at that definition.

    E. <u>**Islam**</u> – Inner war (*Jihad*), Wahhabism
    Critics of Islam and Muslims, intent to harm or ignorant of good, often give a negative meaning to the term *jihad*. While I include it in this conflict section, the conflict may be more the distortion that opponents or extremists give to "holy war." For Muslims, war may be just or unjust; Islam calls nothing "holy" except God. The multi-layered doctrine of *jihad* results from diverse teachings and teachers, applied through history. Noted author John Esposito says that the Qur'an refers to armed struggle as either defensive or expansionist, against nonbelievers.[31] It provides directives for dealing with conflict:
- Who is to fight and who is excused from battle. (48:17; 9:91)
- When to end warfare. (2:192)
- When to make peace, suggested by the other. (8:61)[32]

    But, the deeper meaning of *jihad* deserves more press. It describes the inner struggle with selfishness. While ascetic Sufis directly oppose war, some Islamic scholars call a battle sacred if it enables people to submit to Allah. A Sufi might see how true, 'holy war' praises God if the enemy of truth *within* a person is destroyed. For, the war that needs fighting is an inner one—getting rid of evil within that opposes God. To strive for Allah's cause (greater *jihad*) is better than armed struggle (lesser *jihad*).To attack others or force them into one's own belief is not Islam. Self-control—to restrain anger, revenge, or jealousy, to get rid of inner thoughts that hurt others—is the war worth waging.[33] Such effort moves toward becoming "true believers."[34]

    A brief glance at Islamic Wahhabism shows intent to defend and preserve tradition. Muhammad ibn Abd al-Wahhab was born to a devout Muslim family in 1703. He was sent from his desert home to Medina to study with a teacher (Shah Wali Allah) who was determined to purify Islam. Driven to restore early Arab thought, Wahhabism linked with the Kharijites, the first Muslim extremists. Internal debate over interpreting the Qur'an, applying law, defining a Muslim, and uniting a community divided by tribes and wars had shaken Islam for fourteen centuries. Wahhabist terrorism, meant to conserve or release from foreign sway, basically simplifies *tawhid*—which refers to God's Oneness and Unity.[35]

    Omid Safi names Wahhabism the "single greatest . . . impoverishment" for current Islam.[36] Presuming that it alone is right or knows Islamic truth, it tries to impose orthodoxy on all Muslims. Many Saudis claim it *as* Islam. Diverse Sunni movements feel that it: 1. counters mysticism and reason, 2. rejects intercession, and 3. often relies on *hadith*, not the Qur'an. Begun in the eighteenth century, Wahhabism bonded with 19th century Salifism by 1970, another group less tolerant of different views.[37]

F. Truth Claims that prompt Exclusion: Cause of Conflict from whatever Religion

Most religions make truth claims. Truth claims give members a foundation or basis for belief; they need not be cause for conflict. Problems emerge when others are denied the right to hold claims that differ or when claims are declared to be only or final or the best, as if other religions are inferior or replaced. When certain that my or our way is the only right view, I treat others as objects to be shaped by that view. For example, Christians who insist that Hindus need Christ to save them from sin fail to perceive that Hindus may not feel or seek such need or help. When others are labeled as wrong through my 'only' language, genuine respect for the good of difference lessens. When certain that my view alone represents God's will, I grow less tolerant of what differs and may threaten violence.

How people comprehend truth and divine will vary. Do truth claims that insist on one way or concept enable greater good will? Can a person be grace-filled toward difference yet firm with what matters for her? Might he, for the sake of greater peace in the world, still learn from other group's claims that differ? Claims like the Hindu *trimurti*— creator Brahma, destroyer Shiva, and sustainer Vishnu? Like Buddhist emptiness (*sunnyata*)? Like Taoist energy or life force that pervades all things?

Questions multiply. Might readers expect to enrich their view of God's *agape* love through Buddhist compassion (*karuna*)? Why or why not? Might Christians call Jesus the Enlightened One, Pathfinder, or guru? Might Islam's call for utter submission to one God increase non-Muslim respect for God's will? Might Hindu or Buddhist practice of *ahimsa* enlarge all understanding of God's "nonviolent resistance to evil on the cross"?[38] How do such options enhance personal peace-building?

Peter Phan, from Asia, lists (among others) how Christians might approach truth claims.
1. Avoid presuming that "Christ is the fulfillment, fullness, or definitive expression of divine revelation."
2. Restore the existence of ancient, plural covenants.
3. Admit that what Christians call the Spirit guided people before Jesus' time and that the same Spirit/Energy/Power continues to engage with rituals, teachings, or practice of any religion.
4. God's plan includes multiple religions, each to meet adherents' needs.
5. Each religion, through dialogue, can enable others to more fully achieve its own intent.

6. Dialogue among religions might be of life (shared joys/sorrows), action (toward freedom), exchange of theology (skilled insight), or sacred experience (like prayer or seeking the Ultimate).[39]

II. Peace-building – Final Word

At a Glance: "Religious plurality—the Creator's Wisdom"

A story of Kabir (1440-1519), the poet-saint who brought peoples' hearts together, speaks. People could not tell if he was Muslim or Hindu; he lived the best of each faith. When he died, Hindus wanted to cremate his body and Muslims wanted to bury the *pir* as they do. On looking under the saint's shroud, each group found "only a heap of flowers." Even his death turned conflict to good will.[40]

How might Christians respond to the fact that Buddha was called "Prince of Peace"? Born into a royal family, the idea holds in more than one way. Further, his wide-spread teaching commends a rule of right living (*dhamma-cakkam*). Buddhism calls for external freedom from conflict or war and for inward peace, "peace that passes understanding." Peace that moves from self-centered being or attachment to peaceful Nirvana, devoid of desire.[41]

"Peace the Divine Gift" is how Monika Hellwig titles a chapter. She notes three points on which world religions agree.

1. Peace, ordained by God, directs people and communities.

2. Because people ever quarrel, peace is a gift of heaven.

3. Personal and group peace depends on inner peace with the self and the divine.[42]

Peace-building through Paradigms:
Hinduism, Judaism, Buddhism, Christianity, Islam

How might religions foster more peace-building?

A. **Hinduism**: 'The Way,' Mira Bai, and *ahimsa*

Shared insight into spiritual themes can enhance good will between Hindus and other living faiths. One theme centers on 'way' or 'path' as known to Hindus and Christians.[43] A popular, spiritual classic text for Hindus is *Bhagavad Gita*. The *Gita* is part of the great epic *Mahabharata*, (the other main epic being the *Ramayana).* In the Sanskrit language, *marga* means 'way.' Three types of seeking or striving for a goal, or a path that leads to God-experience, mean liberation: *jnana-marga*, the way of knowledge or intuition, *karma-marga*, the path of action, and *bhakti-marga*, the road of deep devotion.[44] Known as his "spiritual reference book," Gandhi credits the *Gita's* teachings for lifting whatever problem he faced, for showing the 'way.'

The long epic tells about a war between the Pandavas and the Kauravas, two branches of a royal family.[45] Just before going to battle, Arjuna, a Pandava, admits that he cannot kill his own friends and relatives. *Gita* teachings present Arjuna and Lord Krishna's exchange, a sacred process through the three *margas*. Krishna (a Vishnu incarnation) guides Arjuna to intense thought about the *ways* of: being, selfless work to benefit all, and loving surrender to Lord Krishna. Those paths will lead Arjuna to *yoga* or union with the Ultimate (what Christians call salvation).

Consider also Mira Bai who lived during the 1500s.[46] A saint, mystic, and famous poet, she exhorts the way of *bhakti*. Fully devoted to Krishna her lover, she gave up her princely husband to live with kindred, devoted *bhaktas* known for equality and care for the poor. She also chose a Muslim to be her guru, one who "knows the secrets of the Divine path."[47] She traveled to many temples sacred to Krishna where she sang and danced her devotion. A "favored symbolic figure" of Gandhi's, Mira Bai's nonviolent non-cooperation "compelled him to become her disciple." She symbolized for him the "power of love."[48]

Ahimsa, usually explained as nonviolence, has meaning broader than not harming a person. A Hindu writer[49] finds the idea of "oneness with all life" or deep compassion in an ancient Upanishad text. Jains then gave *ahimsa* a central place in thought and practice; they neither kill an insect nor buy silk. Western peace movements rarely practice nonviolence to the Hindu point of unity of all things. Vedic philosophy sees everything as pervaded by divine power (*Sat*) or Brahman (pure consciousness).[50] Another Hindu break-off, Buddhism later applied the practice of *ahimsa* to relations between people. Each person's duty to help, not even despise another, re-shaped the term into positive action. Monika Hellwig suggests that western religions could cultivate a deeper empathy with all living beings for its peacemaking and ecology focus, learning from eastern *karma* about moral cause and effect.[51]

B. Judaism – Genesis 18, Hospitality

I first learned about the hospitality that Abraham and Sarah showed at their tent by the oaks of Mamre when reading my mother's "talks." Her first public speech, given in her home church when age 13, notes this text. How intriguing, that she who hosted more people than anyone I know, including strangers, who credited the Divine as ever-present, chose this ancient account of God's visit!

As with the Hindu poet Tulsidas' counsel to treat all people well lest they be the divine in disguise, such a surprise visit appears in diverse world religions.[52] Three unknown visitors appear to elderly Abraham and Sarah. Gracious, he offers water for thirst and foot-washing and suggests that they rest while he garners the household ('tent-hold') to ready a meal of calf, bread, milk, and butter. He passes God's test of piety (hospitality) that preserves strangers. Here is warmth of welcome and deep respect offered at midday. Whether Yahweh appeared in all three commoners but spoke as one, mystery pervades. After appearing to eat, the guests attend to their 'task': reporting that Sarah would birth a child before another year had passed. That prediction was enough to make the eavesdropper inside the tent flaps laugh. The guests depart having pointedly asked: "Is anything too hard for God?"

The call to entertain strangers recurs. Thirty-six Hebrew texts remind hearers to "love the stranger."[53] That fact reflects basic peace-building, for strangers will be loyal to diverse faith traditions. Risks will be taken and empathy offered when making space for difference. A question lingers: Will Christians see God's image in those whose faith and ideals differ? Rabbi Jonathan Sacks suggests that if we fail this test, we "make God into [our] image instead of allow God to remake us in God's image."[54]

Self-righteous members might negate the stranger in a pluralist context, might set a fence around her. Such absolutists wish to keep their own people separate. They fear that strangers will undermine their values. Martin Marty, in *When Faiths Collide*, supports Darrell Fasching: "To welcome the stranger involves passing over into the other's life and stories and coming back into our own [religion] enriched."[55]

C. **Buddhism** – Engaged Buddhism, Thich Nath Hanh

Sallie King calls 'Engaged Buddhism' "Gandhi's *ahimsa* in Practice."[56] Engaged Buddhism appears as social activism, building peace through transformed systems, or acting out Buddhist basic values. The Four Noble Truths explain suffering, or what results from self-attachment. Factors that cause or remove suffering include compassion, selflessness, interdependence, and *karma* (seeds in actions that shape future fruit). Its precepts counter harming another, stealing, lying, sexual offense, or being drunk.

Sallie King names[57] Buddhist mentors of lived nonviolence like Tibet's Dalai Lama. Consider also Maha Ghosananda, born in the 1920s. He joined a monastery at age ten and came to be known as "Cambodia's Gandhi." The entire family of this humble monk died in the Khmer Rouge holocaust of his country; he died not long ago. Spiritual leader of the masses who walked with him thousands of miles, his wisdom and compassion taught many. His moral sense that revenge only repeats itself grew from intense practice of meditation.

Although Hindus and Muslims persecuted Buddhism in India during the ninth century, when many monks fled to Nepal, a more recent peace-builder there was B. R. Ambedkar. He labored hard to reform India's social system of caste. Born a Hindu Untouchable and ever an advocate for them, he helped write the Indian constitution and was a cabinet minister in the new government. Weeks before his death, he with a half million converted to Buddhism. Buddha's Way, which has become Engaged Buddhism, affirms mutual dependence among all beings.[58]

Perhaps some Americans first became aware of Thich Nhat Hanh (known as "Thay") from actions of monks during the Viet Nam war. Over one hundred monks and nuns set themselves on fire to protest that war.[59] Born in 1926 and a monk for six decades, Nhat Hanh now lives in France, since exiled from Viet Nam. He founded Plum Village in 1982. His peace effort begins with mindfulness and a smile. For Buddhist Nhat Hanh, all violence is injustice, its main corrective being compassion combined with understanding.[60]

Mindfulness restores a person to the present moment, to insight. It centers in awareness of what is going on. It depends on breath which connects life to consciousness, which brings together body and thoughts. Mindfulness, a kind of energy, exists in all that is done. This 'Buddha nature' might be called Spirit, the seed which exists in all people. To practice right mindfulness, Buddhists look to others who live by Buddha teachings—their community or *sangha*. Core members within a *sangha* "observe at least sixty days of mindfulness within a year."[61]

A religious life for Nhat Hanh includes reverence for life, nonviolence, and communion—with people or an absolute.[62] Nonviolence means "to act with love and compassion." By contrast, war, which no one wins, is based on wrong perceptions of a situation. "Thay" contends that killing another person means seeing that one as a beast. To transform such anger into love, or to heal, requires meditation, a core practice of Buddhism.[63]

Asked what he would say if he met Osama bin Laden, Nhat Hanh explained: he would listen, taking strong listener friends along. He would try to understand what suffering may have led bin Laden to be cruel. After a break to absorb the information gleaned, he would calmly respond to each of bin Laden's points in order to "gently but firmly" prompt him to find what he had failed to understand.[64]

D.   Christianity – Peacemakers: 1. Thomas Merton.

As an English teenager, Thomas Merton first read a book on Buddhism. Five years later he met the Hindu monk Bramachari; he also joined the Roman Catholic Church. Attitudes, his and those around him, during his early years at the Abbey of Gethsemani were negative toward other living faiths. Some things changed; others did not. His book titled *Peace in the Post-Christian Era*, ready to be printed in 1964 was published in 2004. Too prophetic, it discusses just war theory, working for peace, and moral issues about nuclear bombs.

At fifty, Merton remained open to the world, people, and God. Learning from interfaith friendships, many through letter writing, Merton was as rooted in his faith as he was free to perceive and receive others.

Peace-building insight from Merton's letters abounds.[65] Writer William Apel begins reporting with Sufi mystic Abdul Aziz. Their exchange is based on 'poverty of spirit'—being humble to learn from the other. Pitting one's God against another's divides and creates idolatry.

Letter writers from different countries and religions appear. Amiya Chakravarty, world citizen rooted in Buddhist wisdom from India, links Christ's limitless love with the Buddha's deep compassion. To love without restraint—have "the mind of Christ"—is like right mindfulness or selfless compassion. Jew Abraham Heschel, writing with Merton, affirms the Hebrew Bible as "God's search for man [sic]." To repent, or re-turn, a person responds to God's seeking. When neither Jews nor Christians reduce or convert the other, their dialogue remains based in covenant.

Another of Merton's Buddhist correspondents was D. T. Suzuki from Japan. Fully aware of inner being, Suzuki reflects on breathing Zen's universal spirit. Both see in Zen deep exchange or communion about life. Both see religious *practice*, not religious doctrine, as the true place for interfaith meeting. Merton, a contemplative Christian monk, shared with his friend the link between Christ's emptying and Zen experience of *sunyata* (emptiness). When Merton wished Suzuki to write the introduction for his book *The Wisdom of the Desert*, censors from his monastic order refused. "A work on the desert fathers could not be introduced by a Buddhist."[66] What Merton knew, they failed to perceive.

D. 2. Joyce Burkhalter Flueckiger, David C. Scott, and Paul F. Knitter

Another source of multifaith peace-building is shared, extensive knowledge of other religions plus respect for religious figures. Three personal friends—Joyce Burkhalter Flueckiger, David C. Scott and Paul F. Knitter—write about and teach World Religions. Joyce and David grew up in India, children of missioners. A Goshen College grad and on the Emory University faculty, one of Flueckiger's books[67] describes her fieldwork over a decade done with Amma, a Muslim healer woman from Hyderabad.

Professional, public religious roles for Muslim women are rare and noticed. Laywomen may practice healing or prayers in homes. Gender roles and arrangements matter for Amma and her teacher husband Abba. She may see, diagnose, and prescribe spiritual forces for Hindu, Muslim, or Christian patients. "They're all the same in the healing room," Amma says. Patients with troubles, her disciples value her charismatic, spiritual teaching and strength. Writing diagnoses on paper "amulets or unleavened bread," she also may pray or recite from the Qur'an.[68] Asked whether Joyce was a disciple, Amma replied: "She loves God and I love God, so we have a connection."

David Scott lived much of his life in India. Retired from
seminary teaching, he spoke several years ago to a group of Methodists
about Christian peace-building with Muslims.[69] To truly know a Muslim
of faith, Scott urges engaging in prayer with her or him, hearing the
Qur'an recited, sharing the Ramadan fast, or absorbing the poetry of
Islam's lived prose. Knowledge enables experience. Islam stems from an
Arabic noun root *aslama* which means to submit. A religion of God, not
Muhammad, Islam depends utterly on God, the Arabic word being *Allah*.
Not a new religion, Islam confirms and culminates what went before—
Abraham, Moses, King Solomon and the Queen of Sheba, prophets and
Jesus. Dependent on the one God, they were all Muslims, all mentioned
in the Qur'an.[70] Muslims explain that as Jesus fulfilled Moses' work, so
Muhammad confirms or fulfills Jesus.

Scott introduces a Muslim approach: they might tell their
children about God's children finding rest and shade at the Oasis of
Moses. When God calls them to journey on, those who refuse because
they wish to stay with Moses are Jews. The rest reach the Oasis of *Isa
Masihu* where they in peace drink at Jesus' feet. Again, called by God to
move on, those who choose to stay with Jesus are Christians. But the rest
follow God to the final seal of prophets, the Oasis of Muhammad.[71]

Paul Knitter's most recent book (*Without Buddha I Could not be
a Christian*) conveys depth of learning about peacemaking from
Buddhism.[72] Several insights:

- Explaining his strong intent in the 1980s to both sit in meditation
and go to El Salvador to stop death squads, a Zen Master taught
him: "You won't be able to stop the death squads until you
realize your oneness with them." (173)
- Joining others to denounce government economic and political
policies, Knitter heard a Buddhist respond: "I'm sorry, but we
Buddhists don't denounce anyone." (176)
- A Tibetan scholar monk asked a Jewish member of the
International Interreligious Peace Council meeting in Jerusalem,
"Why need people remember the Holocaust or hold fast to
memories of suffering?" From meeting Chinese in Tibet, he had,
when present to the moment, awakened to innate wisdom; he felt
compassion on all sides, including for Chinese ignorance. (183)
- Knitter also drew from Thich Nhat Hanh's call to "be peace" if
one expects to "make peace." To be peace inwardly means to
practice mindfulness (accept and embrace what is), remove the
ego from peacemaking, and work to reconcile, in part by not
taking sides. (184-87)

Having passed over to Buddhist wisdom, Knitter explains
passing back to his Christian heritage. He then affirms and enriches truth

about God's kin-dom—its human interconnection, its being already and yet to come. He renews faith in Jesus as his example to both oppose and embrace oppressors. He declares: "When we love those whom we oppose as perpetrators of injustice *as they are*, not *for what we want them to be*, then, maybe only then, are we providing them a chance to become something different." (210)

E. Islam – 1. Riffat Hassan - Interpreting Scripture, Messianiam
   Riffat Hassan who teaches at the University of Louisville was born in Pakistan. Her articles often focus on direct content from the Qur'an, women in Islam, peace concerns, or interreligious dialogue. An important article of hers responds to: "What Does It Mean to Be a Muslim Today?"[73] For Hassan, it means this and more:
   - Belief in Allah, serving Allah and humanity;
   - Being Allah- and Creature-conscious—to understand the interconnection of all life;
   - Following the Shari'ah (Divine law/will of Islam);
   - Knowing that the Qur'an is the charter of human freedom;
   - Developing a way to interpret fundamental teachings separate from additions; [like *hadith*]
   - Heeding Allah's decree that diversity is for knowing each other while being Allah-conscious;
   - Being on a journey toward achieving peace.

   Hassan perceives that accurate insight into Islam depends on careful attention to the prime text, the Qur'an. Her discovery of God's justice and compassion toward women as taught in the Qur'an, compared to the injustice faced by many in life, has shaped her thirty-five year study.[74] With other educated women, Hassan sees how religion is often used to oppress more than liberate. So, they no longer accept myths and arguments given. As Christian and Jewish women scholars learned the value of disciplined, textual study, some Muslim feminists feel driven to be duly informed. For peace-building purposes, Christians in dialogue with Muslims will believe the pain and read others' religious texts.[75]
   Riffat Hassan's discussion of <u>messianism</u> also prods openness with Muslims.[76] "People of the Book" anticipate redemption through a messiah figure—Jews of one to come publicly within the community and Christians with the return of one to bring spiritual, inner change. Qur'an content does not expect such a savior. It avoids points like redemption, intercession, or a figure with charisma.[77]
   Might sensitive Christians not expect Muslims to talk about terms not part of Islam and to hear their distinct concepts? Islam does not claim that one bears the sins of another; all people strive and must answer for their own choices and actions. Yet, most Shi'a and Sufi

Muslim history contains a concept of savior. Together they spread messianism to protest Muslim corruption. Shi'a messianism centers in the Karbala tragedy (680 C.E.) in which Husain the third imam and 100 relatives of Muhammed's died. Oppressed and suffering Shi'as rally around Husain as 'savior of Islamic values.'[78] A couple centuries later, the twelfth Shi'a imam disappeared as a child. Known as the "Mahdi," he will return just before the end of time, after "a long period of chaos and ungodliness." He will save creation and all people, conquer the earth, and avenge Husain's blood.[79]

E. 2. Mahmoud Ayoub

Mahmoud Ayoub, a fine Muslim thinker, wrote essays comparing Muslim with Christian views. Irfan Omar edited some of these into one volume.[80] Christian peace-building will be strengthened when taking others' religious thought as seriously as Ayoub does Christian faith. Not only does he show how one person can display respectful dialogue; he conveys Islamic integrity and conviction along with deep knowledge of a faith not his own. Naming how the two religions differ without judging either, Ayoub helps readers to learn about both in order to better understand each.

Born in South Lebanon in 1935, Mahmoud Ayoub received degrees in Beirut and at Harvard. For twenty years he has been professor of Islamic Studies at Temple University, Philadelphia. His essays in *A Muslim View of Christianity* benefit readers as through details of difference that Ayoub names. Consider the Qur'an's view that Jesus did not die—that Jesus remains with God until his return. (Surah 3:54, 4:157)[81] That stance directly differs from the basic Christian belief that Jesus died on a cross and rose again before ascending. Will adherents honor the other's right to a view that differs while remaining loyal to their own stance, to foster good will between religions? To argue over positions not likely to shift helps little. If texts leave no choice but to differ, might members extend friendship, knowing that partial agreement matters, even if not over key beliefs, as about Jesus or Trinity?[82]

Prior to the Crusades, some good will prevailed. Muslims and Christians at first saw each other as people of faith, the other's religion as God-inspired. They started with similar goals of love and openness; each wished to reform society. They believed in God's being universal, in each faith as meant for all. The recited Qur'an called all 'people of the Book' to "worship no one except God." (Surah 3:64)

Yet, the two groups that claimed to supersede those before them became exclusive. Ayoub explains that while the Qur'an values religious diversity, some commentaries grew exclusive.[83] Without doctrines of sin and redemption, Muslims resent Christian mission efforts that stress salvation in Christ alone. Enmity grew. Christians refused looking to the Qur'an as a guide. They disowned Prophet Muhammad as final revelation. While Christians charged Islam as 'inspired by the devil,' Muslims labeled Christians as polytheist, due to ideas of the Trinity.[84]

Ayoub sees the current challenge to be whether Jews, Christians, and Muslims can hear God's voice through each other's scriptures. Will Christians, for the cause of peace, credit God as revealed in Islam, Muhammad as God's prophet, and the Qur'an as a Book of God? Will both admit the polemics created through fear and distrust, the problems that follow from judging another's by one's own standards?[85] Ayoub encourages parties to "listen to and obey the voice of God as it speaks to all communities through faith traditions."[86]

E. 3. Badshah (Abdul Ghaffar) Khan

Most readers know of M. K. Gandhi. A kindred spirit, also with nonviolence as his driving passion, was Abdul Gaffar (called Badshah) Khan. Khan, a part of the small, Afghani/Pakistan <u>Pathan</u> tribe and a faithful Muslim, died twenty years ago at the age of 98. (Gandhi had died forty years earlier.) Khan and Gandhi[87] bonded through nonviolent effort for twenty-five years prior to India's independence and the bloodshed of Partition.

Tribal life breeds distinct features. Its social code includes honor for guests: "An unknown traveler is a guest sent to us by God."[88] Badshah's father seldom missed hosting strangers or the five daily periods of Islamic prayer. His mother's piety often turned into long periods of silent prayer. Considered warlike by the brutal British, Pathans were taught by Khan to live without revenge. He proved that combining *nonviolence* with *Pathan* was not an oxymoron, despite their ignorance, poverty and fear. Yet, the British held him in prison many years.

For the two 'Gandhis,' these two servants of God, their task became "to serve and to suffer in the cause of truth." Khan asked for a province in Pakistan where all Pathans could by united. Within a year, he was jailed by a Muslim government that faulted him for being pro-Hindu. That Gandhi was killed by another Hindu who resented his pro-Muslim stance compares. Both devout in their own religion yet most respectful of other living faiths, each was misunderstood by those of his own religion. Ingrained, self-righteous disdain for difference prevailed.[89]

F. Conclusion

A question remains: are peace-builders ready for religious pluralism designed by God? Will members loyal to any religion hold lightly yet with conviction, rather than utterly, to ideas that matter? Does the cause of peace and good will matter enough to cut through barriers, to honor convincingly the neighbor? Might integrity be honored saying, "The truth that you teach gives you meaning. I wish to learn from it to enhance being faithful to mine. For, God's truth is 'bigger' than either of us claims."[90] With such a rule, open minded folk of faith will apply learned truth as appropriate to their beliefs, while they grow in empathy for others.

Peter Phan commends others familiar with diverse religions. Wilfred Cantwell Smith sees each religion as an image, or "idol," of God. When an "idol" becomes exclusive, it turns into "idolatry." It replaces God with an image or idea. Aloysius Pieris (Sri Lanka) and Paul Knitter (U.S.) state that faith claims are best <u>lived</u> through actions that favor the poor, not absurd, debated, verbal statements of faith.[91]

One of Thich Nhat Hanh's many small books, titled *Interbeing*, explains the fourteen Guidelines for Engaged Buddhism.[92] Those most related to peace-building reinforce a Buddhist secret: "There is no way to peace; peace is the way."[93] The first precepts move toward freedom from attachments, including devotion to views. To cling to dogma (or require others to adopt your views) prevents further learning from others and prompts conflict.[94] *Interbeing* truth, or confluence of relating, suggests:

- Help diminish suffering.
- Avoid wealth when others hunger.
- Address and resolve factions.
- Be truthful and protect life.
- Do not kill or let others kill, by might, thoughts, or way of life.
- "Possess nothing that should belong to others."

Might such guidelines be a useful format for stating truth, instead of exclusive claims of only/best/first/or final?

We are reminded that people define <u>peace</u> in diverse ways: as contrast to conflict; as a state of inner being; as genuine interest in knowing others' sacred meanings. Interfaith friends become a sign of peace. Not doubting that the Creator's Wisdom includes plural diversity, we greet one another: *Salam alaykum:* "Peace be with you."

Endnotes:

[1] Antony Copley. *Religions in Conflict Ideology, Cultural Contact, and Conversion in Late Colonial India.* New Delhi: Oxford Univ Pr, 1997.

Mark Juergensmeyer. *Terror in the Mind of God The Global Rise of Religious Violence.* (Updated edition) Berkeley: Univ of Calif Pr, 2000.

John L. Esposito. *The Islamic Threat Myth or Reality?* (3rd edition) NY: Oxford Univ Pr, 1999 or *Unholy War Terror in the Name of Islam.* NY: Oxford Univ. Pr., 2002.

Satish Kumar. *The Buddha and the Terrorist.* Chapel Hill: Algonquin Bks, 2006.

Clayton Crockett, ed. *Religion and Violence in a Secular World Toward a New Political Theology.* Charlottesville: Univ of Virginia Pr, 2006.

S. Wesley Ariarajah. "Religion and Violence A Protestant Christian Perspective." *Ecumenical Review*, April, 55/2, 2003, 136-43. [my copy a handout of 8 pp.]

Walter Dietrich. "The mark of Cain: violence and overcoming violence in the Hebrew Bible," *Theology Digest*, 52/1, Spr 2005, 3-11.

Francois Houtart. "The Cult of Violence in the Name of Religion: A Panorama," in *Religion as a Source of Violence*. Wim Beuken and Karl-Josef Kuschel, eds. Maryknoll, NY: Orbis, 1997, 1-9.

Oliver McTernan. "Religion and the Legitimization of Violence," in *Religion in an Age of Conflict*. Maryknoll, NY: Orbis, 2003, 45-76.

Jack Nelson-Pallmeyer. "Religion and Violence," in *Is Religion Killing Us? Violence in the Bible and Qur'an*. Harrisburg: Trinity Pr International, 2003, 13-25.

Vimal Tirimanna. "Does Religion Cause Violence?" *Studies in Interreligious Dialogue*, 17/1, 2007, 5-19.

[2] In certain circles Mennonites are known for peacemaking theory and action. Hopefully, Historic Peace Church members (Quaker, Church of the Brethren, and Mennonite) do not presume to have "a corner" on peace Wisdom. Nor should I overlook important analysis, experience, or case work done by Mennonite leaders like John-Paul Lederach, Joe Liechty (Ireland), Ed Metzler (Nepal), Lisa Schirch, Alain Epp Weaver (Middle East), David W. Shenk, or Kathryn Aschliman (children). Most of these might have learned from peace activist Atlee Beechy's example and life review (*Seeking Peace*).

Beechy in turn had thrived in contexts of peace-work—Europe, Africa, Vietnam—and through denominational heritage. Mennonite Confessions of Faith between 1527 and 1975 reveal that rejection of revenge was their "most central emphasis." Further, Urbane Peachey counted 230 peace and social concern statements by four Mennonite groups and Mennonite Central Committee during the first three-quarters of the 1900s. Leo Driedger & Donald B. Kraybill. *Mennonite Peacemaking From Quietism to Activism*. Scottdale, PA: Herald Pr, 1994, 30-31.

Some current voices directly attest to how other religions teach us Mennonites about faith and peace-building. While a few 'armchair theologians' without sustained experience as minority Christians might explain group views toward religious pluralism, peace-building or dialogue, voices from sustained encounters persist: Doug Hostetter (present M.C.C. staff member at the United Nations, former leader at Fellowship of Reconciliation and peacekeeper during wars in Vietnam and Bosnia), Brice H. Balmer (*Meeting Our Multifaith Neighbors*), or Wallace and Evie Shellenberger with experience in Iran http://www.newperspectivesgoshen.org. Also effective are programs like Eastern Mennonite University's Center for Justice and Peacebuilding and ecumenical effort such as Gene Stoltzfus and Dorothy A Friesen (Christian Peacemaker Teams vision) or Fernando Enns (World Council of Churches). A recent resource *Peace-Building by, between, and beyond Muslims and*

Evangelical Christians (edited by Mohammed Abu-Nimer and David Augsburger) includes Mennonite writers' intent to listen to strong Muslims like Riffat Hassan, Osman Bakar, and Abdul Rashied Omar. Not intent to negate past efforts, my goal is to strengthen peace-building conviction via the richness and Wisdom of other living faiths.

[3] Discussion of such fundamentalist groups can be found in multiple places; I drew from Gabriel A. Almond, R. Scott Appleby & Emmanuel Sivan. *Strong Religion The Rise of Fundamentalisms around the World.* Chicago: Univ of Chicago Pr, 2003, 136-37, 176.

Since Independence (1947), Indians have struggled with their chosen term *communal*—to retain equal value for or distance from the center for each religious group in the country—for governing.

[4] Arundhati Roy. "Fascism's Firm Footprint in India," in *Nothing Sacred Women Respond to Religious Fundamentalism and Terror.* Betsy Reed, ed. NY: Thunder's Mouth Pr, 2002, 179-84. The Booker prize winner for *The God of Small Things*, Roy also addresses the Godhra incident in *War Talk.* Cambridge, MA: South End Pr, 2003.

See also "Voices of Hindutva: Creating and Exploiting Religious Binaries" by Sameer Malik (pseudonym) in *Interreligious Dialogue.* http://irdialogue.org/wp-content/uploads'2009/05/voices-of-hindutva-12.pdf, retrieved 1-14-10.

[5] Dietrich, 3-4.

[6] In Peter C. Phan. *Being Religious Interreligiously Asian Perspectives on Interfaith Dialogue.* Maryknoll, NY: Orbis, 2004, 3rd Printing 2008, 199.

According to church historian Roland Bainton, "Violence in God's name is the worst violence done on the planet." (former Professor of Peace Studies Goshen College Ruth E Krall's correspondence to me, June 25, 2009).

[7] John Ferguson details Hebrew practice and vision in *War and Peace in the World's Religions*, Oxford Univ Pr, 1978. Part of the oldest Hebrew text, Exodus 15:3 states: "Yahweh is a warrior; Yahweh is his name." Joshua 24 tells of God's destroying the Amorites. When Israel fought citizens of Jericho, the Perizzites, Canaanites, Hittites, Girgashites, Hivites, and Jebusites, God "handed them over to Israel." Maimonides, the first to write a systematic code of all Jewish law said, "The primary war which the King wages is a *religious war*." Such wars, whether against the seven tribes, Amalek, or other enemies, differed from *optional war*, fought to extend Israel's borders or increase her prestige. 85, 91. See also *Yahweh is a Warrior* by Millard C. Lind. Scottdale: Herald Pr 1980.

[8] Charles Selengut. *Sacred Fury: Understanding Religious Violence.* Oxford: Alta Mira Pr, 2003, 21, 23 in Tirimanna 9.

[9] Peter W. Macky. *Violence: Right or Wrong?* Waco, TX: Word Book Pub., 1973 in Tirimanna, 9.

[10] Susan Niditch. *War in the Hebrew Bible A Study in the Ethics of Violence.* NY: Oxford Univ Pr, 1993, 28-149, in Leo D. Lefebure. *Revelation, the Religions, and Violence.* Maryknoll, NY: Orbis, 2000, 58-59.

[11] Lloyd Steffen. *The Demonic Turn The Power of Religion to Inspire or Restrain Violence.* Cleveland: Pilgrim Pr, 2003, 182-91.

[12] Charles Kimball. *When Religion becomes Evil.* San Francisco: Harper, 2002, 156-57.

[13] Susannah Heschel. *Abraham Geiger and the Jewish Jesus.* Chicago: Univ of Chicago Pr, 1998. Also see Adele Reinhartz' *Befriending the Beloved Disciple A Jewish Reading of the Gospel of John.* NY: Continuum, 2001.

Those who doubt 'just war' thought and wish to hear more 'just peace' belief may question President Obama's approach in accepting the Nobel Peace Prize, Dec 2009. I regret late receipt of John Howard Yoders' further thought on 'just war' and nonviolence. (See Stassen 2009 resource.) See also Yoder's *When War is Unjust Being Honest in Just-War Thinking.* Eugene Or: Wipf and Stock Pub, 2001.

[14] *Ibid.,* 6, 9, 13.

[15] Roy C. Amore. "Peace and Non-violence in Buddhism," in *The Pacifist Impulse in Historical Perspective.* Harvey L. Dyck, ed. Toronto: Univ of Toronto Pr, 1996, 244.

[16] Amos Yong. *Hospitality & the Other Pentecost, Christian Practices, & the Neighbor.* Maryknoll, NY: Orbis, 2008, 3-7.

[17] *Ibid.,* 8-9.

[18] Eva K. Neumaier. "Missed Opportunities: Buddhism and the Ethnic Strife in Sri Lanka and Tibet," in *Religion and Peacebuilding.* Harold Coward and Gordon S. Smith, eds. NY: State Univ of NY Pr, 2003, 69-92.

[19] *Ibid.,* 70.

[20] *Ibid.,* 74.

[21] Ariarajah, 4-5.

[22] *Ibid.*

[23] Justus Baird. "Waging Holy Peace." *Auburn Views*, Auburn Seminary, Spr 2009, 4.

[24] Theodore J. Koontz and Andy Alexis-Baker, eds. *Christian Attitudes to War, Peace, and Revolution.* John Howard Yoder. (Seminary course created/taught for 30 years by Yoder.) Grand Rapids, MI: Brazos Pr, 2009, 110.

[25] Ferguson, 108.

[26] Roelf Kuitse. "Living in the Global Community," 45-51 in *Weathering the Storm Christian Pacifist Responses to War.* n.a. Newton, KS: Faith & Life Pr., 1991, 49.

[27] W. Eugene March. *The Wide, Wide Circle of Divine Love A Bible Case for Religious Diversity.* Louisville: Westminster John Knox Pr, 2005, 7.

[28] Richard Fletcher. *The Cross and the Crescent The Dramatic Story of the Earliest Encounters between Christians and Muslims.* NY: Penguin Bks, 2003, 77-82, 92.

[29] Koontz and Alexis-Baker, 110-11.

[30] March, 6.

[31] Esposito. *Unholy War. . . ,* 65.

[32] *Ibid.*, 32.

[33] M. R. Bawa Muhaiyaddeen. *Islam & World Peace Explanations of a Sufi.* Phila: The Fellowship Pr., 1ˢᵗ Printing 1987; 5ᵗʰ Printing 1999, 44, 48.

[34] Omid Safi, ed. *Progressive Muslims On Justice, Gender, and Pluralism.* Oxford: One World, 2003, 106.

[35] Reza Aslan. *No god but God The Origins, Evolution and Future of Islam.* NY: Random House, 2005, 241-42, 247-48.

[36] Safi, 8.

[37] *Ibid.*, 27, 49-53, 57.

[38] Phan, 118-19.

[39] *Ibid.*, 142-45.

[40] N. A. Palkhivala. *Essential Unity of All Religions.* Mumbai, India: Bharatiya Vidya Bhavan, 2003, 7.

[41] K. N. Jayatilleke. *Buddhism and Peace.* Kandy, Sri Lanka: Buddhist Pub Society, 1962, 1969, 1983. (Talk given April 8, 1961 at International Fellowship of Reconciliation Seminar, Oxford Univ.), 3, 10, 20.

[42] Monika Hellwig. *A Case for Peace in Reason and Faith.* Collegeville, MN: The Liturgical Pr., 1992, 42.

[43] According to A. M. Joseph Ethakuzhy, the RSV translation of the Bible uses 'way' over 550 times and 'ways' about 200 more times—*derek* in Hebrew texts and *hodos* in Greek. The word can suggest a route of travel, a course to pursue wisdom, or God's will or saving deeds. The word reflects Jesus' pattern of teaching en route, a disciple's conforming to Christ, or Jesus' offer of access to God. "'The Way' in the Bible and in the Bhagavad Gita," *Indian Theological Studies* 45, 2008, 462.

[44] *Ibid.*, 465, 468-72.

[45] *Ibid.*, 466-67. More about the *Gita* story: When the oldest brother (Yudhisthira) of the Pandavas returned from being exiled, the opponent leader refused to return the Pandavas throne and kingdom to him. Krishna, a chief and incarnation of Vishnu, one of the three main forms of Hindu Deity (*trimurti*), tried to resolve the conflict. With war the 'last resort,' Krishna became charioteer for Arjuna, a Pandavas. All three of the 'ways'—intuition of the inner Divine, unattached action that does God's work, and devoted surrender to a personal God—attain release from the cycle of birth and death (*samsara*). Such liberation, or awakening to the self as part of the Absolute, reflects salvation. The *Gita* or 'Gospel' of Hindu religion prompts a never-ending quest for the divine.

[46] Madhu Kishwar and Ruth Vanita. "Poison to Nectar: The Life and Work of Mirabai." *Manushi*, Nos. 50, 51, 52, 1989, 74-93.

[47] Bankey Behari. *The Story of Mira Bai.* Gorakhpur: Gita Pr., 2006, 53.

[48] Kishwar & Vanita, 86-87.

[49] Palkhivala, (in Chandogya Upanishad), 8, 15.

[50] Sunanda Y. Shastri & Yajneshwar S. Shastri. "*Ahimsa* and the Unity of All Things: A Hindu View of Nonviolence," in *Subverting Hatred The*

Challenge of Nonviolence in Religious Traditions. Daniel L Smith-Christopher, ed., Cambridge, MA: Boston Research Center for the 21st Century, 1998, 70.

[51] Hellwig, 50. Buddhism explains *karma* less in the Hindu way of past life experience shaping the present but as good or evil acts prompting current pleasant or unpleasant results. So also, Jayatilleke explains, 16.

[52] This Hebrew story perhaps builds on a Greek saga about Zeus, Poseidon, and Hermes' visit to a childless Hyrieus. Von Rad, 205. Having checked commentaries by Gordon J. Wenham and Terence E. Fretheim, I learned most from Gerhard von Rad's *Genesis.* Phila: Westminster Pr, Revised SCM Pr Ltd., 1972, 203-09.

[53] Jonathan Sacks. *The Dignity of Difference How to Avoid the Clash of Civilizations.* NY: Continuum, 1st Printing 2002; reprint 2003, 58.

[54] *Ibid.,* 201.

[55] Martin E. Marty. *When Faiths Collide.* Malden, MA: Blackwell Pub, 2005, 10, 13, 103, 132.

[56] Sallie B. King. "Engaged Buddhism: Gandhi's *Ahimsa* in Practice," in *Nonviolence for the Third Millennium.* G. Simon Harak, ed. Macon, GA: Mercer Univ Pr., 2000, 101.

[57] *Ibid.,* 101-05.

[58] The concept of <u>harmony</u> is ancient in Asian religions and cultures. Confucius (551-479 BCE) urged governments and individuals to preserve peace. In order to achieve unity or agree with self, others, Heaven and Earth, people were to follow the Way (Tao). He urged them toward peace through virtue, not law and violence. Phan, 199-203.

[59] Jennifer Schwamm Willis, ed., *Thich Nhat Hanh, A Lifetime of Peace Essential Writings by and about Thich Nhat Hanh.* NY: Marlowe & Co, 2003, 113.

[60] *Ibid.,* 264.

[61] Thich Nhat Hanh. *Interbeing. Fourteen Guidelines for Engaged Buddhism.* Edited by Fred Eppsteiner, New Delhi: Full Circle, 1997 New edition, 76.

[62] Willis, 44.

[63] *Ibid.,* 126.

[64] *Ibid.,* 261-262.

[65] Thanks to William Apel for making *Signs of Peace The Interfaith Letters of Thomas Merton* available. Maryknoll, NY: Orbis, 2006.

[66] *Ibid.,* 91.

[67] Joyce Burkhalter Flueckiger. *In Amma's Healing Room Gender and Vernacular Islam in South India.* Bloomington: Indiana Univ Pr, 2006.

[68] *Ibid.,* 17, 42, 68, 70, 86 142, 154, 168.

[69] David C. Scott. "Bridges of Hope: Muslims and Christians Alive to God." United Methodist Church Mission Gathering & Forum, Evanston, Aug 2007, 5 pp.

[70] *Ibid.,* 2.

Even humor speaks: On reaching heaven Muhammad was told by God to have followers pray fifty times a day. When Moses learned what God had required, he exploded, "Forget it; people won't do that. Go back; get God to reduce the demand." Muhammad went back often, each time God reduced the amount by five. Down to five, Moses told Muhammad, "Good luck; go for it."

Again, in heaven, God tells the Prophet to choose one of three vessels set before him—one each with wine, milk, or honey. Loyal to Islam's sound, middle position that combines from others without deserting itself, Muhammad chose milk, neither of the two extremes. Not a new religion, Islam with gratitude "absorbs and integrates" from signs of God's goodness in earlier revelations.

[71] *Ibid.*, 4.

[72] Paul F. Knitter. "Making Peace and Being Peace," in *Without Buddha I Could not be a Christian.* Oxford: One World, 2009, 167-212.

Earlier, Knitter wrote "Buddhist and Christian Attitudes toward Other Religions: A Comparison," European Society of Buddhist-Christian Studies, German Publisher, Salzburg, Austria, June 11, 2007, sent to me by Knitter 12-28-08, 48 pp.

In this article, Knitter asks four questions; he then explains how each might be answered by Buddhists and Christians. First, "The Many Religions: a Problem or a Blessing?" Is religious diversity something to solve or enjoy? Christianity looks for a final oneness or unity of religions. But, as the Trinity never becomes one, religious pluralism abides in its move toward unity. Knitter states: "God may will unity; but that doesn't mean that God doesn't also will diversity." (5) Buddhists know reality as something always new, always more. The whole of religious many-ness credits the parts involved without clinging to either. For dialogue then, the common ground is groundlessness. "No common denominator is the common denominator."(8)

For the second question: "Do the Many Hold Anything in Common?" Knitter finds Buddhist and Christian answers to be both yes and no. His two other questions with discussion follow: 3rd – "Among the Many Does One Excel?" and 4th – "Does 'Many' Mean 'Any'? From an ethical call to compassion, Knitter expects Christian love for others to link with justice and Buddhist "compassion [to] be grounded in the wisdom of enlightenment." (44)

[73] Riffat Hassan. "What does It Mean To Be a Muslim Today?" *Cross Currents,* 40-3, Fall 1990, (Originally Feb, 1990, *New Blackfriars*), 10 pp; http:www.crosscurrents.org/hassan.htm; Retrieved 2/8/2004.

[74] Islamic tradition bases its views on multiple sources: the *Qur'an* (God's Word passed unchanged from angel Gabriel through Prophet Muhammad to the first Muslims), the *hadith* (oral sayings ascribed to the Prophet), *Sunnah* (practices of the Prophet), *fiqh* (law), and Shari'ah (code to regulate life).

[75] Riffat Hassan observes that the biblical Genesis 3 "fall" account does not appear in the Qur'an. The latter speaks of self-conscious choice, of freedom as a condition of goodness. But, misogyny persists with a myth of female evil. Other details follow. With no 'fall' in the Qur'an, no idea of original sin appears

nor does a human need to be "redeemed" or "saved." Without an idea of redemption, no person functions between the believer and creator. A key Islamic belief states: "each person—man and woman—is responsible and accountable for his or her individual actions." Knowing such details affects exchange. Conflict builds when meanings for concepts differ and either party in exchange presumes that one (their) meaning rules for both. Accurate information avoids unfair judgment or conclusions. The ability to accept difference helps peace-building. Riffat Hassan. "Feminism in Islam," in *Feminism and World Religions.* Arvind Sharma and Katherine K. Young, eds. Albany: State Univ of NY Pr, 1999. 259-60, 268.

[76] Riffat Hassan. "Messianism and Islam," *Journal of Ecumenical Studies*, 22:2, Spring 1985, 261-91.

[77] *Ibid.*, 266, note 14. Quoting Fazlur Rahman. *Major Themes of the Qur'an.* Chicago: Bibliotheca Islamica, 1980, 31.

[78] Hassan, "Messianism . . .," 272.

[79] *Ibid.*, 276, notes 53 & 55. Quoting Mahmoud Ayoub. *Redemptive Suffering in Islam.* The Hague: Mouton, 1978.

[80] Irfan A. Omar, ed. *A Muslim View of Christianity Essays on Dialogue by Mahmoud Ayoub.* Maryknoll, NY: Orbis, 2007.

[81] *Ibid.*, 156, 176.

[82] *Ibid.*, 117, 123, 130, 159, 170.

The Qur'an includes an amazing amount of Hebrew/Christian scripture, notably about prophets. But, difference recurs. Holy Mary, lone woman mentioned by name, appears in over thirty Surahs. [*Ibid.*, 120] Roman Catholics and Protestants in dialogue with Muslims might differ in approach to that fact. Muslims deny that Jesus was divine. Yet, Sufis declare him the 'perfect man' who will unify religions and bring people nearer to God. Christians deny the Islamic view that Paul taught that Jesus, God, and Mary were all gods. While Christians describe Jesus as God's son, the idea of "only-begotten son" or God's having an offspring creates major offense for Muslims. They think that "Jesus was created through the verb 'be' which God conveyed to Mary through the angel Gabriel." They strongly believe in "God's absolute Oneness" (*tawhid*), without a consort to bear a child.

[83] *Ibid.*, 191-92.

[84] *Ibid.*, 36, 38, 68.

[85] *Ibid.*, 66, 209, 212, 218.

[86] *Ibid.*, 69.

[87] Returning from South Africa, Gandhi garnered his nonviolent resistance movement among Indians. His message to Britain in 1942, "Quit India," led to the arrest of many; by the end of that year sixty thousand Indians were jailed. Eknath Easwaran. *Nonviolent Soldier of Islam Badshah Khan, A Man to Match His Mountains.* Tomales, CA: Nilgiri Pr, 1984, 1999, 175. Khan spent fifteen years in jail, often in solitary confinement.

Not always endorsing nonviolent tactics, the Congress Working Committee (India) wished to keep Hindus and Muslims united in India. At the end of March 1947, however, they conceded with Lord Mountbatten that India would be divided. The British were often thought of operating on the principle of "divide and rule."

[88] *Ibid.*, 30.

[89] The Muslim reformer and Hindu lawyer continue to mentor us, whether for sedition or as God's servants among disadvantaged folk. Whether in jail with Muslim, Sikh, Hindu, and Christian prisoners, where they studied each other's scriptures, or practicing "pure faith and austere ways," these servants of God pursued nonviolence. They fed the hungry and shared clothes. Khan called the Pathans whom he taught Khudai Khidmatgars (servants of God). Not literate but armed with discipline and faith, their nonviolent resistance had caused the British more fear than their violence. Khan believed that all faiths duly inspire adherents, and that "God sends messengers for all nations and people. Hindus were no less 'Men [sic] of the Book' than Jews and Christians."*Ibid.*, 145.

As Badshah Khan felt mentored by Gandhi his friend toward nonviolent resistance, who mentored Gandhi? His nephew Arun [Arun Gandhi. "Who Influenced Gandhi?" in Harak, 10, 20-21] credits three informally educated women: his mother Putliba, nanny Rumbha, and wife Kastur(bai). His mother instilled a genuine respect for diverse religions plus strength of discipline. His nanny told stories—whether about parental love or king Harischandra, akin to the Hebrew account of Job. And Kastur(bai) lived out active resistance to injustice. She helped him perceive how to change prejudiced people—through love, not conflict. Basics for nonviolent action emerged as Gandhi observed.

Gandhi also sought out friends through letter writing, whether a local Muslim Sheikh Mehtab or Russian Leo Tolstoy. Anthony Parel credits Mahatma (the "Great Soul") with putting into practice Tolstoy's insight into Gospel ethics and state obstacles. And Graeme MacQueen notes his worthy, universal insight. Gandhi mixed ancient Indian asceticism with English vegetarianism, Hinduism with Tolstoy, and the Sermon on the Mount with his own *Gita*. Anthony Parel. "Nonviolence: The Tolstoy-Gandhi Legacy," in Harak, 41, 44.

[90] Phan, 118-19.

[91] *Ibid.*, 88.

[92] Nhat Hanh/Eppsteiner,. *Interbeing;* 14 Guidelines; Willis, 171-73.

[93] *Ibid.*, 6.

[94] *Ibid.*, 20, 22.

Appendix:
Texts of Influence

Undoubtedly, some Christians, on reading this book, will caution, "Yes but, Jesus said, 'I am the Way. . .'" (John 14:6) or "In the book of Acts chapter 4. . ." The 'staying power' of such texts leaves some Christians intent to conclude that only the Christian faith truly links with God. Or, rather than value anew the Hindu, Buddhist, or Muslim faith, as does content in this book, a news feature of a negative action done by some Muslims in one country might persuade a hearer to continue to doubt the integrity of most Muslims. To change views can cause fear—of what to believe, of who I become as a result. To resist letting new, positive information re-shape traditional bias, as about scripture, may be easier.

How to interpret sacred texts prompts diverse opinion and action. Content that follows, with minor edits, appears in my 2007 *Mission Focus Annual Review* article about biblical texts that engage across religious groups. That lecture was first given to the Association of Anabaptist Missiologists in Winnipeg in 2007. Used here with permission, it highlights commentaries and other resources.

Feminist, multifaith, and Asian voices shape my viewpoint. Carter Heyward, known for embodied, experience-based Christology, believes that God's incarnations are many and varied.[1] Some Korean women scholars think of Jesus as co-sufferer known for healings. He is often imaged as a shaman or big sister, not "Lord of all" or "only Son of God." Because Jesus respects them or bestows self-worth and dignity, they know hope.[2] Multifaiths value common views and uphold difference. Rather than hold God captive—through presumed right teachings or ways to worship—most discover God beyond particular limits. Ovey Mohammed, a Jesuit, notes many features that Jesus and Krishna have in common.[3] Jeannine Hill Fletcher states, ". . . ever-new perspectives on the mystery of God might constitute the ultimate human experience of salvation."[4]

> While most Christians find orientation to the world through the story of 'God,' 'Christ,' and 'salvation,' people of other

faiths describe the world in different terms . . . A Buddhist may talk about 'Nothingness' and 'Nirvana.'. . . A Hindu describes the multiplicity of forms through which God incarnates in the world. . . . And Muslims and Jews defend the radical monotheism whereby none is God but God.[5]

While Gandhi valued Jesus the Jewish model for non-resistant living and Sermon on the Mount ethics, he found Hindu thought and practice adequate. He faulted many Christians for failure to imitate their model Teacher. Michael Amaladoss stresses that *God* saves, not religion. Some Asian Roman Catholic bishops explain *saving* as uniting people of different cultures and religions to create love and peace; they understand *Jesus the saviour* as Jesus the union builder."[6] Wesley Ariarajah wishes that the church would "contemplate the possibility that God may have many ways of bringing people to their intended destiny, the Christian way being one of them."[7] His strategies for interpreting the Bible include: admit that others may not comprehend the distinct Israelite perspective; emphasize God's universal covenant with all nations and Christ's salvation available to all; pay attention to biblical encounters between people of different faiths; and value Christian witness along with dialogue.[8]

. . . .

John 14:6 – When Thomas admitted not knowing how Jesus would reach God's dwelling, Jesus provided a <u>confession</u> for believers. He confided, Follow my path of rejection and suffering. *Jesus said to Thomas, "I am the way, and the truth, and the life. No one comes to the Father except through me."*[9]

The teaching of chapters 14-17 of John, called the Farewell Discourse, took place following the Last Supper. The context of the writer decades after the Supper was marked by conflict between Jesus' followers and some leaders within Judaism. Most Christians to whom John wrote sorely disliked opposition toward their movement. They knew injustice when driven from the synagogue. By 'lumping' all "the Jews" into one despised group and faulting all for the actions of "some," John caused further negative reaction, while commending belief in Jesus.

During the Last Supper, a close meal with the Twelve (minus one or perhaps plus more), John's text records Jesus actions: he washes their feet, predicts his betrayal, warns that the world may hate them, and tries to comfort them. He says that he would soon return to God. His intent was to prepare room for believers to relate further with God before returning to mark the end-of-time. He said, "I go." How could he refuse to take them along? Thomas, often a figure to represent common views, later declares "My Lord and my God." Here he admits lack of knowledge for reaching God. "How do we know the way if we don't know where you're going?" (Let alone, if you have not gone there before.) They presumed that the end was imminent, that getting to God might require more than a simple map. They feared how they would manage or survive without their Leader for whom they had left all else. Whether Jesus' response registered—but you do know how to go; at least, I've been telling you for three years—remains unclear.

Jesus turns destiny into route. Not boasting or setting up a dictum to denounce world religions, Jesus claims to be the *way* to God for all who follow him (Jesus). For loyal Christians, he shows and *lives* the *way* of suffering love. Having *lived* intimately with God, he shares *truth* learned from God. For example, God is impartial; no one is favored over others. For the *way* which is open to God's Ways lets *God* decide whom and how to include. Even Thomas would see the idolatry of trying to decide about others, in God's stead, I think.

The writer uses questions to allow Jesus to explain further. Jesus' way of suffering and future cross and the uncharted way for believers are linked as people look to eternal life with God. Robert Kysar calls Jesus the medium. Jesus reveals God's love so that people understand and relate with God in peace. Either *truth* and/or *life* explain *way* or *way* names the goal, which is *truth* and *life.*

Interpreters provide varied schemes for the trio of words. Raymond Brown suggests that the disciples' *way* is already their goal; *truth* is the divine reality; and *life* is reality shared by all people. The center of interest becomes the disciples' going. Barnabas Lindars concludes: to follow Jesus, even to death, is the *way* to believe in Jesus, as one sent by God is *truth*; and to relate with God, enabled by Jesus, is *life*. For Leon Morris, Jesus is the way as he redeems, as he connects God with people. Jesus' actions and being are ever dependable—the truth of the gospel. Jesus is also life and source of life. Recall Psalms 86:11:"Teach me your way, O Yahweh, that I may walk in your truth; give me an undivided heart to revere your name."

For Craig Koester, "Jesus is the way" is "one of Christianity's most essential teachings." For Jesus to *go* the way to God and back, via dying and rising, means for him to *be* the way. Koester believes that the phrase "no one comes to God except through me" serves to level people. Not a Christian privilege of being in, in contrast to those loyal to other faiths being excluded, sin separates all people from God.

For James Charlesworth, early church conflict with segments of Judaism forever shaped the meaning of this text. He calls the portion about Jesus being the only way to God "Jew-hating." Imagine the setting: Jews convinced of their on-going covenant with God being told that Jesus himself excluded their tie with Yahweh of Hosts. Offence *par excellence*! Imagine mostly Jewish Christians telling the majority Jews, "You do not know God!" That judgment conveyed spite and delusion. It continues to justify anti-Jewish thought among Christians. Charlesworth believes that "negative views of Jews and exclusive, divisive words reflect later alterations" to texts. *Not* Jesus' words or reflective of his attitudes, the denial of salvation or a way to God other than through Jesus "violates much of biblical theology." Whereas Jesus' claim as way/truth/life condemns no one who believes in the Divine, the 'no one comes' phrase betrays Jesus' core welcome and limits whom *God* may choose to include. Another option might be: since for Christians God invites all through Jesus, the expression "no one" means "none of you," according to Thomas Thangaraj. None of you 'insiders' will reach God except through a life of self-sacrifice. Non-Christians are not addressed.

Charlesworth raises questions for us. Will Christians value being exclusive about the One God? Why? Especially when based on a phrase that Jesus our Mentor perhaps never uttered? What internal need prompts feeling superior to others? What power issues are raised? What makes power and privilege attractive? Why distort the God of all nations to insist that only Jesus saves? When salvation or wholeness is at stake, why might people wish to usurp divine tasks?

Others have studied this key text. D Moody Smith also notes the polemic between Christ-confessing and Christ-denying Jews. He wonders if people presumed to say that no way to God existed until Jesus opened one (Hebrews 10:20). Not a universal statement for all time, verse 6 for Robert Kysar reflects the Johannine group's intent to affirm their leader over against Judaism, as part of a survival technique. David Scott warns against using any text as a pretext, hiding the real reason with a false one. Mixed intense emotions shape the context of John 14:6.

Not posing triumphant, Jesus invites followers to discover the way of the Cross with courage.[10] Through deep intimacy with God, Jesus assures them that the truth of a suffering God leads to life in its fullness. Knowing that he soon would hang on a cross, he declared himself en route to God. John nudged his Jewish Christian audience, those who already accepted Jesus, to continue their belief. He did not aim his words toward people with other faith loyalty. Devotion or undivided commitment to *God's* kin-dom of justice does not provide space to negate or bow to other gods, even as they might reflect on the One God.

Other voices: Paul Knitter suggests that first generation Christians, when afraid that they might not survive the nearby Jewish majority or the vast Roman Empire, may more easily have overstated features about Jesus. Deep commitment likely prompted them to nudge others to take Jesus seriously, to declare him worthy to reveal the One God. For them or Christians today to confess commitment to Jesus the Christ rather than imply that no one else deserves commitment enables more open exchange with believers "equally committed to their saviors."[11] Arvind Nirmal expressed concern that a plan of salvation that allows for only one way presents God as stingy. Furthermore, it deprives God of the freedom to pursue and achieve salvation in chosen way(s).[12] To re-define the plan could mean to value the place that world religions have within God's richly diverse Being. Sri Lankan Nirmal expects different world religions to correct and enrich each other.

Others speak: Cynthia Campbell, President of McCormick Theological Seminary, urges readers to focus what or who *Jesus* is, not to go beyond what is stated such as to status of or difference in other religions. She sees John's purpose in part to move believers toward a unique doctrine of the triune God; Jesus is a window into the Mystery of three-ness in one.[13] Edward Kessler, involved with Jewish-Christian Relations in the United Kingdom, wishes for Christian faith to be distinct from Judaism without acting triumphalist, without either opposing Jews or presuming to fulfill Judaism.[14] That the church derives from Israel does not mean that God's covenant with Israel breaks down. While Jesus expressed Jewish concerns, John 14:6b rejects claims that rivaled Jesus. But in 10:16 Jesus refers to other sheep, not of his fold, who will listen to his voice when he "lays down his life for them."

An important Asian writer is M. Thomas Thangaraj, Professor of World Christianity at Candler School of Theology, Atlanta.[15] He finds Fourth Gospel material more a sermon on Jesus than what Jesus actually said. The author places words in Jesus' mouth that convey the confession of the early faith community. In the Synoptics, Jesus never claimed anything for himself, titles or statements like John 14:6. In fact, he responded to one who called him Good Teacher, "No one is good but God alone." (Mark 10:17-18) *Context* in the Fourth Gospel finds Jewish and Hellenistic Christians trying to define themselves. So, a text like 14:6 defines what being a follower of Christ means. Thangaraj believes that judging the destiny of all people beyond church walls based on this text totally misrepresents its intent and the context. Thangaraj offers two ideas from John for a multi-religious context: 1. "that God is accessible to all through <u>God's</u> own reaching out to humanity through the Logos," and 2. that readers should look for where Jesus begins to proclaim being <u>the way</u>. To Peter's question "Where are you going?" (chapter 13), Jesus explains the way of suffering love. So, 14:6 points to the central place of sacrifice for the sake of others as the way, truth, and life for reaching God.[16]

May Christians approach John 14:6 and the one from Acts to be examined next with a humble spirit, open to multiple insights rather than use them to insist that only Jesus Saves.

Acts 4:12 – When asked by Jewish religious officials by what power or name he and John had healed a man lame for forty years, Peter said, "There is healing in Jesus Christ. Listen to this Jesus!" Or translated,

"There is salvation in no one else, for there is no other name under heaven given among mortals by which we must be saved."[17]

The context was a Jewish healing event. As Peter and John enter the temple, they meet a man lame from birth. Peter offers all that he could for the circumstance—"in the name of Jesus, walk." Peter offers a symbol of Jesus' presence—healing. Responding to the act, Jewish temple leaders ask, "By what power or name did you do this?" *Name* suggests another's presence to liberate. The miracle symbolized wholeness, being healed or saved.

Convinced that God's Spirit had acted through Jesus' *name*— through life, death, and resurrection—followers like Peter *confess* how he had transformed them. Spirit-filled, they celebrate faith. They express love language, like the child who confesses, "My parents are the best in the world!" Not knowing all parents, and far from all-knowing about how God relates to people of all nations, the child or Peter or we believers confess to the extent that we are able: Jesus is the one through whom Christians best know God. Not for privilege or power and not with freedom to oppress or exclude, Peter confesses the name of Jesus the Healer.

Biblical scholars find the religious rulers and elders to be 'worn down' or upset as Peter and John influence hearers about Jesus and resurrection. Arrested, the two came to testify, to defend the healing, before the Sanhedrin known for contempt. The Greek root word used here, not *soteria*, is *sothenai* which means healed or "made whole" (as translated in 4:9.) The term can be translated either *saved* or *healed.* Thangaraj notes that Peter's confession relates directly to the healing. He cautions: "We would violate the integrity of the passage if we were to place it within today's multi-religious setting and draw conclusions."[18]

Cynthia Campbell notes Beverly Gaventa's comment about the phrase "by which we must be saved." This attempts to translate *dei* which means "it is necessary," a word that Luke uses for things that occur according to God's will.[19] Campbell, Hans Conzelmann, Joseph Fitzmyer, and Paul Knitter all see the context here as God's gift of wholeness. It was not an occasion to negate or compare religions or to imply that God could or would never work in people's lives through other means. Rather, fearful yet convinced early believers call others to both listen to and accept the power available in Jesus—the power to mend, make whole. That too does not suggest that no one else should be heard or a valid teacher of religious truth. Selvanayagam believes that those who base an exclusive view on this text fail to study it carefully. The ultimate aim of life and liturgy is to praise or enjoy God, not make absolute claims . . . To note Jesus' qualities is to confess faith; people of other living faiths project their confessions.[20]

Stanley Samartha's study of segments of Acts 3 and 4 is forceful. This being a healing text reminds him of the link between poverty and religion. Implications of this story for Samartha affect general suffering among people, the beggar healed, and power relations between the church and other religions. For the healed of the text, there is freedom to move, new independence, new self-respect and dignity. God's saving act restores total *wholeness*—personal, social, and cosmic. To claim salvation in no one other than Christ negates and judges neighbor religions. It divides people into 'we' and 'they' in ways that disrupt common tasks. Combined with economic, political, and military power, it prompts tension and warfare. From the context of multifaiths, Samartha declares:

> Exclusive claims, coupled with power destroy the religions and cultures of other people. . . . But people of different faiths and opinions are all to receive God's healing power. Peter and John confess on behalf of Jesus' name, not against others. . . . To shift the crucified Christ into the Christ who conquers leads Christians to pride and self-right-ness. Exclusive claims for one's own faith put fences around God's mystery. They stress power over others and mar respect for cherished beliefs of those others. Such claims threaten world peace. So, Christians who wish to invite others to God's healing must express commitment without negating others.[21]

. . .

Concluding Remarks

Clearly, religions deal with Mystery. Mystery suggests that not all is known. I believe that God, also called Yahweh or Allah or Brahman, is the Way for all nations. But I do not claim to know the breadth of God's form nor how the Way transpires for all. Nor do I choose to limit God's Wisdom in offering wholeness.

To confess that Jesus truly saves and makes salvation available on a universal scale does not limit God from providing other channels for wholeness. Unique and universal do not exclude each other. To confess Jesus as unique Lord and Christ need neither counter dialogue with world religions nor claim that all religions say the same thing or achieve the same goal. As Peter confessed what he knew—the name of Jesus the Healer—I know and confess Jesus as the one who best mediates to me God's healing and freeing power. With Paul Knitter, I confess that "Jesus *truly* embodies and expresses God's love," not that he does so *only*, *solely*, or *fully*. Not the *whole* of God, Jesus is *wholly* God."[22] Other people of faith know other ways that give life deep meaning or wholeness for them. With need to care for oppressed people and earth, I will confess my experience, not negate people loyal to diverse religions.

Endnotes:

[1] Carter Heyward. *The Redemption of God: A Theology of Mutual Relation* (Lanham, MD: Univ Pr of America, 1982, 163 quoted in Lisa Isherwood. *Introducing Feminist Christologies*. Cleveland: The Pilgrim Pr, 2002, 62.

[2] Isherwood. 88-92.

[3] Ovey Mohammed. "Jesus and Krishna," in *Asian Faces of Jesus*. R. S. Sugirtharajah, ed. Maryknoll, NY: Orbis Bks, 1995, 9-24.

[4] Jeannine Hill Fletcher. *Monopoly on Salvation? A Feminist Approach to Religious Pluralism*. NY: Continuum, 2005, 136.

[5] *Ibid.*, 106.

[6] Arevalo. From the FABC (Federation of Asian Bishops' Conferences) Documents from 1970-1991 published as *For All the Peoples of Asia*. eds. Gaudencio B. Rosales and C. G. Arevalo. (Philippines: Claretion Publica, 1992), 163, in *Christ of the Asian Peoples Towards an Asian Contextual Christology*. A. Alangaram, Bangalore: Asian Trading Corp, 2001, 89.

[7] S. Wesley Ariarajah. "Power, Politics, and Plurality, The Struggles of the World Council of Churches to Deal with Religious Plurality," in *The Myth of Religious Superiority A Multifaith Exploration*, Paul F. Knitter, ed. Maryknoll, NY: Orbis Bks, 2005, 189; reviewed by Dorothy Yoder Nyce *Mission Focus Annual Review*, vol. 14, 2006, 211-30.

[8] Kwok Pui-lan. *Discovering the Bible in the Non-Biblical World*. Eugene, OR: Wipf and Stock Pub.s, 1995, 59, from Ariarajah's *The Bible and People of Other Faiths*. Maryknoll, NY: Orbis Books, 1989, 39-47, hereafter, *The Bible. . .*

[9] With many resources to explore, those that I examined were: S. Wesley Ariarajah. *The Bible. . .* ; Cynthia M. Campbell. *A Multitude of Blessings A Christian Approach to Religious Diversity*. Louisville: Westminster John Knox Pr, 2007, 46-48; James H. Charlesworth. "The Gospel of John: Exclusivism Caused by a Social Setting Different from That of Jesus (John 11:54 and 14:6)," in *Anti-Judaism and the Fourth Gospel.* Reimind Pieringer, Didier Pollefeyt, and Frederique Vandecasteck-Vannauville, eds. Louisville: Westminster John Knox Pr, 2001, 247-77; Gospel of JOHN Commentaries by: Raymond Brown, Robert Kysar, Barnabas Lindars, Andrew T. Lincoln, Leon Morris, Gail R. O'Day, Gerald Sloyan, and D. Moody Smith; G. Fackre: "Appendix: John 14:6, Bible, Community and Spirit," *Horizons in Biblical Theology*, 21, 1999, 77-81; Reta Halteman Finger. "Where's the map?" *Mennonite Weekly Review*, Feb 5, 2007 1 pg; Marie-Louise Gubler. "I am the way, the truth and the life" (Jn 14:6) *TD* 41:2 (Summer, 1994), 147-51; Edward Kessler. "'I am the Way, the Truth & the Life' (John 14:6) and Jewish-Christian Dialogue," *Interreligious Insight*, 1/3, July 2003, 25-31; Craig R. Koester. "Jesus the Way, the Cross, and the World according to the Gospel of John," *Word & World*, xxi/4, Fall 2001, 360-69;

James R. Krabill. "I am the way, the truth, and the life"—words from Jesus that spell relief, in *Is It Insensitive to share Your Faith?* Intercourse, PA: Good Books, 2005, 36-41; Lucius Nereparampil. "The Johannine Understanding of Salvation and the World Religions," *Indian Journal of Theology*, 30/3-4, July-Dec. 1981, 146-51; David C. Scott. "I am the Way," in *Biblical Insights on Inter-Faith Dialogue*. Israel Selvenayagam, ed, Bangalore: The Board for Theological Text-book Programme of South Asia, 1996, 203-06; Wilbert R. Shenk. "Is Jesus the only way to God?" *Vision*, 7/1, Spr 2006, 77-85; M. Thomas Thangaraj. "Pre-Text, Text and Post-Test: Discovering Biblical Warrant for Inter-Religious Dialogue," in *Hermeneutical Explorations in Dialogue*, Anantanand Rambachan, A. Rashied Omar & M. Thomas Thangaraj, eds. Delhi: ISPCK, 2007, 42-51; R. E. O White. 'No One Comes to the Father but by Me,' *The Expository Times*. 113/4, Jan 2002, 116-17.

[10] Scott, 205.

[11] Paul F. Knitter. *No Other Name? A Critical Survey of Christian Attitudes Toward the World Religions*. Maryknoll, NY: Orbis Books, 1994, 185-86. See also his sermon: "Jesus: The Way That is Open to Other Ways," First Presbyterian, New Canaan, NY, retrieved 5/6/2009, 3 pp http://www.tcpc.org/library/article.cfm?library-id=518

[12] Arvind Nirmal. "Redefining the Economy of Salvation," *Indian Journal of Theology*. 30/3-4, July-Dec 1981, 211.

[13] Campbell, 47-48.

[14] Kessler, 27-28, 31.

[15] Thomas M. Thangaraj. *Relating to People of Other Religions What Every Christian Needs to Know*, (1997); *The Common Task A Theology of Christian Mission,* (1999); and *The Crucified Guru An Experiment in Cross-Cultural Christology,* (1994). All published at Nashville: Abingdon Pr.

[16] Thangaraj. *Relating . . .*, 105.

[17] Resources used for this text: Campbell, 48-49; Commentaries by: F. F. Bruce, Hans Conzelmann, Joseph A. Fitzmyer, Beverly Roberts Gaventa, Ernst Haenchen, Johannes Munch; Paul F. Knitter. *Jesus and the Other Names Christian Mission and Global Responsibility*. Maryknoll, NY: Orbis Books, 1996, 43, 69-70; W. Eugene March. "In Jesus' Name," in *God's Tapestry*. Louisville, KY: WJK Pr, 2009, 48-55; Stanley J. Samartha. "Religion, Culture and Power—Three Bible Studies," *Religion and Society*, xxxiv/1, March 1987, 74-79 (Samartha addresses related content in *One Christ—Many Religions Toward a Revised Christology*. Maryknoll, NY: Orbis and Bangalore: South Asia Theological Research Institute, 1992); Israel Selvanayagam. "No Other Name?" in his *Biblical Insights . . .* 223-28; Thangaraj, *Relating . . .* 106-7; Christopher J. H. Wright. "The Christian and other religions: the biblical evidence," *Themelios*, 9/2, Jan 1984, 13-14.

[18] Thangaraj, *Relating . . .* 106.

[19] Campbell, 48.

---

[20] Selvanayagam, 223, 227.

[21] Samartha, "Religion . . .," 78-79. [summary of Samartha's paragraphs, not a direct quote.]

[22] Paul F. Knitter. *Introducing Theologies of Religions*. Maryknoll, NY: Orbis, 2002, 122-23 and DMin class discussion [1st year of my 2nd DMin study], United Theological Seminary, Dayton, Ohio, Oct. 2004.

Glossary (Spellings vary in sources.)

ahimsa – nonviolence or non-injury; oneness with all of life

Allah-o-Akbar - "God is Great" or Unity of God

ashram(a) – place of spiritual retreat

atman – Self underlying reality; inner soul/essence; Cosmic Spirit

Aum/om – Vac (spoken word); cosmic/eternal sound

avatar – descent to earth, as 10 descents of Vishnu, to restore goodness

Ayodhya – city important historically to both Hindus (prince Rama) and Muslims (Mughul mosque); major destruction/conflict 2002

Bharata Natya – classical Indian dance form originating in south India

bhajan – devotional song

bhakti – deep devotion to Divine; major path to liberation

bodhisattva – Buddhist destined for enlightenment who helps others toward Nirvana before own goal fully realized

Brahman – Absolute/Ultimate Reality; divine source behind all else;

brahmin – Hindu priest, first of four main caste groupings

communal – combining exclusive attachment to own religion with deep hostility against others; government keeps equal distance between

darshan(a) – seeing; to see/be seen by deity; point of view/philosophy

Dhammapada – Buddha's life and teachings

dharma – religious way of life/moral duty/justice; divine law/order

dukkha – Buddhist thought about suffering; unsatisfactory life

enlightenment – to see/comprehend truth; freed of ignorance/prejudice

ghat – place: to land along river or step into water for ritual bathing

Gita (*Bhagavad Gita*) – "Song of the Lord"; best known scripture epic; part of *Mahabharata*; avatar Krishna & warrior Arjuna converse

guru – one who knows/teaches religious knowledge; spiritual guide

Guru Granth Sahib – Sikh sacred text, understood as the present Guru

hadith – added literature; oral sayings ascribed to Prophet Muhammad

Hindutva – "Hinduness'; prime Hindu loyalty sought

jihad – to struggle/strive; inner struggle with selfishness

jnana - knowledge/insight into spiritual meaning; a path to liberation

karma – deed; work/ritual that produces fruit; cause and effect

karuna – compassion; wish that others be free of suffering

kirtan – singing praise to god in devotional gathering, led by Cantor

lakh – 100,000
linga – Shiva stone symbol; sign of cosmic/creative energy
Mahabharata – Hindu epic dealing with duty; longest poem in world
mantra – sacred sound; ritual formula of praise; most sacred: Gayatri
marga – road/way; paths of salvation – knowledge, action, devotion
mindfulness – Buddha nature; attention to present; deep energy/breath
mridranga and **tabla** – drums for Indian classical and popular music
Nirvana – to be Enlightened; beyond birth and death, suffering/craving
pithos/pithoi - ancient storage jars
prajna – wisdom/intelligence; highest knowledge through yogic insight
prasad – blessed food, distributed with worship event
Qur'an /Koran – most sacred text of Islam
Ramayana – earliest, major Hindu epic; story of Rama and wife Sita
Rig Veda – ric = verse; veda = revealed knowledge; oldest praise book
samhita – collection (as of texts or hymns)
samsara – rebirth; ongoing round of birth and death, shaped by karma
sangha – Buddhist order of monks and nuns; community
sannyasi – one who takes vows of poverty to renounce world (as sadhu)
sati/suttee – former practice of Hindu widow cremated on funeral pyre of husband; Sati – great goddess/Daksha's daughter/Shiva's wife
shakti – "female energy/principle of creation"; power/Spirit/force
shanti - peace
sishya – disciple who learns religious truth from guru
smriti - remembered texts, (not revealed)
sruti – revealed texts; that which was heard
stupa – Buddhist domelike burial shrine; symbol of Buddha's Nirvana
sunyata – emptiness; void of essence; interbeing, not independence
surah – verses in Qur'an
tanpura – stringed instrument for drone sound
tawhid – Allah's absolute oneness
trimurti – Hindu major trinity: Brahma/Creator; Shiva/Destroyer; Vishnu/Sustainer
Tripitaka – Buddhist Pali canon (3 baskets)
Upanishad – Hindu philosophical/mystery writing; rhythm, accent, sequence; known by elite, contrast to popular epics
varna – color; scheme for original caste divisions
xenophobia – fear of difference
yajna – sacrifice; worship through offering to god
yoga – discipline to unite mind/body/soul with Ultimate/higher reality

Resources:

This listing has two parts. Part I combines sections of books and articles that enriched study for chapters 3 and 12; Part II is for other chapters.

Part I – Books: [For chapters 3 and 12]

Abu-Nimer, Mohammed & David Augsburger, eds. *Peace-Building by, between, and beyond Muslims and Evangelical Christians*. NY: Lexington Books, 2009.

Aleaz, K. P. *Theology of Religions Birmingham Papers and other Essays*. Calcutta: Moumita Publishers, 1998.

Almond, Gabriel A., R. Scott Appleby, & Emmanuel Sivan. *Strong Religion The Rise of Fundamentalisms around the World*. Chicago: Univ of Chicago Pr, 2003.

Apel, William. *Signs of Peace The Interfaith Letters of Thomas Merton*. Maryknoll, NY: Orbis, 2006.

Armstrong, Karen. *The Battle for God*. NY: Ballantine Bks, 2000.

Aschliman, Kathryn. *Growing Toward Peace*. Scottdale, PA: Herald Pr, 1993.

Aslan, Reza. *No god but God The Origins, Evolution and Future of Islam*. NY: Random House, 2005.

Balmer, Brice H. *Meeting Our Multifaith Neighbors*. Scottdale, PA: Herald Pr, 2006.

Bauman, Chad M. *Christian Identity and Dalit Religion in Hindu India, 1868-1947*. Grand Rapids, MI: Eerdmans Pub Co, 2008.

Behari, Bankey. *The Story of Mira Bai*. Gorakhpur: Gita Pr, 2006.

Bennet, Sage. *Wisdom Walk Nine Practices for Creating Peace and Balance* from the *World's Spiritual Traditions*. Novato, CA: New World Library, 2007.

Borg, Marcus and Ross Mackenzie, eds. *God at 2000*. Harrisburg, PA: Morehouse Pub, 2000.

Boys, Mary C. *Has God Only One Blessing? Judaism as a Source of Christian Self-Understanding*. NY: Paulist Pr, 2000.

Campbell, Cynthia M. *A Multitude of Blessings A Christian Approach to Religious Diversity*. Louisville: Westminster John Knox Pr, 2007

Cartwright, Michael G. & Peter Ochs, eds. *The Jewish-Christian Schism Revisited*. John Howard Yoder. Grand Rapids, MI: Eerdmans Pub, 2003.

Chappell, David W., ed. *Buddhist Peacework Creating Cultures of Peace*. Boston: Wisdom Publ, 1999.

Clooney, Francis X. *Hindu Wisdom for All God's Children*. Eugene, OR: Wipf & Stock Publ, 1998.

Cobb, John B., Jr. (Edited/introduced by Paul F. Knitter) *Transforming Christianity and the World A Way beyond Absolutism and Relativism*. Maryknoll, NY: Orbis, 1999.

Copley, Antony. *Religions in Conflict Ideology, Cultural Contact, and Conversion in Late Colonial India*. New Delhi: Oxford Univ Pr, 1997.

Crockett, Clayton. ed. *Religion and Violence in a Secular World Toward a New Political Theology*. Charlottesville: Univ of VA Pr, 2006.

Driedger, Leo and Donald B. Kraybill. *Mennonite Peacemaking From Quietism to Activism*. Scottdate, PA: Herald Pr, 1994.

Dula, Peter and Alain Epp Weaver. *Borders & Bridges Mennonite Witness in a Religiously Diverse World*. Telford, PA: Cascadia Pub House & Scottdale, PA: Herald Pr, 2007.

Easwaran, Eknath. *Nonviolent Soldier of Islam Badshah Khan, A Man to Match His Mountains*. Tomales, CA: Nilgiri Pr, 1984, 1999.

Eck, Diana L. *Darsan Seeing the Divine Image in India*. Chambersburg, PA: Anima Pub, 1981.

_____ *Encountering God A Spiritual Journey from Boseman to Banaras*. Boston: Beacon Pr, 1993.

Enns, Fernando, Scott Holland & Ann K. Riggs. *Seeking Cultures of Peace A Peace Church Conversation*. Telford, PA: Cascadia Pub House, WCC, & Herald Pr, 2004.

Esposito, John L. *The Islamic Threat Myth or Reality?* (3rd edition) NY: Oxford Univ Pr, 1999.

_____ *Unholy War Terror in the Name of Islam*. NY: Oxford Univ Pr, 2002.

Farber, Seth. *Radicals, Rabbis and Peacemakers Conversations with Jewish Critics of Israel*. Monroe, ME: Common Courage Pr, 2005.

Ferguson, John. *War and Peace in the World's Religions*, NY: Oxford Univ. Pr, 1978.

Fletcher, Jeannine Hill. *Monopoly on Salvation? A Feminist Approach to Religious Pluralism*. NY: Continuum, 2005.

Fletcher, Richard. *The Cross and the Crescent The Dramatic Story of the Earliest Encounters between Christians and Muslims*. NY: Penguin Bks, 2003.

Flueckiger, Joyce Burkhalter. *In Amma's Healing Room Gender and Vernacular Islam in South India*. Bloomington: Indiana Univ Pr, 2006.

Fredericks, James L. *Buddhists and Christians Through Comparative Theology to Solidarity*. Maryknoll, NY: Orbis, 2004.

Gopin, Marc. *Between Eden and Armageddon The Future of World*

Religions, Violence, and Peacemaking. NY: Oxford U. Pr, 2000.

Gopin, Marc. *Healing the Heart of Conflict.* US: Rodale, 2004.

Groff, Weyburn W. *Satyagraha and nonresistance A Comparative study of Gandhian and Mennonite nonviolence.* Elkhart, IN: Inst of Mennonite Studies, (PhD Dissertation 1963), 2009.

Gross, Rita M. *Buddhism After Patriarchy A Feminist History, Analysis, and Reconstruction of Buddhism.* Albany: SUNY Pr, 1993.

_____ *Soaring and Settling Buddhist Perspectives on Contemporary Social and Religious Issues.* NY: Continuum, 2000.

Gross, Rita M. & Rosemary Radford Ruether. *Religious Feminism and the Future of the Planet A Buddhist-Christian Conversation.* NY: Continuum, 2001.

Hammer, Joshua. *A Season in Bethlehem Unholy War in a Sacred Place.* NY: Free Pr, 2003.

Harak, G. Simon, ed. *Nonviolence for the Third Millennium.* Macon, GA: Mercer Univ Pr, 2000.

Heim, S. Mark, ed. *Grounds for Understanding Ecumenical Resources for Responses to Religious Pluralism.* Grand Rapids, MI: Eerdmans Pub, 1998.

Hellwig, Monika. *A Case for Peace in Reason and Faith.* Collegeville, MN: The Liturgical Pr, 1992.

Herr, Robert & Judy Zimmerman Herr. *Transforming Violence Linking Local and Global Peacemaking.* Scottdale, PA: Herald Pr, 1998.

Heschel, Susannah. *Abraham Geiger and the Jewish Jesus.* Chicago: Univ of Chicago Pr, 1998.

Hick, John and Paul F. Knitter, eds. *The Myth of Christian Uniqueness Toward a Pluralistic Theology of Religions.* Maryknoll, NY: Orbis, 1987.

Hopkins, Jeffrey, ed. *The Art of Peace* Nobel Peace Laureates discuss Human Rights, Conflict and Reconciliation. Ithaca, NY: Snow Lion Pub, 2000.

Isherwood, Lisa. *Introducing Feminist Christologies.* Cleveland: The Pilgrim Pr, 2002.

Jayatilleke, K. N. *Buddhism and Peace.* Kandy, Sri Lanka: Buddhist Pub Society, 1962, 1969, 1983.

Jeanrond, Werner G. & Aasulv Lande, eds. *The Concept of God in Global Dialogue.* Maryknoll, NY: Orbis, 2005.

Jensen, David H. *In the Company of Others A Dialogical Christology.* Cleveland: The Pilgrim Pr, 2001.

Juergensmeyer, Mark. *Terror in the Mind of God The Global Rise of Religious Violence* (Updated) Berkeley: Univ of Calif Pr, 2000.

Kakar, Sudhir. *The Colors of Violence Cultural Identities, Religion, and Conflict*, Chicago: Univ of Chicago Pr, 1996.

Karkainen, Veli-Matti. *Introduction to the Theology of Religions.*

Downers Grove, IL: InterVarsity Pr, 2003.

Kelsay, John. *Islam and War A Study in Comparative Ethics*. Louisville: WJK Pr, 1993.

Kennedy, Robert. *Zen Gifts to Christians*. NY: Continuum, 2000.

Kimball, Charles. *When Religion Becomes Evil*. San Francisco: Harper, 2002.

Kniss, Fred. *Disquiet in the Land Cultural Conflict in American Mennonite Communities*. New Brunswick, NJ: Rutgers Univ Pr, 1997.

Knitter, Paul F. *Introducing Theologies of Religions*. Maryknoll, NY: Orbis, 2002.

_____ *Jesus and the Other Names Christian Mission and Global Responsibility*. Maryknoll, NY: Orbis, 1996.

_____ *No Other Name? A Critical Survey of Christian Attitudes Toward the World Religions*. Maryknoll, NY: Orbis, 1985, 7th 1994.

_____ *One Earth Many Religions Multifaith Dialogue & Global Responsibility*. Maryknoll, NY: Orbis, 1995.

_____, ed. *The Myth of Religious Superiority A Multifaith Exploration*. Maryknoll, NY: Orbis, 2005.

_____ *Without Buddha I Could not be a Christian*. Oxford: One World, 2009.

Koontz, Theodore J. & Andy Alexis-Baker, eds. *Christian Attitudes to War, Peace, and Revolution*. John Howard Yoder's seminary course. Grand Rapids, MI: Brazos Pr, 2009.

Kumar, Satish. *The Buddha and the Terrorist*. Chapel Hill: Algonquin Bks, 2006.

Kurlansky, Mark. *Non-Violence The History of A Dangerous Idea*. NY: The Modern Library, 2008.

Lannstrom, Anna, ed. *Promise and Peril The Paradox of Religion as Resource and Threat* Notre Dame: Univ of Notre Dame Pr, 2003

_____ *The Stranger's Religion Fascination and Fear*. Notre Dame, IN: Univ of Notre Dame Pr, 2004.

Lederach, John Paul. *Building Peace Sustainable Reconciliation in Divided Societies*. Wash D. C.: US Inst. of Peace Pr, 1997, 2004.

Lefebure, Leo D. *Revelation, the Religions, and Violence*. Maryknoll, NY: Orbis, 2000.

Macky, Peter W. *Violence: Right or Wrong?* Waco, TX: Word Book Pub, 1973.

March, W. Eugene. *God's Tapestry Reading the Bible in a World of Religious Diversity*. Louisville: WJK Pr, 2009.

_____ *The Wide, Wide Circle of Divine Love A Bible Case for Religious Diversity*. Louisville: WJK Pr, 2005.

Marty, Martin E. *When Faiths Collide*. Malden, MA: Blackwell Pub, 2005.

McDaniel, Jay. *Gandhi's Hope Learning from Other Religions as a Path to Peace*. Maryknoll, NY: Orbis, 2005.

McFague, Sallie. *Models of God Theology for an Ecological, Nuclear Age*, Phila.: Fortress Pr, 1987.

Muhaiyaddeen, M. R. Bawa. *Islam & World Peace Explanations of a Sufi*. Phila: The Fellowship Pr, 1987, 1999.

Musser, Donald W. & D. Dixon Sutherland, eds. *War or Words? Interreligious Dialogue as an Instrument of Peace*. Cleveland: The Pilgrim Pr, 2005.

Niditch, Susan. *War in the Hebrew Bible A Study in the Ethics of Violence*. NY: Oxford Univ Pr, 1993.

Omar, Irfan A., ed. *A Muslim View of Christianity Essays on Dialogue by Mahmoud Ayoub*. Maryknoll, NY: Orbis, 2007.

O'Neill, Maura. *Mending a Torn World Women in Interreligious Dialogue*. Maryknoll, NY: Orbis, 2007.

Palkhivala, N. A. *Essential Unity of All Religions*. Mumbai, India: Bharatiya Vidya Bhavan, 2003.

Phan, Peter. *Being Religious Interreligiously Asian Perspectives on Interfaith Dialogue*. Maryknoll, NY: Orbis, 2004.

Pui-lan, Kwok. *Discovering the Bible in the Non-Biblical World*. Eugene, OR: Wipf and Stock Pub1995.

Pope-Levison, Priscilla & John R. Levison. *Jesus in Global Contexts*. Louisville, KY: W/JK Pr, 1992.

Reinhartz, Adele. *Befriending the Beloved Disciple A Jewish Reading of the Gospel of John*. NY: Continuum, 2001.

Roy, Arundhati. *War Talk*. Cambridge, MA: South End Pr, 2003.

Sacks, Jonathan. *The Dignity of Difference How to Avoid the Clash of Civilizations*. NY: Continuum, 2002.

Safi, Omid, ed. *Progressive Muslims On Justice, Gender, and Pluralism*. Oxford: One World, 2003.

Sampson, Cynthia and John Paul Lederach, eds. *From the Ground Up Mennonite Contributions to International Peacebuilding*. NY: Oxford Univ Pr., 2000.

Selengut, Charles. *Sacred Fury: Understanding Religious Violence*. Oxford: Alta Mira Pr, 2003.

Selvanayagam, Israel, ed. *Biblical Insights on Inter-Faith Dialogue*. Bangalore, INDIA: BTTBPSA, 1995.

Shenk, David W. *Global Gods Exploring the Role of Religions in Modern Societies*. Scottdale, PA: Herald Pr, 1995, 1999.

Sharpe, Eric J. *Faith Meets Faith Some Christian Attitudes to Hinduism in the 19th and 20th Centuries*. London: SCM Pr, 1977.

Sinn, Simone, ed. *Deepening Faith, Hope and Love in Relations with Neighbors of Other Faiths*. Geneva, SW: LWF, 2008.

Singh, Pashaura. *The Guru Granth Sahib Canon, Meaning and Authority*. New Delhi: Oxford Univ Pr, 2000.

Sivaraksa, Sulak. *Seeds of Peace A Buddhist Vision for Renewing Society*. Berkeley, CA: Parallax Pr, 1992.

Smith-Christopher, Daniel, ed. *Subverting Hatred The Challenge of Nonviolence in Religious Traditions*. Cambridge, MA: Boston Research Center for the 21st Century, 1998.

Smock, David R. *Religious Perspectives on War Christian, Muslim, and Jewish Attitudes Toward Force*. Washington, D. C.: US Inst of Peace Pr, 1992, 2002.

Song, C. S. *Tell Us Our Names Story Theology from an Asian Perspective*. Maryknoll, NY: Orbis, 1989.

Stassen, Glen, Mark Thiessen Nation, & Matt Hamsher, eds. *The War of the Lamb The Ethics of Nonviolence and Peacemaking*. John Howard Yoder. Grand Rapids, MI: Brazos Pr, 2009.

Steffen, Lloyd. *The Demonic Turn The Power of Religion to Inspire or Restrain Violence*. Cleveland: Pilgrim Pr, 2003.

Stern, Jessica. *Terror in the Name of God Why Religious Militants Kill*. NY: HarperCollins Pub, 2003.

Suchocki, Marjorie Hewitt. *Divinity & Diversity A Christian Affirmation of Religious Pluralism*. Nashville: Abingdon Pr, 2003.

Sugirtharajah, R S ed. *Asian Faces of Jesus*. Maryknoll, NY: Orbis, 1995

Thangaraj, M. Thomas. *Relating to People of Other Religions What Every Christian Needs to Know*. Nashville: Abingdon Pr, 1997.

Thich Nhat Hanh *Interbeing Fourteen Guidelines for Engaged Buddhism*. Fred Eppsteiner, ed. New Delhi: Full Circle, 1997, 2000.

Trible, Phyllis & Letty M. Russell, eds. *Hagar, Sarah, and Their Children Jewish, Christian, and Muslim Perspectives*. Louisville: Westminster John Knox Pr, 2006.

Tzu, Lao. *Tao Te Ching*. NY: Penguin Group, 2001.

Varshney, Ashutosh. *Ethnic Conflict and Civic Life Hindus and Muslims in India*. New Haven: Yale Univ Pr., 2002.

Von Rad, Gerhard. *Genesis*. Phila; Westminster Pr, 1972.

Waskow, Arthur, Joan Chittister & Saadi Shakur Chisti. *The Tent of Abraham Stories of Hope and Peace for Jews, Christians, and Muslims*. Boston: Beacon Pr, 2006.

Willis, Jennifer Schwamm, ed. *Thich Nhat Hanh, A Lifetime of Peace Essential Writings by and about Thich Nhat Hanh*. NY: Marlowe & Co, 2003.

Wink, Walter, ed. *Peace is the Way Writings on Nonviolence from the Fellowship of Reconciliation*. Maryknoll, NY: Orbis, 2000.

Yoder, John Howard. *When War is Unjust Being Honest in Just-war Thinking*. Eugene, OR: Wipf and Stock Pub. 2001.

Yong, Amos. *Hospitality & the Other Pentecost, Christian Practices, & the Neighbor*. Maryknoll, NY: Orbis, 2008.

Part I – Articles or chapters: [For chapters 3 and 12]

Amore, Roy C. "Peace and Non-violence in Buddhism," in *The Pacifist Impulse in Historical Perspective*. Harvey L. Dyck, ed. Toronto: Univ of Toronto Pr, 1996, 240-59.

Ariarajah, S. Wesley. "Power, Politics, and Plurality, The Struggles of the World Council of Churches to Deal with Religious Plurality," in *The Myth of Religious Superiority*. Paul Knitter, ed., Maryknoll, NY: Orbis, 2005, 176-93.

_____ "Religion and Violence A Protestant Christian Perspective." *Ecumenical Review*, April 55/2, 2003, 136-43. Also in *Dialogue* (NS) vol. xxix, 2002, Colombo, 58-69. [handout of 8 pp.]

Baird, Rabbi Justus. "Waging Holy Peace," *Auburn Views*, Auburn Seminary, Spr 2009, 4.

Coward, Harold. "The Modern Christian Encounter," in *Pluralism Challenge to World Religions*. Maryknoll, NY: Orbis, 1985.

Dietrich, Walter. "The mark of Cain: violence and overcoming violence in the Hebrew Bible," *Theology Digest*, 52/1, Spr 2005, 3-11.

Eck, Diana L. "Honest to God: The Universe of Faith," in *God at 2000*, Marcus Borg and Ross Mackenzie, eds., Harrisburg, PA: Morehouse Pub, 2000, 21-41.

Erickson, Victoria Lee. "We Have the Faith to Make Life Our Own," in *Still Believing Jewish, Christian, and Muslim Women Affirm Their Faith*, Victoria Lee Erickson & Susan A. Farrell, eds., Maryknoll, NY: Orbis, 2005, 89-101.

Ethakuzhy, A. M. Joseph. "'The Way' in the Bible and in the Bhagavad Gita," *Indian Theological Studies*. 45, 2008, 461-74.

Fletcher, Jeannine Hill. "Shifting Identity—the Contribution of Feminist thought to Theologies of Religious Pluralism," *Journal of Feminist Studies in Religion*, 19/2, Fall 2003, 5-24.

Gandhi, Arun. "Who Influenced Gandhi?" in *Nonviolence for the Third Millennium*. G. Simon Harak, ed. Macon, GA: Mercer Univ Pr, 2000, 3-22.

Geffre, Claude. "Double Belonging and the Originality of Christianity as a Religion," in *Many Mansions? Multiple Religious Belonging*. Catherine Cornille, ed. Maryknoll, NY: Orbis, 93-105.

Gross, Rita M. "Religious Identity and Openness in a Pluralistic World," *Buddhist-Christian Studies* 25, 2005, 15-20.

Harris, Elisabeth J. "Double Belonging in Sri Lanka," in *Many Mansions? Multiple Religious Belonging and Christian Identity*. Catherine Cornille, ed. Maryknoll, NY: Orbis, 76-92.

Hassan, Riffat. "Feminism in Islam," in *Feminism and World Religions*. Arvind Sharma & Katherine K. Young, eds. Albany: State Univ of NY Pr, 1999. 248-78.

Hassan, Riffat. "Messianism and Islam," *Journal of Ecumenical Studies*, 22/2, Spring 1985, 261-91.

_____ "What does it Mean To Be a Muslim Today?" *Cross Currents*, 40/3, Fall 1990. retrieved 2/8/2004, 10. http://www.crosscurrents.org/hassan.htm

Hill, Knitter, Madges. "Religions—Why So Many?" and "Understanding Theology," in *Faith, Religions, and Theology A Contemporary Introduction*. Brennan R. Hill, Paul Knitter, and William Madges. Mystic, CT: Twenty-third Pub, 1997, 191-218, 285-318.

Houtart, Francois. "The Cult of Violence in the Name of Religion: A Panorama," in *Religion as a Source of Violence*. Wim Beuken and Karl-Josef Kuschel, eds. Maryknoll, NY: Orbis, 1997, 1-9.

Khan, M. A. Muqtedar. "American Muslims and the Rediscovery of America's Sacred Ground," in *Taking Religious Pluralism Seriously Spiritual Politics on America's Sacred Ground*. Barbara A. McGraw & Jo Renee Formicola, eds. Waco, TX: Baylor Univ Pr, 127-48.

King, Sallie B. "Engaged Buddhism: Gandhi's *Ahimsa* in Practice," in *Nonviolence for the Third Millennium*. G. Simon Harak, ed. Macon, GA: Mercer Univ Pr, 2000, 101-19.

Kishwar, Madhu & Ruth Vanita. "Poison to Nectar: The Life and Work of Mirabai." *Manushi*, Nos. 50, 51- 52, 1989, 74-93.

Knitter, Paul F. "Between a Rock and a Hard Place: Pluralistic Theology Faces the Ecclesial and Academic Communities," *Journal of Theology*, Summer 1997, 79-102.

_____ "Buddhist and Christian Attitudes toward Other Religions: A Comparison," Salzburg, Austria: European Society of Buddhist-Christian Studies, June 11, 2007, 48 pp typed.

_____ "Making Peace and Being Peace," in *Without Buddha I Could not be a Christian*. Oxford: One World, 2009, 167-212.

_____ "My God is Bigger than Your God!" *Studies in Interreligious Dialogue*, 17/1, 2007, 100-18.

_____ "Toward a Liberative Interreligious Dialogue," *CrossCurrents*, Winter 1995, 451-68.

Kronemer, Alex. "White Hats and Black Hats," *Harvard Divinity Bulletin*, Autumn 2007, 63-64.

Kuitse, Roelf. "Living in the Global Community," in *Weathering the Storm Christian Pacifist Responses to War*. n.a. Newton, KS: Faith & Life Pr, 1991.

McTernan, Oliver. "Religion and the Legitimization of Violence," in *Religion in an Age of Conflict*. Maryknoll: Orbis, 2003, 45-76.

Nelson-Pallmeyer, Jack. "Religion and Violence," in *Is Religion Killing Us? Violence in the Bible and Quran*. Harrisburg: Trinity Pr International, 2003, 13-25.

Neumaier, Eva K. "Missed Opportunities: Buddhism and the Ethnic Strife in Sri Lanka and Tibet," in *Religion and Peacebuilding*. Harold Coward & Gordon S. Smith, eds. NY: State Univ of NY Pr, 2003, 69-92.

Nyce, Dorothy Yoder. "Faithful and Pluralistic," *CrossCurrents*, Summer 2003, 214-30.

_____ "Sharing God's Gift of Wholeness with Living Faiths: Biblical Examples," *Mission Focus: Annual Review*, vol. 15, 2007, 52-72.

_____ "Wisdom or Folly: Thoughts of Religious Superiority," [Review Essay of *The Myth of Religious Superiority*. Paul F. Knitter, ed*]*, *Mission Focus: Annual Review*, v. 14, 2006 211-30.

Panikkar, Raimundo. "The Myth of Pluralism: The Tower of Babel—A Meditation on Non-violence," *CrossCurrents* 29, 197-230.

Phan, Peter C. "If Jews are Saved by Their Eternal Covenant, How are Christians to Understand Jesus as Universal Savior?" http://www.bc.edu/research/cjl/meta-elements/sites/partners/ccjr/phan0, retrieved 11/25/2007, 7 pp.

Platcher, William C. "What about Them? Christians and Non-Christians," in *Essentials of Christian Theology*, William C. Platcher, ed., Louisville: Westminster John Knox Pr, 2003, 297-327 & notes 407-10.

Roy, Arundhati. "Fascism's Firm Footprint in India," in *Nothing Sacred Women Respond to Religious Fundamentalism and Terror*. Betsy Reed, ed. NY: Thunder's Mouth Pr, 2002, 179-84.

Scott, David C. "Bridges of Hope: Muslims and Christians Alive to God," United Methodist Church Mission Forum, Evanston, Ill, August 2007, 5 pp.

Selvanayagam, Israel. "The Bible and Non-Christian Scriptures," *Epworth Review*, Jan. 2002, 49-57.

Singh, Dharam. "Sikhism and Religious Pluralism," in *The Myth of Religious Superiority*, Paul F. Knitter, ed., Maryknoll, NY: Orbis, 2005, 62-74.

Tirimanna, Vimal. "Does Religion Cause Violence." *Studies in Interreligious Dialogue*, 17/1, 2007, 5-19.

Wuthnow, Robert. "How Pluralistic Should We Be?" in *America and the Challenges of Religious Diversity*. Princeton: Princeton Univ Pr, 2005, 286-314 & notes 348-49.

Part II - Books: [For all chapters except 3 and 12, with no repeats from Part I]

Agrawala, Vasudeva S. *The Glorification of the Great Goddess* (Devi Mahatmayam). Varanasi: All-India Trust, 1963.

Amaladoss, Michael. *Making All Things New Dialogue, Pluralism & Evangelization in Asia.* Maryknoll, NY: Orbis, 1990.

Ariarajah, S. Wesley. *Hindus and Christians A Century of Protestant Ecumenical Thought.* Currents of Encounter, vol. 5, Grand Rapids: Eerdmans, 1991.

_____ *The Bible and People of Other Faiths.* Geneva: World Council of Churches, 1985.

Berling, Judith A. *Understanding Other Religious Worlds A Guide for Interreligious Education.* Maryknoll, NY: Orbis, 2004.

Bharat, Sandy & Jael. *A Global Guide to Interfaith Reflections from around the world.* Washington: O Books, 2007.

Boucher, Sandy. *Discovering Kway Yin, Buddhist Goddess of Compassion.* Boston: Beacon Pr, 1999.

Cassidy, Edward Idris Cardinal. *Ecumenism and Interreligious Dialogue Unitatis Redintegratio, Nostra Aetate.* NY: Paulist Pr, 2005.

Chatterji, J. C. *The Wisdom of the Vedas.* Wheaton: Quest Books, 1992.

Cornille, Catherine. *The im-Possibility of Interreligious Dialogue.* NY: The Crossroad Pub Co., 2008.

Cracknell, Kenneth. *In Good and Generous Faith Christian Responses to Religious Pluralism.* Cleveland: The Pilgrim Pr, 2005.

Das, Lama Surya. *Awakening to the Sacred Creating a Spiritual Life from Scratch.* NY: Broadway Books, 1999.

(Department of Tourism). *The Temples of India.* Delhi: Publications Division, 1964.

Diwakar, R. R. and S. Ramakrishnan, eds. *Upanishads in Story and Dialogue.* Bombay: Bharatiya Vidya Bhavan, 1st ed. 1960, 1981.

Eck, Diana L. *A New Religious America* How a "Christian Country" Has Become the World's Most Religiously Diverse Nation. San Francisco: Harper, 2001.

Feldhaus, Anne. *Water & Womanhood Religious Meanings of Rivers in Maharashtra.* NY: Oxford Univ Pr, 1995.

Fenton, John Y., Norvin Hein, Frank E. Reynolds, Alan L. Miller, and Niels C. Nielsen, Jr., eds. *Religions of Asia.* NY: St. Martin's Pr, 1983.

Filliozat, Jean. *India The Country and its Traditions.* Englewood Cliffs, NJ: Prentice-Hall, 1961.

Ford, J. Massyngberde. *Revelation.* The Anchor Bible, Garden City, NY: Doubleday & Co, 1975.

Francis, T. Dayanandan & Franklyn J. Balasundaram, eds. *Asian Expressions of Christian Commitment.* [See V. Chakkarai, P. D.

Devanandan, S. J. Samartha chapters], Madras: CLS, 1992.
Friesen, J. Stanley. *Missionary Responses to Tribal Religions at Edinburgh, 1910*. Studies in Church History # 1, NY: Peter Lang, 1996.
Gnanadason, Aruna, ed. *Future of the Church in India*. [See chapters by P.C. Alexander and Padmasani Gallup] Nagpur: NCCI, 1990.
Griffiths, Bede. *The Cosmic Revelation: The Hindu Way to God*. Springfield, Ill: Templegate Pub, 1983.
Haddad, Yvonne Yazbeck & John L. Esposito. *Daughters of Abraham Feminist Thought in Judaism, Christianity, and Islam*. Miami: Univ Pr of Florida, 2001.
Hadley, Judith M. *The Cult of Asherah in Ancient Israel and Judah*. Cambridge, UK: Cambridge Univ Pr, 2000.
Huyler, Stephen P. *Meeting God Elements of Hindu Devotion*. New Haven: Yale Univ Pr, 1999.
_____ *Painted Prayers Women's Art in Village India*. NY: Rizzoli, 1994.
Idliby, Ranya, Suzanne Oliver, & Priscilla Warner. *The Faith Club A Muslim, A Christian, A Jew*. NY: Free Pr, 2006.
Kalman, Bobbie. *India, the Culture*. NY: Crabtree Pub., 1990.
Kaufman, Gordon D. *God, Mystery, Diversity Christian Theology in a Pluralistic World*. Minneapolis: Augsburg, 1996.
Kaufmann, Walter. *Life at the Limits*. NY: Reader's Digest Pr, 1978.
Klostermaier, Klaus K. *A Survey of Hinduism*. Albany, NY: SUNY Pr, 1989.
Knitter, Paul F & Chandra Muzaffar, eds. *Subverting Greed Religious Perspectives on the Global Economy*. Maryknoll, NY: Orbis, 2002.
Krieger, David J. *The New Universalism Foundations for a Global Theology*. Maryknoll, NY: Orbis, 1991.
Lahiri, Jhumpa. *The Namesake*. Boston, NY: Houghton Mifflin Co. 2003.
Laughlin, Paul Alan. *Getting Oriented What Every Christian Should Know about Eastern Religions, but Probably Doesn't*. Santa Rose, CA: Polebridge Pr, 2005.
Lopez, Donald S., Jr., ed. *Religions of India in Practice*. Princeton, NJ: Princeton Univ Pr, 1995.
Mann, Gurinder Singh, Paul Numrich, & Raymond Williams. *Buddhists, Hindus, and Sikhs in America A Short History*. NY: Oxford Univ Pr, 2001, 2008.
McCarthy, Kate. *Interfaith Encounters in America*. New Brunswick: Rutgers Univ Pr, 2007.
McFague, Sallie. *Metaphorical Theology Models of God in Religious Language*. Phila: Fortress Pr, 1982.
Miller, Barbara Stoler. *Exploring India's Sacred Art*. Phila: Univ of

Pennsylvania Pr, 1983.

Mitter, Sara S. *Dharma's Daughters*. New Brunswick, New Jersey: Rutgers Univ Pr, 1991.

n.a. *India Calling A Country Between Covers*. Visit India, Tourist Year, 1991.

Nabar, Vrinda. *Caste as Woman*. New Delhi: Penguin Bks, 1995.

Otto, Rudolf. *The Idea of the Holy*. NY: Oxford Univ Pr, 1950.

Panikkar, Raimundo. *The Vedic Experience Mantramanjari*. Berkeley: Univ of California Pr, 1977.

Patai, Raphael. *The Hebrew Goddess*. NY: Avon Bks, 1967.

Pui-lan, Kwok. *Postcolonial Imagination & Feminist Theology*. Louisville: WJK, 2005.

Punja, Shobita. *Daughters of the Ocean Discovering the Goddess Within*. New Delhi: Viking, 1996.

Rambachan, Anantanand, A Rashied Omar & M. Thomas Thangaraj. *Hermeneutical Explorations in Dialogue: Essays in Honour of Hans Ucko*. Delhi: ISPCK, 2007.

Russell, Letty M. *Just Hospitality God's Welcome in a World of Difference* (J. Shannon Clarkson & Kate M. Ott, eds.) Louisville: WJK Pr, 2009.

Sahni, Bhisham. *Tamas*, New Delhi: Penguin Bks, 1974, Revised English Translation, 1988.

Samartha, S. J. *One Christ—Many Religions Toward a Revised Christology*. Maryknoll, NY: Orbis, 1991, Bangalore: SATRI, 1992.

Sanford, Elias Benjamin, ed. *A Concise Cyclopedia of Religious Knowledge*. Hartford, CN: S. S. Scranton Co., 1912.

Scott, David C. *New Relationships in Religious Pluralism*, Manganam: TMAMOC, 1991.

Sharma, Arvind & Kathleen M. Dugan, eds. *A Dome of Many Colors Studies in Religious Pluralism, Identity, and Unity*. Harrisburg, PA: Trinity Pr Internat, 1999.

Sharma, Arvind & Katherine K. Young, eds. *Feminism and World Religions*. NY: SUNY Pr, 1999.

Sister Vandana. *Waters of Fire*. Bangalore: Asian Trading Corp., 1989.

Smith, Wilfred Cantwell. *The Meaning and End of Religion A New Approach to the Religious Traditions of Mankind*. NY: Macmillan Co., 1962.

Swami Ajaya, ed. *Living with the Himalayan Masters Spiritual Experiences of Swami Rama*. Honesdale, PA: Himalayan International Institute of Yoga Science & Philosophy, 1978.

Swami Prabhavananda. *The Spiritual Heritage of India*. Garden City, NY: Doubleday & Co, 1963.

Tagore, Rabindranath. *My Reminiscences*. Calcutta: Rupa & Co, (First published by Macmillan & Co, 1917), 1991.

Thangaraj, M. Thomas. *The Common Task A Theology of Christian Mission*. Nashville: Abingdon Pr., 1999.

_____ *The Crucified Guru An Experiment in Cross-Cultural Christology*. Nashville: Abingdon Pr., 1994.

Viswanathan, Ed. *Am I a Hindu?* San Francisco: Halo Bks, 1992.

Werner, Karel. *A Popular Dictionary of Hinduism*. Chicago: NTC Pub Group, 1994.

Young, Serinity, ed. *Encyclopedia of Women and World Religion*. 2 vol, NY: Macmillan Ref USA, 1999.

Zimmerli, Walther. *Ezekiel*. vol. 2, Phila: Fortress, 1983.

Part II Articles and Misc.: [For all chapters except 3 and 12]

Aleaz, K. P. "Church in the Indian Pluralistic Context: Challenges and Opportunities," *NCC Review*, cxv/8, 1995, 659-68.

Allman, T. D. "The Eternal City of Benares," *Asia*, Jul/Aug, 1981, 54, 44-49, 54.

Anthonysamy, S. J. "Christian Mission in the Context of Many Religions Today," *Indian Theological Studies*, 30/2, June 1993, 93-107.

Ariarajah, S. Weslay. "Asian Christian Theological Task in the Midst of Other Religious Traditions," *CTC Bulletin*, xviii/1, Apr 2002, 14-30.

_____ "Interfaith Dialogue," World Council of Churches Dictionary of the Ecumenical Movement article. http://www.oikoumene.org/en/resources/documents/wcc-programmes/in retrieved 3/1/2010, 7 pp.

Balasundaram, Franklyn J. "Crisis of Secularism in India," *The South India Churchman*, May 1994, 1 p.

Berman, Shelley. "Comparison of Dialogue and Debate," Adapted from discussions of the Dialogue Group of the Boston Chapter of Educators for Social Responsibility, Winter 1993, 1 p.

"Bharatanatyam, the Art," Program notes of Classical Dance Performance, Siri & Sita Sonty, Wilmette, IL, June 19, 1999.

Bhargava, Simran. "Tamas, An Emotional Odyssey," *India Today*, Dec 31, 1987, 86-87.

Binger, Tilde. "Ashera in Israel," *Scottish Journal of Theology*, 9/1, 1995, 3-18.

Bobb, Dilip. "Soldiers of Secularism," *India Today*, Mar 15, 1993, 38-41

Burke, T. Patrick. "Must the Description of a Religion be Acceptable to a Believer?" *Religious Studies*, 20, 631-36.

Camp, Claudia V. "1 and 2 Kings," in *The Women's Bible Commentary*, Carol A. Newsom and Sharon H. Ringe, eds., Louisville, KY: Westminster/John Knox Pr., 1992, 96-109.

Correspondent, *The Hindu.* "An enjoyable fare," Aug 14, 1998, 28; SVK "Deep trust in God," July 19, 1998; "Making music," Nov 21, 1998, 11; "Music Festival, a Feature," Dec 1, 1998, A-H (11 articles/writers); "Perfect blend of philosophy and music," Oct 30, 1998.

Das, Somen. "Globalisation from a Biblical-Theological Perspective," *Religion and Society*, xli/2, June 1994, 2-15.

Davis, Richard H. "A Brief History of Religions in India, Introduction," in *Religions of India in Practice*. Donald S. Lopez, Jr., ed. Princeton, NJ: Princeton Univ Pr, 1995, 3-52.

Day, John. "Asherah in the Hebrew Bible and Northwest Semitic Literature," *Journal of Biblical Literature,* 105/3, 1986, 385-408.

Devarajan, Arthi. "Embodying Text and Dancing the Word: Reflective Opportunities through the Non-Discursive Text of Classical Indian Dance," in *Hermeneutical Explorations in Dialogue: Essays in Honour of Hans Ucko*. Anantanand Rambachan, A. Rashied Omar & M. Thomas Thangaraj, eds. Delhi: ISPCK (Indian Society for Promoting Christian Knowledge), 2007, 89-104.

Dever, William G. "Asherah, Consort of Yahweh? New Evidence from Kuntillet Ajrud," *Bulletin of the American Schools of Oriental Research* # 255, Sum 1984, 21-38.

Duraisingh, Christopher. "A New Expression of Identity," *Religion and Society*, xxvi/4, Dec 1979, 95-101.

_____ "Alternate modes of theologising now prevalent in India," *Religion and Society*, xxvii/2, Je 1980, 81-101.

Eck, Diana L. "India's *Tirthas*: 'Crossings' in Sacred Geography," *History of Religions*, 20/4, May 1981, 323-44.

_____ "Myth, Image, and Pilgrimage," Lecture #8 of Video "Hindu, Buddhist, Muslim, Sikh: The Religions of India," Great World Religions: Beliefs, Practices, Histories. The Teaching Company Limited Partnership, 1994, 45 min.

_____ "Neighboring Faiths—How Will Americans Cope with Increasing Religious Diversity?" *Harvard Magazine*, Sept-Oct 1996, 38-44.

_____ *"The Religions of India: Points of View," Video, Lesson 1 (of 10), Great World Religions Part V, The Teaching Company Limited Partnership, 1994.*

_____ "The River Ganges and the Great Ghats," in *Banaras City of Light*. Princeton: Princeton Univ Pr, 1982, 211-51, 390-92.

Eliot, T. S. "Little Gidding," in *Collected Poems*. NY: Harcourt, Brace & World, 1963, 200-09.

Faria, Stella. "Feminine Images of God in Our Traditional Religions," *In God's Image*, June 1989, 7-17.

Fiorenza, Elisabeth Schussler. "Introduction" and "Justa—Constructing

Common Ground: To Speak in Public: A Feminist Political
Hermeneutics," in *But She Said, Feminist Practices of Biblical
Interpretation*, Boston: Beacon Pr, 1992, 1-14, 102-32.

Flueckiger, Joyce Burkhalter. "Storytelling in the Rhetoric of a Muslim
Female Healer in South India" in *Spiritual Traditions Essential
Visions for Living*, David Emmanuel Singh, ed., Bangalore,
India: United Theological College, 1998, 226-52.

Freedman, David Noel. "Yahweh of Samaria and his Asherah," *Biblical
Archaeologist*, 50/4, Dec 1987, 241-49.

Gaventa, Beverly Roberts. "'What God has Cleansed': Conversion in
Luke-Acts (Part 2)," in *From Darkness to Light Aspects of
Conversion in the New Testament*, Phila: Fortress, 1986, 96-129.

Gnanadason, Aruna. "Living in Harmony with Each Other: A Feminist
Perspective," *The Conrad Grebel Review*, Winter 1996, 91-98.

Gupta, Lina. "Kali, the Savior," in *After Patriarchy Feminist
Transformations of the World Religions.* Paula M. Cooey,
William R. Eakin, Jay B. McDaniel, eds., NY: Orbis, 1991, 15-
38.

Gyan, Satish C. "Gospel and Culture: Reflections on Worship and
Liturgy," *NCC Review*, cxvi/2, Feb 1996, 109-19.

Hackett, Jo Ann. "Can a Sexist Model Liberate Us? Ancient Near
Eastern 'Fertility' Goddesses," *Journal of Feminist Studies in
Religion*, 5/1, Spr 1989, 65-76.

Hadley, Judith M. "The Khirbet El-Qom Inscription," *Vetus
Testamentum,* xxxvii/1, 1987, 50-62.

_____ "Some Drawings and Inscriptions on Two Pithoi from Kuntillet
'Ajrud," *Vetus Testamentum,* xxxvii/2, 1987, 180-213.

Heiderer, Tony. "Sacred Space, Sacred Time, India's Maha Kumbh Mela
Draws Millions," *National Geographic*, 177/5, May 1990, 106-
17.

Hestrin, Ruth. "Understanding Asherah, Exploring Semitic
Iconography," *Biblical Archaeology Review*, xvii/5, Sept/Oct
1991, 50-59.

Indian Preparatory Group. "An Indian Search for a Spirituality of
Liberation," in *Asian Christian Spirituality Reclaiming
Traditions*, Virginia Fabella, Peter K. H. Lee & David Kwang-
sun Suh, eds. Maryknoll, NY: Orbis, 1992, 64-84.

India Today (weekly journal), n. a. Multiple articles in issues titled:
"Ayodhya, Nation's Shame," "Savagery in Bombay," Dec 31,
1992, Jan 31, 1993.

Kalidas, S. "Eternal Enchantress," Sept 7, 1998, 83; "Flamboyant
Flautist," July 6, 1998, 66-67, *India Today*.

Kinsley, David. "Introduction," "Durga, Warrior Goddess and Cosmic
Queen," "Laksmi, Goddess of Abundance and Luck," "Sita, the

Ideal Wife," in *The Goddesses' Mirror Visions of the Divine from East and West,* NY: SUNY, 1989, ix-xix, 3-24, 53-70, 91-112.

Kripal, Jeffrey J. "Kali's Tongue and Ramakrishna: 'Biting the Tongue' of the Tantric Tradition," *History of Religions*, 34/2, Nov 1994, 152-89.

Kulandran, Sabapathy. "The Rise of Hindu Theism," in *Grace A Comparative Study of the Doctrine in Christianity and Hinduism*, London: Lutterworth Pr, 1964, 115-44.

Mahmood, Cynthia Keppley. "Rethinking Indian Communalism," *Asian Survey*, 33/7, Jul 1993, 722-37.

Menon, Ramesh & Soutik Biswas. "The Rumour Mills," *India Today*, Feb. 28, 1993, 15.

n.a. "After the slaughter, what hope?" India's Hindus and Muslims, *The Economist* March 9, 2002, 45-46.

n.a. "India's cultural ambassador Ravi Shankar," *Indian Reporter*, Feb 5, 1999.

n.a. "Search for my Tongue," Program notes, Oct 30, 1998.

Nyce, Dorothy Yoder. Personal Journal, Madras, India, June 15, 1988.
_____ *Strength, Struggle and Solidarity: India's Women.* Goshen, IN: Pinch Penny Pr, 1989, 43-46.

Pandey, Gyanendra. "In Defense of the Fragment: Writing about Hindu-Muslim Riots in India Today," in *A Subaltern Studies Reader, 1986-1995*, Ranajit Guha, ed., (Reprinted from *Representations* 37, winter 1992), Minneapolis: Univ of MN Pr, 1997, 1-33.

Panikkar, Raimundo. "The Jordan, the Tiber, and the Ganges Three Kairological Moments of Christic Self-Consciousness," in *The Myth of Christian Uniqueness Toward a Pluralistic Theology of Religions.* John Hick and Paul F. Knitter, eds. Maryknoll, NY: Orbis, 1987, 89-116.

Parikh, Manju. "The Debacle at Ayodhya," *Asian Survey*, 33/7, Jul 1993, 673-84.

Patai, Raphael. "The Goddess Asherah," *Journal of Near Eastern Studies*, 24, 1965, 37-52.

Pelikan, Jaroslav. "The Rig Veda," *On Searching the Scriptures—Your Own or Someone Else's*, NY: Quality Paperback Book Club, 1992, 37-42; (Also, Introduction to vol. 5 of *Sacred Writings Hinduism: The Rig Veda*, NY: with Motilal Banarsidass, 1992, ix-xii).

Pentuker, Ramchander. "Saying It with Flowers," *Discover India*, June 1988, 4-15.

Personal interviews: Roelph Kuitse, November 2, 1993; David Lindell, November 4, 1993; Raj Biyani, January 8, 1994; Rita Paul Raj, June 12, 1996, and Eve Ricketts (multiple times).

Purie, Aroon. "From the editor in chief" *India Today*, Dec 31, 1992, 1.

Rhoads, David. "Jesus and the Syrophoenician Woman in Mark: A Narrative-Critical Study," *Journal of the American Academy of Religion*, lxii/2, 343-75.

Samartha, S. J. "Christian Community in a Pluralist Society—Towards a Revised Self-Understanding," *NCC Review*, cxvi/3, Mar 1996, 153-64.

Schiffman, Richard. "The Wisdom Teachings of India," in *Living Wisdom Vedanta in a World Community*. Pravrajika Vrajaprana, ed. Madras: Sri Ramakrishna Math, 1995, 63-70.

Scott, M. Corinne. "Poor Slum Women's Oppression and Sources of Strength: A Feminist Ethical Perspective," MTh Thesis, Serampore College, April 1993.

Scott, David C. Multiple correspondence.

Smith-Christopher, Daniel L. "Gandhi on Daniel 6: Some Thoughts on a 'Cultural Exegesis' of the Bible," *Biblical Interpretation*, 1/3, Nov 1993, 321-38.

Smith, Mark S. "God Male and Female in the Old Testament: Yahweh and His 'Asherah,'" *Theological Studies*, 48, 1987, 333-40.

Sugirtharajah, R. S. "The Bible and its Asian Readers," *Biblical Interpretation*, 1/1, 1993, 43-66.

Taylor, J. Glen. "Was Yahweh Worshiped as the Sun?" *Biblical Archaeology Review,* 20/3, May-June 1994, 52-61, 90-91.

Taylor, Joan E. "The Asherah, The Menorah and the Sacred Tree," *Journal for the Study of the Old Testament*, 66, 1995, 29-54.

Thakur, Ramesh. "Ayodhya and the Politics of India's Secularism," *Asian Survey*, 33/7, Jul 1993, 645-64.

Vedantam, Vatsala. "From the Godhra Station," *Christian Century* March 13-20, 2002, 8-9.

Zaehner, R. G. "Introduction," *Hindu Scriptures*, London: J. M. Dent & Sons, (Everyman's Library 1938), 1966, v-xxii.

About the Author

Ever since living in India from 1962-65, plus on seven further assignments there, Dorothy Yoder Nyce has been drawn to study and absorb the richness of multifaiths alongside Christian loyalty. This book reflects her effort to respect, understand and ever-learn from key religions. As the number of people loyal to diverse religions grows in the United States, her hope deepens for adherents to be welcomed. This book also reflects Dorothy's thanks to those who have mentored her religious being—her Mother's habit of ever-humming hymns of faith, international friends, key professors of world religions, and numerous writers of interfaith Wisdom.

An advocate for diverse justice issues, Yoder Nyce values disciplined research and the rigor of writing. A teacher at heart, she values sharing what she learns. Retired from secondary, college and seminary teaching (part-time), Dorothy's fondness for religions deepened through increased exposure and changes that enhanced personal faith. She invites Christians to promote God's inclusive kin-dom through openness to sacred difference, ecumenical or interfaith.

In addition to dozens of articles, Dorothy Yoder Nyce earlier wrote or edited books: about women (*Rooted and Branching Women Worldwide*, *To See Each Other's Good*, and *Which Way Women?*); or about theology (*Jesus' Clear Call to Justice*, *Mission Today Challenges and Concerns*—with Abraham Athyal—and *Weaving Wisdom: Sermons by Mennonite Women*) plus booklets or collections of articles about death and grief, sexual or spiritual diversity, and family history.

Academic degrees that Yoder Nyce has earned are: BA - Goshen College, Goshen, Indiana; MDiv - Associated Mennonite Biblical Seminaries, Elkhart, Indiana; DMin - Western Theological Seminary, Holland, Michigan.